语言教学新环境丛书

# Developing Online Language Teaching

Research-Based Pedagogies and Reflective Practices

# 开发在线语言教学

## 基于研究的教学法和反思实践

edited by **Regine Hampel**
and **Ursula Stickler**

上海外语教育出版社
外教社 SHANGHAI FOREIGN LANGUAGE EDUCATION PRESS
www.sflep.com

图书在版编目（CIP）数据

开发在线语言教学——基于研究的教学法和反思实践 / （英）雷金·汉佩尔（Regine Hampel），（英）乌苏拉·斯提克勒（Ursula Stickler）编. — 上海：上海外语教育出版社，2020
（语言教学新环境丛书）
ISBN 978-7-5446-6372-4

Ⅰ.①开… Ⅱ.①雷… ②乌… Ⅲ.①语言教学—网络教学—教学研究—英文
Ⅳ.①H09

中国版本图书馆CIP数据核字（2020）第052549号

出版发行：**上海外语教育出版社**
（上海外国语大学内）　邮编：200083
电　　话：021-65425300（总机）
电子邮箱：bookinfo@sflep.com.cn
网　　址：http://www.sflep.com
责任编辑：奚玲燕

印　　刷：**浙江临安曙光印务有限公司**
开　　本：890×1240　1/32　印张 6.875　字数 253千字
版　　次：2020 年 4 月第 1 版　2020 年 4 月第 1 次印刷
印　　数：2 500 册

书　　号：ISBN 978-7-5446-6372-4
定　　价：**25.00** 元

本版图书如有印装质量问题，可向本社调换
质量服务热线：4008-213-263　电子邮箱：**editorial@sflep.com**

# 出 版 说 明

随着网络技术的发展,教学技术的革新也与时俱进,在线学习、数字游戏化学习、慕课、翻转课堂等新的学习范式应运而生,打破了课堂教学的时空局限,改变了传统的教学理念,以多元化的形式满足学习者的个性化需求。

由于语言的交际特性,这些技术革新对语言教学,尤其是外语教学领域的影响尤为显著。外语教师除了在日常教学中广泛运用网络、多媒体等技术外,还开始关注和研究非正式学习中新技术带来的挑战,研究者们也将更多目光投向技术革新和新的学习范式对外语教学的作用。

上海外语教育出版社引进推出的这套“语言教学新环境丛书”,正是聚焦新的技术环境下,以学习者为中心的语言教学的实践经验和理论发展,探索分析新技术对语言教学课堂内外的深远影响。需要特别说明的是,作为研究的一部分,作者在书中所附的网站链接可为读者提供教学资源和参考,其中内容还须读者注意甄别。

这套丛书展示了国际学界在新环境下语言学习与教学领域的研究动态和成果,相信它们的出版能抛砖引玉,为国内的研究者提供方向和参考。

# Developing Online Language Teaching

## Research-Based Pedagogies and Reflective Practices

Edited by

Regine Hampel and Ursula Stickler
*The Open University, UK*

# Contents

*List of Figures and Tables*                                      v

*Series Editor's Preface*                                       vii

*Notes on Contributors*                                        viii

1   Introduction: From Teacher Training to
    Self-Reflective Practice                             1
    *Regine Hampel and Ursula Stickler*

2   European Language Teachers and ICT: Experiences,
    Expectations and Training Needs                      12
    *Aline Germain-Rutherford and Pauline Ernest*

3   Part-Time and Freelance Language Teachers and their
    ICT Training Needs                                   28
    *Ursula Stickler and Martina Emke*

4   Online Language Teaching: The Learner's Perspective    45
    *Linda Murphy*

5   Transforming Teaching: New Skills for Online Language
    Learning Spaces                                      63
    *Ursula Stickler and Regine Hampel*

6   Free Online Training Spaces for Language Teachers      78
    *Joseph Hopkins*

7   Sharing: Open Educational Resources for
    Language Teachers                                    96
    *Anna Comas-Quinn and Kate Borthwick*

8   Online Communities of Practice: A Professional
    Development Tool for Language Educators              113
    *Aline Germain-Rutherford*

9   Theoretical Approaches and Research-Based Pedagogies
    for Online Teaching                                 134
    *Regine Hampel*

10  Developing Online Teaching Skills: The DOTS Project        150
    *Mateusz-Milan Stanojević*

11   Using DOTS Materials for the Professional Development
     of English Teachers in Turkey: Teachers' Views                    163
     *Süleyman Başaran, Emrah Cinkara and Neşe Cabaroğlu*

*Bibliography*                                                          183

*Index*                                                                202

# List of Figures and Tables

## Figures

| | | |
|---|---|---|
| 1.1 | Skills pyramid | 5 |
| 2.1 | Most frequent profiles | 24 |
| 5.1 | Skills pyramid (adapted) | 66 |
| 5.2 | Skills pyramid for reflection | 76 |
| 6.1 | Nik Peachey's Learning Technology Blog | 87 |
| 6.2 | Russell Stannard's video tutorial on creating podcasts | 88 |
| 6.3 | Dave's ESL Café's Computer-Assisted Language Learning Forum | 90 |
| 8.1 | Home page of the Middlebury Interactive Teachers Community | 125 |
| 8.2 | Level of activity (views and posts) by participants in the DOTS Online Community | 128 |
| 8.3 | Level of activity (views and posts) per member of the Regional Croatian Online Community | 129 |
| 8.4 | A visual representation of participants' answers generated by the software 'Wordle' | 132 |
| 9.1 | Action research spiral | 144 |
| 10.1 | Modified action research spiral | 161 |
| 11.1 | Accessibility of computer and smart board at state schools in Diyarbakır | 170 |
| 11.2 | Availability of projectors in classrooms | 171 |
| 11.3 | Availability of regular access to the Internet in classrooms | 171 |
| 11.4 | Availability of Learning Management System | 172 |
| 11.5 | School management support for development of ICT skills | 172 |
| 11.6 | Overall rating of the workshop | 173 |
| 11.7 | Improved confidence in and knowledge of using ICT in the classroom | 174 |
| 11.8 | Willingness to use ICT after the workshop | 175 |

11.9   Willingness to keep up with technological development
       after the workshop                                        176

11.10  Skills in identifying and applying appropriate
       ICT tools                                                 177

11.11  Capability to act as a multiplier and promote the use
       of ICT tools to others                                    177

11.12  Enhanced ability to identify and apply appropriate
       DOTS tools                                                179

11.13  The ability to promote the use of DOTS tools             179

11.14  Perceived quality of materials provided during
       the workshop                                             180

11.15  Perceived quality of DOTS materials provided
       during the workshop                                      181

## Tables

2.1   Teacher profiles                                           23

4.1   Survey sample and responses in 2008 and 2011               51

4.2   Age profile of respondents in 2008 and 2011               52

4.3   Highest previous educational level of respondents
      in 2008 and 2011                                           52

4.4   Taxonomy category ranking in 2011 and highest
      ranked features within each category where 1 = highest
      and 5 = lowest rank                                        53

5.1   Technical and pedagogical knowledge and skills for CALL    67

6.1   Typology of freely available training resources            81

6.2   Syllabus for task-based language teaching with digital tools   85

6.3   Son's (2011) tool categories                               86

6.4   Recommendations for a teacher self-development plan        93

8.1   Participants' activity in the library of the ACTFL
      Language Educators Community                               122

8.2   Activity types in the ACTFL Language Educators
      Community                                                  123

# Series Editor's Preface

The 'New Language Learning and Teaching Environments' book series is dedicated to recent developments in learner-centred approaches and the impact of technology on learning and teaching inside and outside the language classroom. It offers a multidisciplinary forum for presenting and investigating the latest developments in language education, taking a pedagogic approach with a clear focus on the learner, and with clear implications for both researchers and language practitioners. Regine Hampel and Ursula Stickler and their authors write persuasively about the need for teachers to develop their ability to successfully teach online, not merely as a set of mechanical skills, but as a pedagogically transformative practice that has the potential to empower both students and teachers. The chapters in this edited book provide many different perspectives that together cover all aspects of this field; learners and teachers, full-time and part-time staff, research and practice. As editor I am particularly pleased to welcome this collection into the series as it deals with a topic that underpins many of the kinds of innovation that modern-day teaching (and the research of teaching) requires. The experiences, knowledge and research findings shared here will certainly inform and support readers in their own thinking and practice in this area.

*Hayo Reidners*
*Auckland, October 2014*

# Notes on Contributors

## Editors

**Regine Hampel** is Professor of Open and Distance Language Learning at The Open University, UK. Her research explores the impact of using new technologies for learning and teaching and the implications for communication, literacy, activity design and teacher training.

**Ursula Stickler** is Senior Lecturer in the Department of Languages at The Open University, UK. She has published in the areas of autonomous and technology enhanced language learning, teacher training and learner preparation for online language learning.

## Contributors

**Süleyman Başaran** is Assistant Professor in the Foreign Languages Department, Dicle University, Turkey. He is the Director of the School of Foreign Languages and Coordinator of the Erasmus, Mevlana and Farabi Exchange Programs. His research interests include educational technology and drama.

**Kate Borthwick** is Senior Academic Coordinator for e-learning at the Centre for Languages, Linguistics and Area Studies, University of Southampton, UK. Her research interests include OERs, open educational practice, technical issues around open resource sharing and communities of open practice.

**Neşe Cabaroğlu** is Lecturer in the English Language Teaching Department at Çukurova University, Adana, Turkey. She received a PhD from the University of Reading, UK. Her research revolves around student-teacher learning, professional development and online teaching and learning.

**Emrah Cinkara** is Instructor in English at Gaziantep University, Turkey, where he received his BA in ELT. His current research interests include ICT in language teaching and second language processing. He is currently completing his PhD on EFL reading.

**Anna Comas-Quinn** is Associate Head of the Department of Languages at The Open University, UK. She publishes on online, blended and mobile language learning, and is currently researching how open resources and practices impact on language learning and teacher development.

**Martina Emke** is an experienced EFL teacher in adult and vocational education in Germany and now works as a project manager in tertiary education. Her research interests focus on learner autonomy and professional development for language teachers.

**Pauline Ernest** is Lecturer in English and Coordinator of English Language courses at the Universitat Oberta de Catalunya (UOC). Her interests include second language acquisition, language learning in virtual environments, training teachers in the use of ICT in the language classroom and computer-supported collaborative work.

**Aline Germain-Rutherford** is Linguistics Professor at Middlebury College in Vermont, USA. She is also the Chief Learning Officer of a company specializing in online language courses. She received a Doctorat de Didactique des Langues at La Sorbonne Nouvelle, Paris, France.

**Joseph Hopkins** is a language teacher/teacher trainer and is currently the Director of the School of Languages at the Universitat Oberta de Catalunya in Barcelona, Spain. His main interests are web-based language learning and computer-mediated communication.

**Linda Murphy** is a part-time consultant and supervisor for the Open University Doctorate in Education programme. Her research has focused on learning and teaching strategies and teacher development to support motivation, self-direction and autonomy in language learning.

**Mateusz-Milan Stanojević** is Assistant Professor in the Department of English, University of Zagreb. His fields of interest include cognitive linguistics, particularly cognitive grammar and conceptual metaphor theory, English as a Lingua Franca, and online teaching and learning.

# 1

## Introduction: From Teacher Training to Self-Reflective Practice

*Regine Hampel and Ursula Stickler*

### Focus of the book

This book has been written to meet the need of language teachers who are keen to engage in online teaching and learning contexts, teacher trainers in search of resources that they can use with their trainees to develop their online teaching skills, and researchers in language pedagogy looking for well-founded studies and recommendations in this area. It integrates technology and pedagogy as well as theory and practice, and will help teachers in formal, non-formal and informal settings to become confident users of online tools and to relate their pedagogical practice to online learning situations as well as giving them a basic understanding of selected theories. Readers will be able to use this volume in the context of independent self-training and pre-service teacher training courses, for in-service staff development and also for establishing their own research projects. As befits the content, the book is modular rather than linear, and certain elements can be taken out of context and used independently for self-training or institutional training events.

When moving towards teaching online, teachers are confronted every day with challenges such as online moderation, establishing social presence online, transitioning learners to online environments and giving feedback online. This book, without explicitly focusing on specific issues, is designed to help teachers consider the skills they have and how they can develop these further. The authors are taking a broad perspective, looking at the need to self-train and the challenges around it, the skills that are required to use information and communication technology (ICT) in language teaching contexts, the online communities that teachers can tap into for support, other resources available for initial training as well as continuing professional development on the internet, and the role of open educational resources. The book also tries to inspire teaching practitioners to do their own research, helping them to position themselves theoretically and methodologically and to find out if what they do online with their students works and how it can be improved. Teacher trainers will find this book helpful for pre-service and in-service training of teachers. All elements of the book acknowledge the need for reflective practice, encouraging readers throughout to place their own experience in context and reflect on developmental options.

Hubbard and Levy (2006a, p. ix) identified a number of themes that recurred in their edited book on teacher education in CALL (computer-assisted language learning):

- the need for both technical and pedagogical training in CALL, ideally integrated with one another;
- the recognition of the limits of formal teaching [in the context of CALL training] because the technology changes too rapidly;
- the need to connect CALL education to authentic teaching settings, especially ones where software, hardware, and technical support differ from the ideal;
- the idea of using CALL to learn about CALL – experiencing educational applications of technology first-hand as a student to learn how to use technology as a teacher;
- the value of having CALL permeate the language teacher education curriculum rather than appear solely in a standalone course.

These themes, on the whole, are still valid today and also guide the approach to CALL that the authors in this book have been following. Almost ten years later some of Hubbard and Levy's (2006a) recommendations still remain to be implemented. In many contexts, there is still insufficient training in CALL, and often the technical and the pedagogical elements are not integrated (see Chapters 2 and 3). Many teachers feel that while they may receive training for using ICT in the classroom, the resources on the ground are still inadequate for them to use computers in their daily practice (see Chapter 11).

In their own teaching, teacher training and research, the authors in this book believe in giving teachers hands-on experience of using ICT and share a learner-focused perspective that helps students to use the computer to connect with others, thus developing their own knowledge. An example of how CALL can help teachers learn about CALL is the DOTS (Developing Online Teaching Skills) project, funded by the European Centre for Modern Languages (ECML). Seven of the book's authors have been involved in this project – which is also at the centre of Chapter 10.

Acknowledging the seminal influence of Hubbard and Levy (2006a), this book adds to their agenda in several ways. Expanding on work done previously (Hampel & Stickler, 2005), it focuses specifically on the skills that teachers have to develop to teach successfully online. It also deals with current issues of sharing and learning together, thus pointing to one way of dealing with the consequences of Hubbard and Levy's second point above. Collaboration has become crucial in the way teachers gather information and develop expertise, work together in communities of practice, and develop and use open educational resources and practices. In addition, the book emphasizes the need for teachers to carry out their own research. Accordingly, it calls for teaching professionals to become aware of the theoretical and pedagogical models that underlie online teaching and learning and to research their own practice.

## Theoretical rationale

The chapters in this book are united by sociocultural and socio-constructivist approaches to teaching online, approaches that go back to the work of the developmental psychologist Lev Vygotsky in Russia in the 1920s. Vygotsky (1978) stressed the importance of the social in learning – an idea that was taken up by Wertsch in his work on sociocultural theory more than half a century later. 'The basic goal of a sociocultural approach to mind is to create an account of human mental processes that recognizes the essential relationship between these processes and the cultural, historical, and institutional settings' (Wertsch, 1991b, p. 6).

Similarly, socio-constructivism brings in the social element to build on constructivism, a theory of knowledge that assumes that humans construct their own knowledge and make sense of the world based on their own experiences in a complex and non-linear process. 'Incorporating influences traditionally associated with sociology and anthropology, this perspective emphasizes the impact of collaboration, social context, and negotiation on thinking and learning' (Hinckey, 1997, p. 175).

In the area of language learning research, in 1997 Firth and Wagner called for an epistemological and methodological broadening of second language acquisition (SLA) that included 'a significantly enhanced awareness of the contextual and interactional dimensions of language use' (Firth & Wagner, 2007, p. 801; see Firth & Wagner, 1997). This formed part of the 'social turn in second language acquisition' as Block (2003) has called it:

> a broader, socially informed and more sociolinguistically oriented SLA that does not exclude the more mainstream psycholinguistic one, but instead takes on board the complexity of context, the multi-layered nature of language and an expanded view of what acquisition entails. (p. 4)

Sociocultural and socio-constructivist ideas can be seen to inform this book in various ways. Chapter 2 focuses on language teachers' needs in terms of training, and Chapter 3 takes account of teachers' institutional contexts as part-time or freelance staff. Chapter 4 shows the relationship between the teacher and the learner in terms of expectations, and in Chapter 5 the importance of the social in the context of language teaching skills is highlighted. Chapters 6 and 7 focus on the impact of sharing resources and practices; an idea that is developed further in Chapter 8 which argues for the central role of peer support through communities of practice. Chapter 9 examines theoretical and pedagogical approaches to online language teaching from a sociocultural perspective, and Chapter 10 shows the importance of shaping training to teachers' needs and of learning collaboratively. Last but not least, Chapter 11 highlights some of the issues that language teachers and learners face within their institutional settings in Turkey.

## A model for online teaching skills

When we were working with teachers in the early 2000s to introduce web conferencing in language courses at the Open University, it became clear to us that teachers had to develop new skills to be able to successfully use the new online tools with which they were expected to teach. Although there were pockets of development in terms of websites, courses and other resources (for example, Graham Davies' ICT4U, the EU-funded Medienpass project, or the Webheads who freely provided in-depth training in the use of web communication tools for EFL/ESL teachers from 2004, see Almeida d'Eça & Gonzáles, 2006), training was not widely integrated into colleagues' practice and the perception was that what worked well in face-to-face settings could easily be transferred to online environments. This, however, had been disproved in some of the early trials that had been carried out at the Open University with various online communication tools (see Hampel & de los Arcos, 2013). So we set about developing a model specifically for online language teaching that tried to bring together the various skills that this form of teaching requires of teachers and integrated pedagogy with technology. This resulted in the skills pyramid in Figure 1.1[1] which will be elaborated in Chapter 5.

Since the mid-2000s the sophistication and choice of ICT for language teachers has proliferated, and teachers (as well as students) are increasingly becoming more familiar with the use of new technologies in the classroom. However, our work with the European Centre for Modern Languages (part of the Council of Europe) and the European Commission has shown that there is still a need for teacher training in CALL. An initial needs analysis carried out in 2008 in the context of the DOTS project showed that while teachers rate ICT highly (for example, in terms of authentic communication, collaboration, access to up-to-date information, exam preparation, development of autonomous learning and critical thinking, and flexibility), only half of the respondents had received formal training. Subsequent evaluation with teaching professionals who attended DOTS workshops has confirmed this initial finding and other reports that have been published (see Chapter 2).

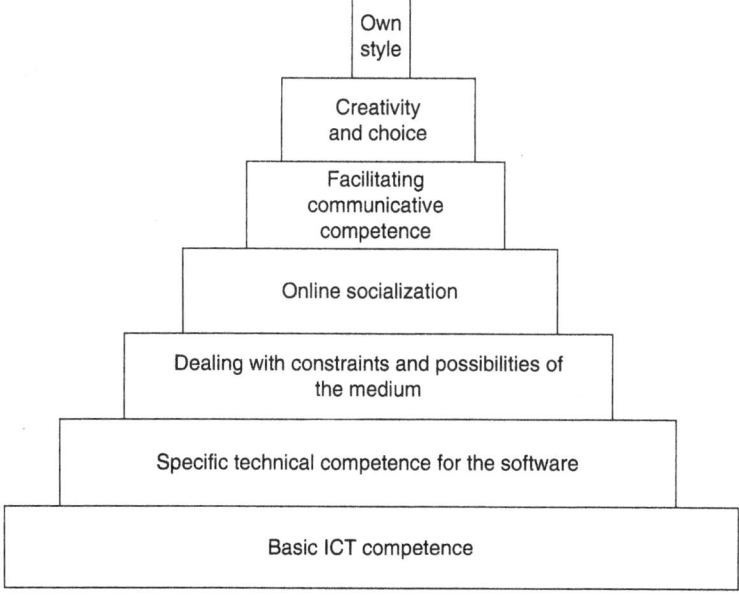

*Figure 1.1* Skills pyramid
*Source*: Hampel & Stickler (2005, p. 317).

## Chapter overview

In terms of its structure, the book can be compared to a travel hand-book, guiding novice online language teachers on a journey towards successful integration of ICT elements into their online or blended teaching. For some readers the first stages will not be necessary, as they are already well aware of their own needs and skills levels. Those readers can explore the more specific suggestions provided later or read the first chapters for information and to compare their own teaching context with those of fellow teachers across Europe and beyond. For others, having a structured approach – from needs to expectations, skills, training suggestions, towards peer support and action research – will provide a valuable means of supporting their progress.

In line with our socio-constructivist approach to learning, every chapter has a reflective task at the end. This should help the reader to engage more deeply with the content matter of the chapter, allow evaluation of progress and depth of understanding, and bring the relevance of the chapter within the reader's own frame of experience.

The book starts with the needs of language teachers who are integrating ICT into their teaching. Rather than taking the expert view from outside (or above), the authors start by inquiring about language teachers' situation with respect to ICT integration, their actual teaching practice and the best practices they are aspiring to and, most crucially, their perceived training needs. Considering a variety of teaching situations, from formal teaching of languages in compulsory and post-compulsory education institutions to informal language mediation in voluntary and migration contexts, and taking into account a scale of different employment contexts (i.e. full-time, part-time, casually employed, or volunteering), the next two chapters present our attempt to understand the emic perspective on the changing situation of language professionals in an increasingly digital world. We hope that in Chapters 2 and 3 every language educator, teacher trainer or trainee teacher will find their dilemmas and challenges reflected to some extent.

Leading on from establishing the needs and challenges of teachers, Chapter 4 then takes the mirroring perspective of language students and asks what learners expect from their online teacher. This perspective helps not only to give the learner a voice in shaping a successful online teaching/learning environment, it also allows teachers to mould their training and preparation to adapt to or adjust the expectations of their learners.

Teaching skills, as they have to be developed and adapted for online language teaching, are the central focus of Chapter 5. That language teachers need to prepare specifically for an environment that, to the novice, may offer little in non-explicit non-verbal communicative cues, has been an established tenet of online language teacher training for more than a decade. Based on our skills pyramid for online teaching (Hampel & Stickler, 2005), we consider the changes in the online world of learning and teaching over the past ten years and how these have influenced the development of online teaching skills. Changes are not only occurring in the form of technical advances and in terms of accessibility and use of online communication tools, but there are also shifts in pedagogic emphasis and the mindset of users, digital natives, immigrants, residents and sojourners. Skills such as basic ICT competence, still a necessary consideration in 2005, are now taken for granted by almost all employers, national agencies for education and by learners themselves (as shown in the changing expectations of students, see Chapter 4). There is, however, now an increased need for the negotiation of online spaces as learning spaces, which will be discussed in Chapter 5.

Having established training needs and necessary skills, Chapter 6 provides some much needed practical guidance on utilising free online resources for self-training and integrating online resources into language classes. The overview of online training resources for language teachers presented in this chapter allows practitioners to select the most suitable format for their own training. Due to the fast-changing nature of internet resources, specific websites are only used to point out types and formats, rather than providing detailed guidance on how to use a particular resource. This is consistent with the fundamental assumptions of our approach to teaching and research exemplified also in other chapters in this book: guiding practitioners towards self-training and reflection is ultimately more beneficial than training activities that focus on technical aspects and the latest 'gadgets'.

This line of thinking is further explored in Chapter 7, where the concept of Open Educational Resources (OER) as simple reusable learning materials that teachers can download and integrate into the next lesson is challenged and extended to a description of 'Open Educational Practices' (OEP), a far more wide-reaching approach to finding, evaluating, using and sharing resources needed for language learning tasks with like-minded colleagues. That this view of open education has the potential to revolutionise teaching across the curriculum has been acknowledged by educational institutions worldwide and is supported by the chapter.

Following on from the idea of a community of practitioners sharing freely their resources and ideas, Chapter 8 introduces communities of practice as a valuable if not necessary tool for the professional development of the online language teacher. Using a number of examples from current online communities, legitimate peripheral participation, peer learning, and sharing as reflective practice are demonstrated and evaluated. Moreover, the chapter provides initial considerations and guidelines for the establishment of successful online communities of practice, the necessary foundations, communication structures, and ongoing support to help teachers become full members of an online community that enables them to develop their online teaching skills in collaboration with peers.

In Chapter 9 the journey of the online language teacher progresses a step further by offering suggestions for self-reflective research. Starting from outlining learning theories that underpin online language teaching, the chapter offers various options for researching one's own teaching. Practitioners, whether novice or established, can use the suggestions for different methodologies, including action research and ethnography, to systematically investigate their online teaching. This chapter will be of interest to researchers wanting to move into CALL or ICT research as it presents an overview of the most commonly used pedagogies, linking them to learning theories on the one hand, and potential areas for research on the other.

Chapter 10 fills in the gaps in the background to this book by presenting the ECML-funded DOTS (Developing Online Teaching Skills) project, as well as the follow-up projects that it has generated. Their history from needs analysis to training workshops and a free online workspace with open educational training resources to, finally, the reflective research presented in this book, mirrors the journey undertaken through Chapters 2 to 9. In addition, practical suggestions on how teachers can use the freely available DOTS resources are provided.

The final chapter serves as proof that DOTS, and the approach it is based on, is already being cascaded successfully: a collegiate of Turkish academics has used the DOTS materials and research instruments to train a number of Turkish teachers of English in the use of ICT tools in their own context. This group of researchers present their findings and the specific challenges encountered in a country that is quite distinct from the majority of European countries where the concept was developed. Their experience shows ways of successfully utilising and adapting DOTS materials (see Chapter 10) and Chapter 11 can be seen as an evaluation of the approach to teaching and researching advocated in this book.

The reflective task in the final chapter invites readers to assess their readiness for online teaching taking into account hindering and enabling factors. It can be seen as a reflection valid for the entire book:

by the end of the journey from needs analysis, via suggestions for self-training and online collaboration, to researching and evaluating their practice, teachers will decide where to go next and what steps to take to enhance their own and their students' online language learning and teaching.

## Future developments

We hope that this book will encourage language teachers to integrate ICT more fully into their teaching and will make them feel better prepared for the challenges ahead. In a fast-moving environment such as computer supported learning, current skills are never enough and the ability to self-train and further develop one's own skills independently becomes indispensable.

In following this independence of approach, we support a move towards adaptive teaching: a responsive balancing of the needs and abilities of learners with the affordances (i.e. the possibilities and constraints) of the tools used and the demands of accreditation and assessment. This adaptive teaching is greatly enhanced by teachers' own research as action researchers in the classroom, with learners acting as participants or even co-researchers. Placing learners firmly in the centre is made easier by a pedagogically sound and confident use of digital media, in particular social media, for communicating, as well as other knowledge management tools for selecting, storing, sharing and retrieving information.

Teachers' research will introduce more realistic insights into the reality of teaching with technology in restricted circumstances; it can generate new ideas of how ICT can help teachers to cope with the pressures of assessment, and how ICT can be used within culturally sensitive contexts, for example for the pairing of native speakers with learners of a language, by selectively using or not using visual images of participants, or by teaching young learners to deal with online communication in the absence of many of the non-verbal cues taken for granted in face-to-face situations. We hope that this book will also encourage teachers to experiment with technology use in particular contexts, for example by making the most of the availability of mobile technology in the absence of institutional computing support ('MALL' instead of CALL).

Finally, a word about the medium used: a (paper-based) book dealing with technology-enhanced teaching might seem a little incongruous. However, our reasons for choosing a medium slightly at odds with what we are promoting are twofold: firstly, we want to reach an audience who might not feel entirely comfortable with a fully online presentation. By offering a traditional format we help readers make the first steps towards ICT integration into language teaching. Most chapters include links to online sites that can support further steps, giving concrete guidance on how to move from theoretical knowledge about ICT in language teaching to practical use of tools, tasks and communities online.

Our second reason for choosing this more fixed format of presentation is more conceptual: although the book only captures a particular moment in time of the development of ICT in language teaching and learning, the underlying principles of our approach, that is, sociocultural theory, a learner-centred approach, and an emphasis on self-development and action research, will continue to apply and thus should be of interest to novice and experienced teachers, teacher trainers, and language teaching researchers today and in the future.

## Acknowledgements

This book would not have been possible without the help of many people and institutions. First and foremost our thanks go to the European Centre for Modern Languages, a division of the Council of Europe and mentioned in several places in the book. Their work on enhancing language education and multilingualism throughout Europe and beyond has supported the projects which have fed into some of the research work described here. Their administrative support, their careful collection of participant feedback and impact surveys have encouraged us to also be more persistent and systematic in evaluating our workshops and our materials. All project members have contributed to this book.

Our thanks also go to the participants in our workshops who generously shared with us their ideas, their enthusiasm and their apprehensions. They willingly answered our questionnaires and engaged with our qualitative research, leading to deeper reflections and insights. In addition, we would like to acknowledge the work of reviewers and proofreaders who carefully perused the chapters and helped to bring the book to completion. These are: Marie-Josée Hamel, Phil Hubbard, Stella Hurd, Agnes Kukulska-Hulme, Marie-Noëlle Lamy, Carlos Montoro Sanjosé, Chris Niblett, Müge Satar, Prithvi Shrestha, Elke StJohn, Thomas Strasser and Cynthia White.

And last but not least, we are grateful to those experts who allowed us to re-use their work and share their images and website details with us:

Middlebury Interactive Languages
Nik Peachey

Dave Sperling
Russell Stannard
Taylor and Francis

## Note

1. Acknowledgement: Figure 1.1 was originally published in the article 'New skills for new classrooms: Training tutors to teach languages online', Regine Hampel and Ursula Stickler, *Computer Assisted Language Learning*, 2005, reprinted with the permission of the publisher (Taylor and Francis Ltd. http://tandfonline.com).

# 2

# European Language Teachers and ICT: Experiences, Expectations and Training Needs

*Aline Germain-Rutherford and Pauline Ernest*

## Introduction

In 2006, as part of its recommendations for lifelong learning, the European Parliament and the Council of the European Union identified Communication in foreign languages, Digital competence, Learning to learn and Cultural awareness and expression as key competences for individuals to develop in order to fully contribute to a knowledge society (Official Journal of the European Union, 2006).

Since then, several reports, initiated and funded by the European Commission, have been published on the topic of language learning practices in formal and informal settings and on the use and impact of online tools on language learners in blended and online environments, and also in learning situations where information and communications technology (ICT) is used in a face-to-face learning environment. The *Study on the impact of information and communications technology (ICT) and new media on language learning* (Stevens, 2009) was commissioned by the Education and Culture Executive Agency (EACEA), and surveyed 2,195 ICT users from eight different European countries. It was followed, in 2010, by a report on *Learning, Innovation and ICT: Lessons learned by the ICT cluster Education & Training 2010 programme,* prepared for the Directorate General responsible for Education and Culture of the European Commission (ICT Cluster, 2010), and then in 2011 by a report on the project *Young people with fewer opportunities learning languages informally: perceptions and uses of ICT and social media,* coordinated by the Universitat Autónoma de Barcelona (Antoniadou et al., 2011). This latter study conducted a survey among 258 young people at a socioeconomic disadvantage or members of minority groups, from six different European countries.

All three reports examine the practices and attitudes of learners and teachers as they increasingly integrate ICT in their learning and teaching habits. They also acknowledge the growing importance of ICT use in formal and informal language learning contexts, and the ways that social media seem to support language learning by promoting informal interaction among learners of second or foreign languages. As Antoniadou and colleagues (2011, p. 7) point out, 'these platforms provide a valid context in which language has a real communicative and interactive purpose, which helps the informants learn by interacting with other multilingual and multicultural counterparts'. Furthermore, most survey participants mention the use of ICT as a motivating factor in learning a language, as they can access more authentic documents and pace their own learning.

However, the use of ICT tools seems less preeminent in formal language settings than it is in informal learning contexts (Stevens, 2009), and the Stevens report identifies several barriers that still impede the use of ICT. Cost and accessibility are often quoted as negative factors, at a national or regional level, even though the ICT Cluster study reports that all the European countries participating in this study have policies to equip most schools with adequate technology and Wi-Fi access. In addition, the belief still shared by many, that learning a language requires physical interaction with others, can slow down the adoption of ICT in schools.

All three reports also highlight the need to provide teachers and educators with appropriate and on-going training support in order for them not only to become digitally competent but most importantly to help them become pedagogically aware of why and how ICT can enhance language learning. It is especially important, as noted in the 2009 report and confirmed by the current research presented in this chapter, to address this need in formal learning settings where the use of ICT for language learning and assessment is still lacking.

> [T]he use of ICT for formal language learning and assessment is not that widespread. Computers/other technologies were the main medium in language courses for less than 10% of the respondents, and a regular course component for about 30%. Similarly, less than one in five respondents had earned formal certification of their language skills using technologies in the exams or in the preparation for them. (Stevens, 2009, p. 29)

Even though the shift from teaching to learning has been aided by the fact that ICT gives learners access to other resources and spaces for interactive practice, many language teachers still need to overcome their resistance to the use of technology in their classrooms (Antoniadou et al., 2011). They also need to receive guidance and training to help them both understand and accept their new role as learning facilitators in this new context. Similar results are highlighted in a 2008 report published by Teachers of English to Speakers of Other Languages, Inc. (TESOL) where it is noted that even in extremely well-equipped schools, 'many classroom teachers never used the computers at all' (Healey et al., 2008, p. 9), reinforcing the need for teacher training.

This lack of engagement of many teachers is not surprising, considering the profound changes that the use of ICT in the classroom entails. As emphasized by Stevens and Shield (Stevens 2009, p. 71), '[t]he scale and depth of the cultural shift for professional educators implied by new ways of learning should not be under-estimated. Changes need professionals to design, deliver and support new modes of learning. Professionals include existing experienced teachers as well as new recruits'.

In this chapter we will examine the results of several surveys on the needs of language educators in Europe, conducted from 2008 to 2014 by a team of language education experts working on three related professional development projects funded by the European Centre for Modern Languages (ECML). The findings from these surveys, combined with qualitative research, have fed into the creation of online training resources and a series of basic profiles of language educators and their attitudes to the use of technology in their professional practice. This practice encompasses work carried out in online courses, blended environments and face-to-face classrooms which integrate online elements.

## Empowering language professionals: a European Centre for Modern Languages (ECML) initiative

The Council of Europe's European Centre for Modern Languages promotes language education in Europe and supports a variety of projects based around the common theme of empowering language professionals. The DOTS (Developing Online Teaching Skills) project 2008–2011, the More DOTS project 2011–2013 (http://dots.ecml.at) and the ICT-REV initiative (http://ict-rev.ecml.at/) from 2013, are three interlinked projects supported by the ECML and led by a team of experts from Croatia, Germany, Great Britain and Spain as well as Canada and the United States (see Chapter 10 for a detailed description of the DOTS, More DOTS and ICT-REV projects).

The overall aim of these three projects has been to develop an open source virtual platform to deliver teacher training at a distance, to offer workshops for teaching professionals based in the 32 countries in Europe and beyond which are ECML members, and to create a community of practice which will promote reflection on and dissemination of the DOTS bite-sized training materials available via the platform (Stickler et al., 2010a). (See Chapter 8 for a discussion of a regional online community of practice within DOTS.) One of the priorities of the projects, and their driving force, has been the implementation of a series of surveys which aim to evaluate the levels of expertise and the training needs, regarding ICT use in their professional practice, of language teachers and teacher trainers across ECML member countries. As shown in Chapter 10, these surveys also served to inform the DOTS project and the DOTS workspace. The survey initially used in 2008 was subsequently revised in 2011 and in 2013 in order to collect data from a wider profile of language teachers: those working in informal and non-formal settings[1] (2011 survey) and teacher trainers (2013 survey). The survey questions can be accessed at http://moodle.dots.ecml.at.

## The 2008 DOTS survey

26 participants, selected by the respective National Nominating Authorities of 25 member states of the European Centre for Modern Languages (ECML) completed the initial version of the DOTS survey in 2008 (Beaven et al., 2010). Six participants worked in higher education, twelve in secondary schools, two in primary schools and six were teacher trainers. The survey asked for feedback on three main areas:

1. Prior knowledge of and experience with ICT used in the language classroom
2. Objectives in relation to the use of ICT in participants' teaching practice
3. Participants' previous experience of teacher training and their current needs.

### Participants' prior knowledge of and experience with new technologies

All participants had some previous experience with ICT in their teaching, but at various levels and with different tools. The most popular tools used (identified by 84–96% of replies) were presentation tools (PowerPoint, beamers/data projectors), reference tools (electronic dictionaries), or tools to gather information and content (Internet, CDs and DVDs). Approximately 60% also used radio and TV shows via the Internet (YouTube), as well as digital audio recorders, to produce content for their language courses. Podcasts and iPods were used, respectively, by 50% and 19% of participants. Only 34–42% reported use of interactive and collaborative online tools such as chats, forums, blogs, wikis and white boards, and only 23% used videoconferencing or webcam tools. Course management platforms were used by a small majority (57%) of the participants, with 38% of these using Moodle and 19% using the commercial platform WebCT.

The most common reason participants gave for using ICT in their teaching practice was the possibility of bringing more diverse and authentic materials (via Internet, YouTube, CDs, DVDs) into the classroom to practise listening skills and to enhance cultural awareness. In addition, such materials were considered to be especially effective in helping students to work on their own and at their own pace, thus fostering individualized learning, as well as skills related to self-reflection, autonomy and independence. These results echo the findings of the three reports mentioned earlier (Antoniadou et al., 2011; ICT Cluster, 2010; Stevens, 2009) and highlight a wide consensus over the use of ICT to give self-paced access to more authentic language and culture uses.

Online tools such as wikis, blogs, forums, chats and email were highlighted as ways of facilitating collaborative work among students in the same class or students in different classes and in different countries. PowerPoint, often used by participants to present lesson material, was also seen by some as a tool for promoting collaborative skills, when groups of students had to present their own material. Collaboration, task-based learning and problem-based learning were also highlighted as positive aspects of using the Internet for language quest and web-quest activities.

In general, use of the Internet and multimedia technologies was perceived by most participants as a way to increase students' motivation – by helping teachers to design more stimulating lessons and use more authentic learning materials, by having students collaborate to produce material (learning by doing) and by helping students become more reflective about their learning (for example, using blogs as journals). By comparison, Moodle was considered to be most useful as a tool for organising and distributing course content.

Despite the generally positive comments on the use of ICT in the classroom, participants also noted that the constraints around computer networks in some schools (for example, firewalls or other security policies) can restrict access to the Internet and to certain software. Other issues raised were the need to constantly update online materials (noted in the Stevens and Shield (2009) report as an important reason for initial and ongoing teacher training), not just to ensure accuracy but also to maintain student motivation, and the need for more classrooms equipped with computers.

### Participants' objectives in relation to the use of new technologies in their teaching practice

The three most highly rated objectives (identified by 88–96% of the participants) all relate to the ways that ICTs helps students to communicate and use the language they have learned in real contexts, outside and inside the classroom, by offering more diverse and authentic learning resources and tasks. As one participant wrote: 'Give them access to a real audience for their language use'. Giving students up-to-date information (76%) and facilitating collaborative work (84%) were also seen as important objectives, while preparing students for exams was considered the least important objective (although still recognized as important by 73% of participants).

When asked to name benefits other than those listed in the survey, participants noted objectives such as enabling students to become autonomous learners, to develop their critical thinking and computer literacy skills and to have more flexibility in terms of when and where to study. One participant highlighted the financial benefit of accessing free course material, and two others saw ICT as facilitating the process of content selection and delivery for the teacher.

Participants were also asked about the technologies that they were currently not using but would like to use in their teaching practice. It is interesting to note that the participants' answers to this question, when compared with the answers they gave in the first section of the survey, clearly demonstrated that they had passed the stage of using ICT just to present learning material and to develop online exercises or quizzes, for example, and that they now wanted to explore, in decreasing order of importance, Web 2.0 tools to foster learning via social interactions and collaboration, tools to create digital audio documents, and course management platforms to organize and distribute course material. Wikis and blogs were the most frequently mentioned tools participants wanted to be able to use for collaborative and interactive learning tasks involving students from within the class and students from other places in the world. In addition, Audacity, podcasts and YouTube were mentioned by many as having great potential not only for creating digital audio material for online use but also for enhancing oral and listening skills. Lastly, in order to organize all the digital material developed for a course, as well as improve communication with students, several participants saw the need to explore course management platforms such as Moodle.

### Participants' previous experience of teacher training and their current needs

30% of the participants had received no or very little training in using ICT for their teaching practice and were therefore mainly self-taught. By contrast, 53% had attended formal training workshops or online tutorials delivered either by their educational institutions or government agencies. The remaining participants had learned via their peers or while collaborating in projects involving the use of online technologies. All but one of the participants said they would like to receive training on specific tools but they would also want to be given an overview of existing tools in order to increase their knowledge of what is currently available. Several participants mentioned the need to blend technical training on the use of specific tools with pedagogical considerations on how to implement the tool in their teaching practice.

Most participants said they would prefer hands-on training, with concrete examples and activities. As regards their preferred format for training, participants could select several options. Blended training, that is, combining online and face-to-face elements, was the first choice for 80% of participants; face-to-face training with guided, hands-on activities was the second choice for 73%, and a fully online training programme was the third choice for 61%. An equal number stated that, irrespective of the format, they would want to be trained by qualified trainers. The following final request was made by one respondent: 'Only educational technologists please! No computer specialists!'

Despite the small sample of this survey, the results reflect the conclusions outlined in the four reports mentioned in the introduction (Antoniadou et al., 2011; ICT Cluster, 2010; Healey et al., 2008; Stevens, 2009). There is clearly a widespread need for language educators to receive systematic and high quality training on the pedagogical uses and best practices of technology for online teaching.

## DOTS: Teachers' attitudes to and beliefs about language teaching and technology

Given the rapid changes which occur in relation to the design and range of ICT tools available, it was clear that the data obtained in 2008 would need to be regularly updated with the help of new surveys which would reflect the changes both in technologies and in the professional practice of language teachers. As stated by Stevens (2009, p. 72), '[o]ne of the major challenges to professionals is the constant evolution of technology and software applications. For some teachers, this situation can result in a concern which is that they are always "behind the times", especially in comparison to their students, resulting in a subsequent diminution of self-confidence'.

Our concern about the need for updating was confirmed by feedback received from participants at the DOTS training workshops held from 2008–2011 in Graz. As a result, the 2008 version of the survey was revised and extended, and the 2011 and 2013 versions have now been completed by 292 participants from Austria, Belgium, Great Britain, Croatia, Finland, Hungary, Norway and Slovenia. As in 2008, most participants were selected by the ECML National Nominating Authority of their respective country. 53 teachers completed the 2011 survey while 221 teachers and 18 teacher trainers completed the 2013 survey. Answers from these three groups were considered separately. Of the 221 teachers, 111 were from Austria, where several in-service DOTS training workshops were delivered at nine different educational institutions.

The 2011 and 2013 surveys share the same questions on three areas related to the attitudes and beliefs of language professionals on language teaching and technology (see points 1 and 3 below). The second section of the survey was added to the original survey in 2011 in order to be able to contrast teachers' beliefs about language teaching with their attitude to and use of technology:

1. Their professional views on the use of computer technology in the classroom
2. Their professional views on language teaching and learning
3. Their individual professional development as a teacher.

The first two sections of the survey are based respectively on Wozney, Venkatesh and Abrami's Technology Implementation Questionnaire (2006) and on Evdokia Karavas-Doukas' survey regarding teachers' attitudes to the communicative approach (1996).

Participants of this survey were mainly secondary school teachers (69%), with 25% from primary schools and 14% from universities. Some participants from Hungary and Belgium indicated that they had worked in both secondary and university settings.

## Professional views on the use of computer technology in the classroom

93% of participants agreed that ICT was a valuable instructional tool, 89% thought that it helped promote the development of communication skills and 77% claimed it increased academic achievement. However, 90% thought that the use of computer technology in the classroom 'is successful only if there is adequate teacher training in the use of technology for learning', 89% claimed that it was successful 'only if technical staff regularly maintain computers', while only 34% believed that it 'demands too much time because of technical problems'. Participants were very positive about the effects of using computer technology on their students' learning and over 90% agreed that this 'helps accommodate learners' personal learning styles' and 'motivates learners to get more involved in learning activities'.

## Professional views on language teaching and learning

In order to better understand the views of these professionals on the use of ICT in language education, we considered it important to relate the opinions outlined above to their beliefs and attitudes regarding language teaching and learning.

Learners' needs, group work activities and error correction are the three main areas highlighted in this section. 86% of participants agreed that 'tasks and activities should be negotiated and adapted to suit the learners' needs rather than imposed on them', and 91% agreed that group work activities 'are essential in promoting opportunities for cooperative relationships and genuine interaction among learners'. However, 12% of participants were still unsure how effective this kind of learning was 'since it is very difficult for teachers to monitor learners' performance and prevent them from using their mother tongue' and 18% also considered that 'learners do best when taught as a whole class by the teachers. Small group work may occasionally be useful to vary the routine but it can never replace sound formal instruction by a competent teacher'.

As regards attitudes to the teaching of grammar, 86% agreed that 'grammar should only be taught as a means to an end and not as an end in itself' and 80% disagreed with the statement that 'by mastering the rules of grammar, learners become fully capable of communicating with a native speaker'. However, there were a variety of opinions on whether 'direct instruction in the rules and terminology of grammar is essential if we want learners to communicate effectively' and also on whether 'the teacher should correct all errors learners make'.

**Individual professional development as a teacher**

Responses to the statement in the survey that 'I am very optimistic that using ICT will allow me to develop my personal teaching style further' were generally very positive: 'Yes, that's true. I strongly feel that new styles and approaches are needed in my classroom'; 'I agree with this statement as it has already transformed how I teach'. However, one participant also highlighted her 'confidence in traditional teaching methods where the teacher can make the choice according to the target group and the educational situation', and another emphasised the fact that her optimism 'depends on the technical supply and support at her school ... There has to be a stable Internet connection and the necessary equipment ... I hate fighting with bad hardware!'

There was general disagreement with the suggestion that 'using ICT will make me insecure in teaching', though participants agreed on the need for adequate preparation, training and support in order to combat possible insecurity. The great majority of participants also disagreed with the statement 'I believe that I will have to change my personal teaching style when I use ICT'. Typical responses were: 'I will never change my personal teaching style. It is more about including ICT in what I already do and like'; 'I believe ICT will supplement and eventually be built into my personal teaching style' and 'using ICT will just make my teaching style richer and more varied'.

Participants' responses to the final statement in this section – 'I believe that my students will know more about ICT than I do (and be able to help me with it)' – were extremely positive and very detailed, as the following examples show:

- 'My experience is that I often know more than the students when it comes to tools, relevant software (MS Excel e.g.) and for example how to efficiently use syntax rules to get precise search results in search engines on the Internet. Students often know more about music, mp3, video etc. and related software and more'.
- 'Students today have a lot of knowledge about ICT, and I will see this as a huge advantage! If students feel that they can actively take more part in their learning – also when it comes to the use of ICT, I am sure they will see their time in the classroom as even more worthwhile'.
- 'My students probably have better general ICT skills than me, yet I believe that I know a lot more than they do when it comes to evaluating sources on the net and finding better ICT resources. I often receive help from my students when it comes to technical problems, and they seem happy to be able to provide assistance'.

## The DOTS surveys: 2008, 2011, 2013

The three DOTS surveys aimed to understand language teachers' awareness of ICT tools and training needs, and the ways that language professionals perceive and use technology in their teaching and training practice. They show that the integration of technology in language teaching, although desired by a growing number, still requires considerable professional development and training.

As mentioned above, there was a large contingent of Austrian teachers who were offered the DOTS training workshops as part of their in-service training (111 of whom completed the survey), and it is interesting to compare them with the 110 teachers and teacher trainers from other countries. 51% of the 110 non-Austrian teachers who completed the 2013 survey considered themselves to be either novice or advanced beginners in the use of ICT, in contrast to the 78% of teacher trainers who said that they use technology all the time or often in their practice. It is interesting, and perhaps not surprising, to note that those teachers with the least experience of using ICT (only 11% of the 111 Austrian teachers who completed the survey said that they actually used ICT tools in their teaching practice) see fewer advantages in using technology. If we compare the results of the Austrian participants with the results of the other teachers and with the teacher trainers (who have most experience with ICT tools), we see that only 62% of the Austrian group, compared with 77% of the other teachers and 99% of the teacher trainers, believe 'that the use of computer technology in the classroom increases academic achievement'. Similarly, only 77% of the Austrian participants, compared to 93% of the other teachers and 98% of the teacher trainers, think that 'technology helps accommodate learners' personal learning styles'. Furthermore, 74% of the Austrian group think that 'tasks and activities should be negotiated and adapted to suit the learners' needs rather than imposed on them', compared with 88% of the rest of the teachers and 98% of the teacher trainers.

It should be noted, however, that the 111 Austrian teachers completed the surveys while attending in-service training seminars delivered by the DOTS team at the teachers' educational institutions throughout the country. For most participants, this training formed part of their obligatory continuing professional development. As a result, their motivation, experience and expectations were slightly different from those teachers and teacher trainers who chose to travel to a central location in their country and participate in a two-day DOTS training workshop specifically aimed at ICT in language teaching.

Although further analysis is required, the results outlined above seem to indicate that attitudes to the usefulness of technology in language learning are closely related to teachers' actual experience of using ICT tools. Incorporating online ICT elements into any teacher training programme, in order to offer participants practical, hands-on experience from a learner's perspective, would therefore seem a very positive step to take. (See Chapter 10 for details of how this has been done by the DOTS project team.)

## ICT user profiles

At the same time as the data obtained from the DOTS surveys served to evaluate the levels of expertise in the use of ICT and the related training needs of language teachers throughout Europe, qualitative data was being collected by the DOTS project team in order to generate more in-depth typical 'ICT user profiles' of language teachers. Seven profiles have been generated from the survey data and from qualitative data on teachers' self-perception and training needs, collected during the workshops delivered by the DOTS team in different European countries since 2008 (Emke & Stickler, 2015). This qualitative data has included comments gathered during the workshops concerning participants' 'perceived strengths as teachers and their most pressing needs' (Emke & Stickler, 2015). In addition, data was elicited with the help of a narrative framework approach (Barkhuizen & Wette, 2008) where participants were asked to write about the use of ICT in their own teaching.

Table 2.1 shows the ICT user profiles, which cover a range of expertise from the most sceptical and unconfident to the most confident, skilled ICT user and language education expert.

These teacher profiles, in terms of ICT use, have been employed in the DOTS workshops as the basis for reflection on participants' attitudes towards using ICT in their own teaching practice. The results from the

*Table 2.1*   Teacher profiles

| Aisha | Bogdan | Carlotta | Dennis | Elisabeth | Fatima | George |
|---|---|---|---|---|---|---|
| Likes computers but only for private use. | Loves teaching but is not confident enough to use computers in class. | Is sceptical about computers in language teaching. | Expert in everything – ICT, language teaching, etc. | Sticks to what the rules and the syllabus say, does what she is told. | Feels she does not have enough time but would like to try out ICT. | Is doing much but would do more if he had the overview. |

workshops obviously vary depending on participants' backgrounds, but we have found that Fatima, Dennis and Bogdan are the teacher profiles with whom participants identify most frequently (see Figure 2.1).

However, at each DOTS workshop, we have encountered teachers at both ends of the spectrum. There are a number of pioneers like Dennis, who are enthusiasts and are expert at implementing innovative teaching approaches and new technologies in their professional practice. At the same time, there are many other teachers who lack both the necessary time to learn about ICT tools and also the self-confidence to actually use the technology in their classes. In addition, these teachers are not always convinced that the use of technology necessarily improves the quality of language learning.

The fact that there are a relatively high number of teachers who are either not confident enough to use ICT or who have a negative attitude towards ICT seems to contradict some of the feedback received via the 2011 DOTS survey. Here, the great majority (92%) of participants said that they considered ICT to be a valuable instructional tool in language teaching. At the same time 33% confirmed that the use of ICT in the classroom 'demands too much time' and participants who commented

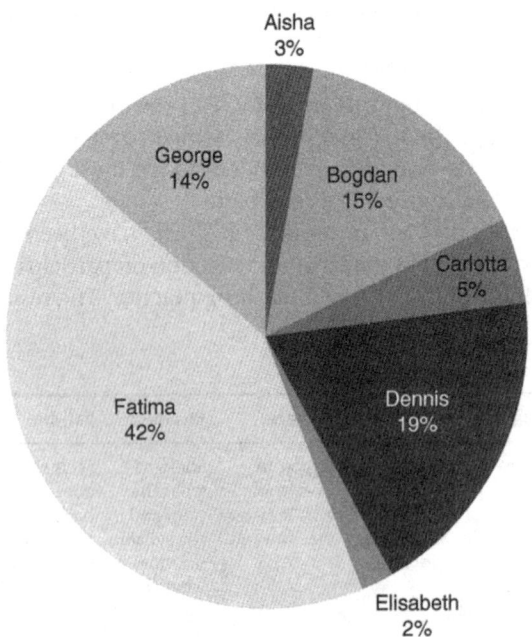

*Figure 2.1*   Most frequent profiles

on the statement 'I fear that using ICT will make me insecure in teaching' expressed their disagreement with this statement. This suggests that there is some discrepancy between the importance participants give to issues involving the overall 'added value' of integrating ICT into language courses and the time and level of confidence required by teachers, both for training in the use of tools and for preparing accompanying materials to use with students. Of course, views expressed via a survey and those which emerge during a two-day training workshop, as a result of reflection and discussion with colleagues on ICT user profiles, may not always coincide. We would recommend that teachers' views on these issues should always be highlighted in any future surveys or training programmes in the use of ICT in language teaching.

## Conclusion

The main objective of the 2008 DOTS survey was diagnostic. The project team wanted to understand which ICT tools participants were using at that time, their objectives in using these and their needs as regards training and experience with further tools. The 2011 and 2013 surveys concentrated more on reflecting the changes in technologies available, and on highlighting the ways this has affected language teachers' professional practice. All the data collected has been used to inform the overall design of the DOTS projects, the training materials available and the content of the training workshops, and it has helped the DOTS team to ensure that these are all truly relevant to participants' needs.

The three DOTS surveys and the qualitative data collected with participants in more than 20 DOTS workshops across Europe have all highlighted similar areas for reflection regarding the potential and the challenges of using ICT in language teaching. As research has shown, for students the use of such tools is seen as a motivating factor, providing access to authentic materials, facilitating both autonomous and collaborative learning and accommodating different learning styles (see Dahlstrom et al., 2013). As regards the teacher, the surveys highlight, above all, the need for high quality, appropriate and ongoing forms of training (online, blended and/or face-to-face), not simply to guarantee technical competence in using new tools but also to ensure that pedagogical considerations as to how and why ICT can enhance language learning are taken into account. Training of this type is seen as crucial in helping to overcome many teachers' resistance to using technology in their teaching and in developing confidence. Such training is also essential for pre-service teachers in order for them to experience the benefits and added value that ICT can bring to language education and enable them to deal with the challenges involved. The results of this research confirm the findings of the four reports mentioned in the introduction to this chapter, and show that training needs for teachers continue to be a priority today. We trust that this overview of European language teachers' experiences, expectations and training needs for ICT will be useful for language educators working in different settings, and that it will help to confirm or challenge their own beliefs and attitudes on using ICT in their professional practice.

## Reflective task

Read the expanded ICT user profiles below and select the one that most closely matches your attitude to using ICT tools with your students. You may discover that none fits your profile. If so, create a new profile which defines your position more accurately.

Note down the following:

- What do you need in order to be able to use ICT (more) successfully in your work? For example: support, time, training.
- What is your greatest strength as a teacher or teacher trainer? For example: being a good communicator; designing effective training materials.

Reflect on what you have written and decide on one action which would lead to and support a change in your professional practice.

### ICT user profiles

*Aisha*

'I love computers. I spend a lot of time on the Internet and often chat with my friends in the US. I shop online and download the latest films. In my language courses I don't like using the computer, because the students aren't supposed to chat online in class. And how am I supposed to play "shopping"? Using the Internet for this is far too dangerous.'

*Bogdan*

'I have taught languages for many years and teaching is a lot of fun. I am really good at it. I only use computers if I have to. My children are much better at it and I can ask them when I need help. But I am not going to make a fool of myself in front of my class! I would never use anything that I haven't mastered completely. That's much too risky in my classes.'

*Carlotta*

'I have taught languages for many years and it's important for me that my students learn the language properly. Once they have mastered the subjunctive for example, we celebrate together, and I am really proud of them. Using computers wouldn't provide any additional benefit.'

*Dennis*

'I have taught languages for many years. I enjoy teaching a lot and I am quite successful. I am also good at using the computer and using new technologies. When I have the time I like helping my colleagues to use digital media in their lessons.'

*Elisabeth*

'The curriculum is planned very carefully and I have to stick to it. If I am told to use computers, I will do so. If I am supposed to do more group work in class, there needs to be more time allocated for this in the curriculum. Otherwise it won't work.'

*Fatima*

'That all sounds really exciting. I would love to create a wiki or a webquest or something like that. But I just haven't got the time for the necessary preparations. We will have started on a completely new topic before I have found enough good material to work on a wiki or webquest.'

*George*

'Actually, I'm using quite a bit already but I'm just not sure of what I'm doing. I certainly don't feel like an expert. I would love to use more diverse tools if anyone had a brilliant idea and could show me exactly what to do. There are just too many different options, I don't have the overview.'

## Notes

1. Non-formal and informal learning settings are defined by the European Commission as follows:
   1) Non-formal learning: Learning that happens outside the formal school/vocational/university system, via planned activities (e.g. with goals and timelines) involving some form of instruction.
   2) Informal learning: Learning that is not organized or structured in terms of goals, time or instruction. This covers skills acquired (sometimes unintentionally) through life and work experience.
   (http://ec.europa.eu/education/lifelong-learning-policy/informal_en_htm).

# 3

# Part-Time and Freelance Language Teachers and their ICT Training Needs

*Ursula Stickler and Martina Emke*

## Introduction

The focus in this chapter is on part-time and freelance teachers of languages. It links to the previous one dealing with online training needs of European language teachers but whereas Chapter 2 explores mainly quantitative data collected from full-time teachers across Europe, this chapter is based on a small sample of qualitative data, collected from selected part-time teachers of languages, representing different cultures and different teaching contexts. In our analysis of these 'vignettes' of language teachers we found similarities and common themes that are typical for the situation of teachers who are not solely associated with one educational institution.

Part-time and freelance language teachers in Europe work in different employment situations: from casually employed teachers, contracted only to deliver a particular course for one semester or term, to fractionally employed 'part-timers', who have the same rights and duties as full-time staff (albeit with a reduced workload). The terminology used to describe part-time language teachers is similarly varied. For the purposes of this chapter we use 'part-time' interchangeably with 'freelance' language teacher.

It is difficult to find exact figures for part-time language teachers in European countries as their numbers are hidden in employment statistics, and often they might not even be recognized as part of the teaching force. Sometimes they are identified as self-employed, independent professionals, or support teachers. From our experience and knowledge of the sector and the little official information that can be found we can assume that the numbers are considerable. The *Volkshochschule* (VHS) in Germany, which is one of the largest adult education providers, and within this market the institution with the highest percentage of language courses in its curriculum (WSF – Wirtschafts- und Sozialforschung, 2005), employs approximately 187,000 part-time teachers and only 3,247 full-time teaching staff (i.e. fewer than 2%). Of the part-time teachers only 0.8% are fully qualified teachers (Huntemann & Reichart, 2013), and there are 'no formal regulations regarding the qualifications of staff in adult education institutions in Germany' (Dausien & Schwendowius, 2009, p. 190). In all German continuing education institutions more than 650,000 people in total are employed on a part-time or casual basis. For the Austrian continuing education sector, numbers are available for the year 2012: more than 92,000 persons were employed, 51,402 of whom had teaching or teaching-related posts. Only 4% of these were full-time employees, the rest were part-time employed (Vater & Zwielehner, 2013). These numbers are across all subject areas, not specific to languages, but they can provide a backdrop to our understanding of the area under investigation.

Despite the important role freelance and part-time language teachers play, particularly in adult and post-compulsory education, their situation is under-researched. There is a need for more information in order to better understand but also to better support the ongoing professional development of these teachers. Large-scale quantitative studies have investigated the situation of teachers in adult education (Buiskool et al., 2009; Research voor Beleid & PLATO, 2008), a sector which is characterized by a high number of part-time staff. Small-scale qualitative studies have explored the professional development of teachers in a similar context (Maier-Gutheil & Hof, 2011). However, none of these studies is particularly concerned with language teaching, a gap that we attempt to fill with this chapter. It presents an exploratory study of part-time language teachers' needs to learn more about the use of Information and Communication Technology (ICT) in teaching and learning, and their understanding of their own position and identity with regards to evolving ICT use and required professional development.

This chapter is informed by our own experience. Both authors have worked as part-time language teachers. Martina worked as a part-time teacher of English at the VHS, at a vocational college, and in companies in Germany. Ursula was a fractionally employed German teacher at various higher and further education institutions in the UK, a language assistant at a new university, and has worked for commercial language schools. Working for up to five employers at the same time, we both have experienced the pressure from different institutions on the part-time teacher, and the expectations regarding continuing professional development (CPD) and developing professional skills.

## Background

Part-time and freelance language teachers' work situation strongly influences the availability of continuing professional development (CPD) courses for them. Generally, teachers in Europe are expected to participate in CPD activities as part of their professional duties (European Commission/EACEA/Eurydice, 2013). Whereas some educational organizations offer a range of courses for professional development to full-time, part-time, and freelance staff, other organizations do not consider the CPD of freelancers a priority. At the same time, the teachers' self-perception influences their attendance (or non-attendance) at training events.

As a background to our own research, we first present findings from other studies that specifically deal with ICT, CPD and teacher identity.

### ICT in language teaching and forms of CPD

That language teachers need a working knowledge of ICT has become evident (see, for example, the introductory Chapter 1 and Chapter 2) and has generally been acknowledged over recent years (Kern, 2006; Motteram, 2013). Computers, like books before them, have become 'normalised' (Bax, 2003, 2011), and the challenge that the 'information society' poses specifically to teacher training has been well documented since the turn of the century (Buchberger et al., 2000). Students now have regular access to a wide variety of tools (Steel & Levy, 2013) although the availability of a certain type of technology might still be limited in some countries and some educational settings.

ICT plays an important role not only in the classroom, where part-time language teachers face the need to acquire the necessary skills to use technology to a similar degree as full-time professionals, but also in the CPD of teachers, where it can be an alternative to face-to-face training. Some teacher educators believe that the use of computer-mediated communication (CMC) can qualitatively change teacher training (e.g. Johnson, 2006) by generating more engagement and equity amongst participants.

The format of CPD can influence how engaged the trainees become. The teacher educator Aileen Kennedy suggests that the more teachers are engaged in the selection and decision making process of their CPD, the higher the level of actual change or transformation is expected to be. She proposes nine different models of CPD for teachers (Kennedy, 2005, p. 3); amongst them a traditional training model, communities of practice, action research and a transformative model.

Action research for language teacher training (see Chapter 9 of this volume) demands high engagement from the teachers and is therefore a highly valuable method (Cabaroglu, 2014). Together with mentoring, coaching, peer observation and reflective activities, it has been recommended as CPD format for experienced part-time teachers in adult education (Rodríguez & McKay, 2010).

Although informal, experience-based learning is clearly important in CPD for part-time teachers, most CPD formats emphasize the formally recognized side of development. Lindsay (2013) offers an alternative model, describing different aspects of CPD: formal learning, informal learning and – even less recognized – personal learning. The recognition of non-formal, less strictly organized formats of CPD for teachers, already predicted in 2000 by the report of the Thematic Working Group on teacher education in Europe (Buchberger et al., 2000) will be of great interest to part-time language professionals. When emphasis is shifted from the cognitive side of CPD to the interpersonal and intrapersonal dimensions, agency and identity become relevant areas for CPD (Lindsay, 2013).

## Identity of freelance teachers

In his extensive meta-study on language teachers' cognition, Borg (2003) found that prior language learning experience and teacher training were shown to have an influence on what teachers believe, what they know, and how they make decisions about what to do in their classrooms. This area of research, also known as 'teacher beliefs', links closely to identity and the way teachers see themselves. Although Borg does not distinguish between full-time and part-time teachers, some of his conclusions are of particular relevance to our group, for example, the influence of contextual factors. As freelance and part-time teachers are potentially exposed to a greater number of institutions, with less power to shape the environment in which they work, they are more constrained by contextual factors. Borg states that '[g]reater understanding of the contextual factors – e.g., institutional, social, instructional and physical – which shape what language teachers do are central to deeper insights into relationships between cognition and practice' (Borg, 2003, p. 106). Another relevant factor, specifically for those freelance teachers who base their expertise on their native speaker competence rather than on pedagogic training or experience as language teachers, is the declarative knowledge of the language or language awareness, and how this influences teaching.

If it is more than just a job, a role the teacher performs in the classroom, something that can be left behind as soon as her or his teaching duties are completed, teaching can be a form of identity – a professional identity (Jephcote & Salisbury, 2009) that has a deeper impact on life and the self. Identity touches the understanding a person has about their own values, beliefs, and the core of their existence (MacLure, 1993), going beyond the cognitive dimension of teaching described by Borg (2003). Identity is never a fixed or given state but is constructed 'in a form of argument rather than description' (MacLure, 1993, n.p.); it is a powerful instrument for understanding the situation of teachers. The identity of language teachers is additionally refracted through their status as native or non-native speakers of the language(s) they teach (L2) and as cultural experts by virtue of longer sojourns in the L2 country or countries or by having grown up there.

What teachers believe works in teaching, their pedagogic tenets, will influence not only the range and frequency of CPD activities they choose (Scheerens, 2010) but also their attitude to the integration of technology (Ertmer et al., 2012; Kopcha, 2012). Ertmer and colleagues (2012) found amongst a group of teachers who were highly valued for their implementation of technology that they use it in one of three distinct ways: to help students learn content and skills, to complement or enrich the curriculum, or to transform their own teaching.

This aspect of teachers' choice links all three of our areas of investigation: CPD, ICT use and teachers' beliefs. When a teacher feels that using up-to-date communication forms a necessary part of his or her teaching, they will make every effort to integrate ICT into their teaching in a meaningful way. By directing the focus of our small exploratory study to the aspects of CPD, teacher identity and ICT training needs for part-time and freelance language teachers, we hope to prompt further investigations in this important but as yet under-researched field.

## Method

In our own working lives and in the DOTS (Developing Online Teaching Skills) workshops which we held across Europe (see Chapter 10) we have met many language professionals and learned about their work and training situations. In this chapter we attempt to systematize and structure this knowledge, supported by additional data collected purposefully where our understanding was lacking. This is in keeping with the sociocultural perspective of this book (see Chapters 1 and 9) and the action research approach taken by some language teachers.

After finding out generally about teachers' needs (see previous chapter), and teachers' attitudes towards ICT (Emke & Stickler, 2015) we felt that we needed to learn more about how part-time teachers describe themselves in a more detailed and individualized fashion. In line with Breuer's (2003) reflexive approach, which sees the person of the researcher and his or her biography as central to the design of the research, we started with interviewing each other to clarify ideas and our own position in relation to the topic. This process led to our focussing the research questions on part-time language teachers' training to use ICT in their teaching. We decided that only a qualitative research design interlinking a number of different data collection tools could do justice to this complex topic with strong individual aspects.

A narrative frame questionnaire (Barkhuizen & Wette, 2008) was sent to ten part-time language teachers from seven different countries (for an overview see Table A3.1 in the Appendix) whom we know either personally or through the DOTS project. Narrative frames attempt to solicit information around particular themes using the format of 'stories' (Barkhuizen et al., 2013) and giving respondents enough space to express themselves in their own way while getting them to focus on particular aspects (Shelley et al., 2013). Narrative frame questionnaires sent by email are a low-threshold approach to data collection, making it easier and quicker for respondents to provide their answers while giving them the time and space to write their stories at their own convenience. Where we lacked information, we requested additional data via email. In addition, three semi-structured interviews were conducted to elicit in-depth information of teacher identities.

Our data analysis followed a grounded theory approach (Glaser & Strauss, 2008 (1967)), as adapted by Charmaz (2000) and Breuer (2003). Rather than relying on pre-formed ideas, we started from the data and looked for emerging categories and themes, reflected in our own biographical interview contributions. We used thematic analysis (Boyatzis, 1998) informed by our understanding of the topic through our own life histories, thus taking a reflexive approach (Mruck & Mey, 2007). In discussions between ourselves and joint readings we formed initial ideas and identified themes from the data, using constant comparative analysis (Charmaz, 2000). Some recurring themes appeared in response to different questions, in different parts of the data. Findings and interpretations were continually checked and re-checked not only against our own biographical self-reflection but also against what our research participants had said. The second stage of analysis was already influenced by our reading and research in related areas such as CPD or CALL (Computer Assisted Language Learning). Themes were confirmed but also expanded, and a pattern emerged that led to our deeper understanding of the subject.

Findings from the data, wherever possible retaining the teachers' own voice, will be presented in the next section; further analysis and our categories and interpretation will follow.

## Findings

Our data show that CPD is important for freelance language teachers for a variety of reasons: they want to keep up to date with the latest developments in the target language, the teaching field and in technology; and they want or need to ensure that they continue to satisfy the demands of the institutions that (potentially) employ them and the needs of their students in an effective way. Heather,[1] a qualified English language teacher working in Spain, very bluntly states the mandatory aspect of CPD for freelance language teachers: 'I need to stay current to get contracts', a view that is shared by Jagda, who teaches English in Croatia. She writes that she is required to 'meet formal conditions for continuing to work in higher education'. Greta, who works as a teacher of English and German in Hungary, states that CPD is important for her because 'language usage and technological devices keep changing'. This view is echoed by several participants. A second reason for the importance of CPD results from the perceived need to 'provide better and possibly more effective teaching' (Emma) to students and 'because students, especially teenagers live in the world of modern technology which is a tricky territory' (Lucy).

Freelance language teachers in our study are interested in CPD courses which address specific needs related to their teaching in a timely fashion. However, the responses indicate that courses offered to them seldom meet their needs. Lucy, an experienced English language teacher who works in Poland, explicitly states that the courses are not 'down to earth – meaning: far from my everyday teaching reality and the needs of my students'. This complaint is supported by other respondents who claim that the courses are 'too basic or focus on technology (whiteboard)' (Greta) or are 'focussed on encouraging me to use a particular course book' (Judith). Consequently, freelance language teachers have to look for suitable training themselves rather than being offered the opportunity, an important distinction made by Heather. The selection of CPD courses is not always successful as 'specific training can be difficult to locate and/or not provided in a suitable timeframe' (Carlton).

In the course of our data analysis, two recurring themes emerged: time and money. The following statement exemplifies the first, addressing a dilemma that many freelance language teachers face with regard to CPD courses: 'I cannot always attend 'cause I am too busy with my students and I don't even have any time for myself (I mean even for sleeping)' (Yasenya). Like Yasenya, a Turkish teacher of English who teaches at two organizations, many part-time teachers work for different institutions, and their timetables may not include specific time-slots for training. Working at multiple institutions increases travel time not only to the teaching venues but also to the institution where the training is offered, and some training courses 'do not allow flexible learning' (Emma). Another participant confirms this impeding factor by claiming that she 'cannot always attend because face-to-face training sessions are a two-hour journey away' (Judith), and Jagda supports this point by stating that in her hometown 'there are not enough workshops and conferences (at least to my knowledge) for ESP teachers'.

A second recurring theme centres on the cost of CPD. Several participants support Lucy's claim that the courses may be 'too expensive' and Greta emphasizes the need for financial support by stating that it is 'almost impossible [...] to get a scholarship to travel to English or German speaking countries' to attend a CPD course abroad. A further impeding factor is the lack of 'the right equipment' (Lucy).

Considering the findings above, it is unsurprising that informal means of CPD are very important for freelance language teachers. Heather mentions that she can get non-formal CPD through her work as an English Language Teaching author and 'by peer observation + discussions, picking the brains of colleagues who have more specialist knowledge than me, reading articles + blogs online'. Another form of CPD mentioned by Greta is 'using the library of my language school, by using internet websites (e.g. Oxford University Press teacher development website, teaching resources websites). I keep checking language book stores to find new course books, materials and I also buy some if I feel I can use them'.

The attitude of freelance language teachers towards CPD is inextricably linked with their self-perception as language teachers. Mehmet from Turkey, a qualified teacher of English, states that teaching 'is more about experience than skills, therefore sharing experiences and ideas helps a lot in developing teaching skills'. Since freelance language teachers often suffer from a perceived 'lack of a formal framework or setting which normally provides some form of professional input' (Heather), a regular exchange with other language professionals becomes a 'great source of inspiration' (Greta) and it is seen as vital to 'learn from them or see some teaching problems in a different light' (Lucy).

Some teachers see CPD as important for reflecting on professionalism and self-development. Judith, another English language teacher working in Spain, states 'Training sessions and workshops also remind me that I AM a professional!', while Mehmet claims that CPD courses prevent him from becoming 'a regular boring teacher'. This view is supported by Greta's statement that professional development 'also means that one can get new ideas, stay open and creative, use new resources, otherwise teaching can become monotonous and just routine'. For Carlton from the UK and Hawk from Turkey, teaching effectively is an important aspect of their role and their view of themselves as teachers. They stress their need for CPD courses that offer 'concrete solutions' (Hawk) to teaching problems encountered and help in 'relating tools/ functions available to appropriate and sound learner-centred teaching and learning' (Carlton).

The use of computers in teaching and for CPD is closely connected to the individual work situation. Whereas some freelance language teachers use computers for and in their teaching regularly, as is the case when teaching online courses (five respondents out of 12), most of the teachers we contacted work in face-to-face (seven) or blended learning environments (five), with some using two or all of these formats for different courses. This is not unusual for the sector. Therefore the perceived ICT training needs cover a range of issues, from technical assistance for 'connecting all the devices for a presentation, learning how to use some software and formatting the text' (Lucy) to practical teaching ideas on 'how to use some technologies which I do not use in teaching, e.g. wikis, vlogs,[2] Survey Monkeys and podcasts' (Jagda). Hawk is predominantly interested in courses that support him in his 'effective way in teaching languages'. The need for an ICT training course that focuses on pedagogy is mentioned by Carlton, an English language teacher with a PhD in an unrelated subject and a long career as an independent bookseller who came to English teaching relatively late in life. His wish is to be offered courses that 'address specific issues of applying language learning pedagogy to online environments'.

## Discussion

In the big picture of language teaching, the part-time language teacher is almost invisible: marginalized in the profession, under-researched in studies, and under-represented in the literature. Even our own first approach to the topic was influenced by a deficit model: what are these teachers' ICT needs, or in other words: what skills do they lack?

The answers to our open enquiry revealed a different and much more complex picture: the tensions between CPD and ICT needs and requirements on the one hand and the teachers' own professional context and identity on the other.

## Part-time teachers' use of ICT and CPD provision

The language teaching contexts in our sample range from fully online courses delivered synchronously or asynchronously (Heather, Judith), to blended models where teachers are expected to participate in online discussion forums or video conferences as well as being present in physical classrooms (Emma, Carlton), to courses taught entirely face-to-face (Greta, Jagda) with the occasional use of a computer room (Lucy) or a computer activity (Lydia, Maria). These teaching contexts are designed often without direct influence from the teachers, although freelance teachers increasingly take more control of their teaching contexts, often choosing the option of becoming self-employed, independent online teachers (Kozar, 2012).

The role ICT plays in language teachers' work also depends on their attitude towards technology. Ertmer and colleagues, for example, asked teachers 'to describe the biggest enablers to their technology integration practices. Five teachers [in Ertmer's study] mentioned internal factors (their own attitudes and beliefs or knowledge and skills) as the strongest contributing factor' (Ertmer et al., 2012, p. 429). In our study, for example, Hawk says: 'I use computers in my teaching for [...] reaching my objectives in a very short time. Using visual and audial facilities (like videos, charts, songs, presentations etc.) is an effective way in teaching languages especially for the young learners'. This exemplifies his teaching strategy of using ICT for efficiency gain. Regardless of whether technology really makes for more effective language teaching or not (Felix, 2005; Golonka et al., 2014), Hawk's beliefs and attitudes lead him towards ICT integration.

In order to be able to use ICT proficiently in teaching, solid training is required (Blurton, 1999). This requirement for ICT-focused CPD is even more relevant today than in the last century. However, there are limiting factors which influence the availability and feasibility of ICT training for freelance or part-time language teachers. Specific characteristics of CPD to be considered in our context are integration, recognition and obligation.

### *Integration of CPD provision into the working schedule*

CPD for ICT is varied and depends on the employer and the employment situation: fully integrated training days, preparation days or teacher days at the beginning of a teaching term are one option. These integrated sessions can be problematic for part-timers, as they might have to participate fully in the length of the training, despite only working part of the time at the institution. On the other hand, relying on part-timers themselves to find and organize their own ICT training also puts more strain on the teacher than is the case in full-time employment where staff development is an integral and integrated part of the employment (Caena, 2011) and any new ICT tool which teachers are expected to be using will be introduced and supported (as Heather mentions). In between these two extremes in terms of integration of CPD, part-timers can find a range of options from institutionally organized but flexible training to offline or asynchronous training that can be flexibly fitted into the timetable of teachers.

CPD is increasingly offered for free, online, by supportive peers (see Chapters 6, 7 and 8). In our own professional development, we have participated in 'Becoming a Webhead' (Almeida d'Eça & Gonzáles, 2006) and the Electronic Village online (Hanson-Smith & Bauer-Ramazani, 2004; Hubbard, 2008), and contributed to DOTS workshops and the DOTS toolkit (Beaven et al., 2010; Stickler et al., 2010).

*Recognition of CPD or training*

Not all formats of CPD are equally recognized (Lindsay, 2013) by employers and official educational institutions. Our respondents list various sources of training, some of them quite informal, for example, reading blogs online. Many of these CPD formats are mentioned in the literature as influential and suitable forms of training (Rodríguez & McKay, 2010; Stickler et al., 2010b). It is clear that the degree to which teachers' needs are met in no way depends on the formality or informality of the source of advice or training. A helpful peer or work colleague often provides the necessary 'just-in-time' support ideal for ICT integration (Carlton). This can engender a change in attitude towards ICT in language teaching, sometimes more effectively than a formal, certified training course. This finding matches our experience throughout the DOTS workshops (see Chapter 10). However, where formal recognition is a requirement for CPD this informal peer-support might not be sufficient.

*Obligation or requirement for training*

Some participants mention the full and up-to-date training records their institutions require (Heather, Jagda). Sometimes part-timers are expected to show the same level of CPD and commitment as full-time employees. Institutional requirements may focus on specific outcomes such as a certificate, or be more process-oriented, requiring only that an employee does undertake some CPD.

The final aspect of obligation under scrutiny here links most closely to identity: a sense of professional pride can act as strong internal motivator for teachers, as a feeling of obligation, not to let their profession down, not to become 'a regular boring teacher' (Mehmet), someone who should not be a teacher any longer. As Judith puts it: 'if you stop learning, you should probably also stop teaching!'

## Professional identity

One might assume that professional identity is defined by professional qualifications and certification. However, for part-time or freelance language teachers who often enter adult education organizations from different professions (Research voor Beleid & PLATO, 2008), professional identity can be based on their experience and biography (Maier-Gutheil & Hof, 2011). Not all have a recognized teaching qualification, although in our small sample, only one of the 12 teachers had no teaching qualification. A special case is the native speaker teacher who has a slightly different teaching identity to non-native speakers (Borg, 2003). The idea of native vs. non-native teachers has been problematized in the past 15 years (Cook, 1999, 2013; Norton, 1997; Selvi, 2011), particularly from the standpoint of the hegemony of a perceived 'native standard' of English. Less attention has been paid to the professional identity of the native speaker who finds himself or herself as a teacher of their language but without the pedagogic qualification. This aspect requires further research.

Even when starting a teaching career relatively late in life (Buiskool et al., 2009), language teachers (like Carlton) – similar to other part-time teaching professionals (Jephcote & Salisbury, 2009) – often strive for professional recognition. This can be expressed through certificates, diplomas or institutionally provided accreditation. For the VHS in Germany, for example, the 'Basisqualifikation Lehren' (Harmeier, 2009) is a basic, subject-specific teaching certificate. Some of our respondents base their teaching on a national qualified teacher status for secondary schools (e.g. Greta, Maria and Hawk) although they no longer teach in this sector.

Professional identity, particularly with reference to CPD and acquiring the new skills necessary for ICT integration, also relies on individual motivation. A strong impetus for being, becoming or remaining a good teacher defines the professional pride of some – though not all – part-timers. In our respondents, motivation often seems to come from positive feedback from learners (Greta, Lucy) and the impression that one's own teaching supports learners in their learning processes (Emma). Professional identity can be shaped by sharing professional knowledge and expertise in the classroom and with colleagues (Greta, Maria). As Greta says: 'Meeting interesting, creative personalities is also a great source of inspiration'. This finding is also confirmed in wider research (Harmeier, 2009; Rosenbladt & Thebis, 2004).

In our sample we found different stories of how someone came to be a freelance or part-time language teacher. Some of these are clearly distinct trajectories. Some teachers, for example, were originally full-time and/or fully qualified language teachers (Greta, Jagda), but for personal, family or other reasons 'shifted out' of the profession and either re-entered as part-timers or never really re-entered formal employment in the profession and are still trying to find their niche in language training/teaching. This we identified as a 'shifted professional identity'.

Another identity not yet found in the literature is the refracted or 'fractured professional identity': teachers who did not start off as language teachers but came from different, maybe related professions (Carlton, Lucy). These teachers may have difficulties identifying themselves as language teachers in the classical sense, and there might be some tensions, some desire to gain additional training and a full 'professional identity'. The impression they give to the outside is different from their self-image.

As some of the research participants show, 'full professional identity' as a language teacher (e.g. Emma, Hawk) where the teacher works part-time but fully identifies as a language teacher, regardless of training or accreditation, can be achieved over time, even starting from a 'fractured' (Ursula, Martina) or shifted professional identity.

That much of the CPD undertaken by part-time language teachers is not fully recognized is in part due to the limited perception of CPD by institutions. Based on Lindsay's model (Lindsay, 2013), we discovered that only those CPD activities are fully recognized which are organized, often certified courses focussing on the cognitive side of professional development rather than on interpersonal or intrapersonal development. These two areas tend not to be recognized either by the institutions or by peers (Heather, Greta), and the associated activities are often linked to informal learning.

Interpersonal aspects of development can take place face-to-face or in online communities of practice (CoPs) (Martina, Lucy, Greta). Recently, some CoPs have been gaining informal recognition through peer badges or self-certification, moving them slightly closer to non-formal or even formal learning and training formats. Even more difficult to formalize are intrapersonal development activities (Judith, Greta), where the teacher who is undergoing the learning is sometimes the only person realising that specific, targeted development activities are taking place. However, these are the activities with the potential to transform a teacher's skills, style, beliefs and even her or his professional identity, as Mehmet mentions. Sharing with other professionals becomes an important means to establish or confirm professional identity, as Hawk does, thanking us for the opportunity to express his 'thoughts about training, using computers and difficulties on training effectively'.

Finally, after investigating the areas of part-time teachers' use of ICT and CPD provision and professional identity separately, the findings of our research suggest that the connections and tensions between these areas determine the ICT training needs for freelance or part-time language teachers. There seems to be a dynamic balance between the various aspects that requires further in-depth research.

## Conclusions

We have shown that the rapidly evolving field of ICT and its integration into part-time language teaching needs more investigation. Working with part-time teachers has shown us how much they appreciate the opportunity and (institutional) support to reflect upon and to further develop their professional identity. This, in turn, influences their motivation to participate in CPD and the value they place on it. Our study also revealed some of the difficulties that part-time and freelance language teachers encounter: their own and their institutions' expectations of continuous training clash with their relative lack of opportunities for fully paid and integrated CPD. They often have to juggle conflicting demands from different institutions, be those logistical, in terms of time and money, or on a more fundamental level of the pedagogy they are expected to employ.

Another area of conflict exists between forms of CPD currently offered and recognized by institutions and those that would be most beneficial for freelance or part-time language teachers. Following Kennedy's (2005) suggestions, we would expect reflective and interactive models to be high on the scale of recognized CPD formats. However, most recognized CPD courses follow a cognitive approach and reflection only plays a minor role in these courses. A way forward is shown by our participants who state that CPD activities make them realize that they are professionals (Heather) and appreciate the space to reflect and report on their own CPD needs and tasks (Hawk).

Based on current literature and data analysed from our small study, we can offer a set of recommendations which may be helpful for empowering both institutions and individual teachers:

- Acknowledging the specific work situations of freelance language teachers, employers can support them by recognizing their CPD even if acquired non-formally and informally.
- It is important for freelance language teachers to raise their own awareness of their professional identity (full, shifted or fractured). Opportunities for solitary or collaborative reflection can aid this process.
- As our examples have shown, professional identity is not a static concept, and a shift from fractured or shifted identity towards a fully developed professional identity is possible. However, freelance language teachers need to take into consideration the dynamic balance between CPD, ICT and teacher identity. Integrating ICT into their teaching and training can be an opportunity as well as a challenge.
- As much of the motivation of part-time teachers comes from the positive responses of their students, meeting their learners' expectations (see Chapter 4) and matching their level of ICT competence is an important factor.
- Peers can be an invaluable form of support and an important source of information.
- A community of practice, online, face-to-face or in a blended format (see Chapter 8), is often the only form of training available to part-time and freelance teachers.
- Just-in-time, to-the-point training is the ideal CPD format for part-time teachers.
- Learning by doing and experimenting with new tools is inspiring for some teachers.
- Online, flexible, open access training materials (OERs) play an important role in the CPD of our research participants (see also Chapters 6 and 7) by fulfilling the need for time and cost efficiency, required by so many part-time teachers.

The reflective task concluding this chapter will focus on creating your own step-by-step development plan for the integration of ICT into your teaching.

## Reflective task

Design a step-by-step plan towards integrating ICT into your language teaching. You can download a template to help you be as detailed and concrete as possible by going to the DOTS Moodle workspace (http://moodle.dots.ecml.at). Start by identifying how ICT could enhance your teaching.

For example, by employing an online survey tool for a student task which involves asking questions and collecting data in the target language.

Evaluate the skills you currently have.

For example, you can use SurveyMonkey but have never created a survey in your class.

The next steps, as detailed in the online template, are: your goal, planned actions, success indicators, obstacles, timing and, finally, reward. It is important to plan a reward for your successful development.

For example, present your successful project to peers and collect badges or positive feedback.

## Appendix

*Table A3.1* Overview of participants

| Name or Pseudonym | Country of origin | Country of teaching | Language(s) taught |
|---|---|---|---|
| Carlton | UK | UK | English |
| Emma | Germany | UK | German |
| Greta | Hungary | Hungary | English/German |
| Hawk | Turkey | Turkey | English |
| Heather | UK | Spain | English |
| Jagda | Croatia | Croatia | English/Russian |
| Judith | UK | Spain | English |
| Lucy | Poland | Poland | English |
| Lydia | UK | Germany | English |
| Maria | Austria | Austria | English/French/Italian |
| Mehmet | Turkey | Turkey | English |
| Yasenya | Turkey | Turkey | English |

## Notes

1. Names have been changed where respondents preferred this, otherwise the real first name of the person is used.
2. A Vlog is a video log, similar to a 'weblog', i.e. blog, but using visual recordings.

# 4
## Online Language Teaching: The Learner's Perspective

*Linda Murphy*

### Introduction

Many institutions are making the transition from primarily face-to-face instruction to online or a blend of face-to-face and online learning across a range of disciplines (Edwards et al., 2011). Languages are no exception, particularly in the light of mounting evidence of the effectiveness of blended approaches to language learning (Comas-Quinn, 2011). The focus of this book is on support for language teachers who are keen to engage in online language teaching and covers theory, practice and tools, tasks, and skills development for teachers in this context. However, awareness of the expectations and responses of language learners is also crucial in developing effective online language teaching. The transition from face-to-face to online teaching represents a substantial change not only for many teachers, but also for the learners, so there is increasing interest in the way this transition impacts on practice and on the learner's experience. For example, does this transition mean adding to the teacher's skills repertoire, or a transformation of existing practice? How does it affect the relationship between the teacher and learner?

This chapter will examine these issues in the light of research carried out at The Open University (UK), where there has been a shift to greater use of online elements in blended language teaching. Traditional print and audio-visual material supported by face-to-face tuition and asynchronous online conferencing has been extended and enhanced through interactive online activities and online tuition using synchronous audio-conferencing. The study explored the language learner's view of the skills and qualities required for effective online/blended tuition, whether these were perceived as different from those expected in classroom and traditional distance learning, and the relationship between learner and teacher in online environments.

## Theoretical background

The skills and qualities required for classroom teaching in general and classroom language teaching in particular have been well researched, as have the generic competencies for distance and online instruction (see examples in Murphy et al., 2011). Tait (2000, p. 289), writing about distance education in general, derived his understanding of learner support from a social constructivist view that knowledge is made and re-made by active participation in learning. He defined three primary learner support functions, each of which is relevant to the teacher role:

1. cognitive: supporting and developing learning through the mediation of the standard and uniform elements of course materials and learning resources for individual students;
2. affective: providing an environment which supports students, creates commitment, and enhances self-esteem; and
3. systemic/administrative: establishing administrative processes and information management systems which are effective, transparent and overall student-friendly.

A study reported by Baumann and colleagues (2008) invited language teachers working in distance education to identify the skills and qualities required for effective teaching in this context and found that the outcomes mapped closely onto Tait's framework (Baumann et al., 2008, p. 384). A follow-up study by Murphy and colleagues (2010), exploring the learner's perspective on the skills and qualities needed for effective distance teaching including online tuition, confirmed the importance of these three functions, finding that the teacher's learner support role was 'strongly underpinned by affective and organisational dimensions of tutor practice' (Murphy et al., 2010, p. 132). Comas-Quinn and colleagues (2012) summarized research on the evolution of teacher roles as teachers move into online learning, highlighting growing awareness of the importance of social roles and research into the skills which teachers need to acquire as they make this transition.

In a widely cited paper, Hampel and Stickler (2005) presented a model or Skills Pyramid to encompass the additional skills which language teachers need to acquire as they make the transition to teaching online (see the introductory chapter to this book and Chapter 5). The layers in this pyramid build from a broad base of general skills to an apex of individual and personal styles. However, Compton (2009) notes in a critique of the pyramid that the skills on each level can be developed concurrently, not only in sequence. Other researchers (for example, Levy et al., 2009; Wang et al., 2010) have focused on the process 'that experienced face-to-face language teachers undergo to become confident and competent online tutors' (Levy et al., 2009, p. 18). They highlight the importance of combining teacher training with hands-on experience, modelling, reflection and feedback in order to move teachers through stages of the skills pyramid and take account of the affective side of the transition to online teaching and its effects on teacher role and identity.

Although there have been numerous studies of the distance learner's perspective on the skills and qualities required for effective teaching (see examples in Murphy et al., 2011), relatively few (such as Hurd, 2006; Murphy et al., 2010; White, 2003) have examined the views of language learners in distance or blended contexts and what they need or expect from their teachers. This is despite widespread acceptance that language teaching differs from other disciplines in that the language is both the subject of, and vehicle for, instruction (Borg, 2006), and recognition that language learning, particularly online, makes significant affective demands (Hurd, 2008). There have also been few comparisons of learner and teacher perspectives regarding distance, blended and online learning. A longitudinal study carried out by Murday and colleagues (2008) investigated learner and teacher views about online learning introduced into a traditional course. Quantitative data showed a trend to increasing satisfaction with online courses, however, in qualitative data from interviews and focus groups, learners reported anxiety in online chat rooms and greater need for direction, motivation and self-regulation. Murday and colleagues (2008) concluded that 'the success of technology driven learning materials may depend as much on the human element as on the sophistication of the technology employed' (p. 137). Murphy and colleagues (2011) gave a critical comparative overview of the findings of two phases of the project mentioned above, which aimed to establish the skills and qualities needed for effective distance language teaching. The first phase (Baumann et al., 2008; Shelley et al., 2006) explored the teacher perspective and the second invited learners to give their views on the taxonomy of essential skills and qualities drawn up by teachers (Murphy et al., 2010). A further investigation phase was felt to be necessary in 2011 because online tuition had been introduced to a far greater extent in the courses previously surveyed. The outcomes of this investigation are the focus of this chapter.

The concern with social roles and the cognitive, affective and systemic or administrative functions of the teacher role online are brought together within the Community of Inquiry (CoI) framework first published by Garrison and colleagues in 2000 and followed up by numerous studies examining its nature and application which are summarized by Garrison and colleagues (2010). The CoI framework is based on collaborative constructivist principles and aims to develop understanding of the complexities of online learning. It consists of three elements: Social Presence; Cognitive Presence and Teaching Presence. These are interlinked in that teaching presence facilitates social and cognitive presence. Each element has been further divided into categories. These categories are exemplified by indicators which also reflect Tait's (2000) affective, cognitive and systemic functions of learner support and develop them in relation to the context of online learning.

Social presence has been defined as 'the ability of participants to identify with the community (e.g., course of study), communicate purposefully in a trusting environment, and develop inter-personal relationships by way of projecting their individual personalities' (Garrison et al., 2010, p. 32). Social presence consists of the categories of open communication, group cohesion and affective expression. Examples of indicators are risk-free expression, encouragement for collaboration and use of emoticons (Garrison & Arbaugh, 2007, p. 159).

Cognitive presence reflects the learning process and is defined by four phases: definition of a problem or task (or triggering event); exploration for relevant information/knowledge; making sense of and integrating ideas; and, finally, testing plausible solutions (Garrison et al., 2010, p. 32). Examples of indicators are a sense of puzzlement, information exchange, connecting ideas and applying new ideas (Garrison & Arbaugh, 2007, p. 159).

Teaching presence is defined as 'the design, facilitation and direction of cognitive and social processes for the purpose of realizing personally meaningful and educationally worthwhile learning outcomes' (Garrison et al., 2010, p. 32). It consists of the categories of design and organization of learning opportunities, facilitation of discourse and direct instruction. Examples of indicators are setting the curriculum and methods, sharing personal meaning and focusing discussion (Garrison & Arbaugh, 2007, p. 159). Garrison and colleagues (2010, p. 32) further explain the responsibilities of teaching presence as establishing curriculum content, learning activities and timelines; monitoring and managing purposeful collaboration and reflection; ensuring that the community reaches the intended learning outcomes by diagnosing needs and providing timely information and direction. They cite research studies, such as Shea and colleagues (2006), suggesting that teaching presence directly influences the creation and sustainability of social and cognitive presence, and that it is a 'significant determinate of student satisfaction, perceived learning and sense of community' (Garrison et al., 2010, p. 32).

In this chapter, the CoI framework together with Tait's functions of learner support have been used to aid understanding of the learner's view of the skills and qualities required for effective online language teaching within a blended learning environment as opposed to face-to-face teaching, whilst also mapping these skills and qualities onto the Hampel and Stickler pyramid of skills. In this way, it is hoped to answer the following questions:

• What qualities and skills do learners perceive as essential for online teaching?
• Do they perceive a difference between the qualities and skills required in online contexts and traditional face-to-face contexts?
• Does the increase in online teaching and learning affect their perceived relationship with their teacher?

Answers to these questions will help to establish whether transition to online teaching requires acquisition of *new skills*, or is more a matter of transforming *existing practice*. The next sections describe how the study was carried out and are followed by presentation and discussion of the findings.

## Background to the study

As indicated above, the research involved three distinct phases. Firstly, distance language teachers at The Open University (UK) worked together to identify the skills and qualities which they felt were essential for effective distance/blended language teaching. At the time when the study was carried out, teachers supported learners participating in a 'blend' of self-study of print and audio-visual material, online asynchronous activities, with a tutorial (*either* synchronous online *or* face-to-face) approximately once a month, and regular spoken or written assignments. The resulting taxonomy was framed by the following eight broad categories within which defining features were identified (see Appendix to this chapter, which shows two excerpts from the questionnaire with the 2008 categories and defining features, and the additional features added for the 2011 survey):

- affective qualities and orientation;
- pedagogical expertise;
- subject matter expertise;
- IT skills;
- interactive support skills;
- organization and self-management;
- group support and management;
- knowledge of institutional systems and distance learning.

Secondly, the views of language learners were sought in relation to the items in this taxonomy (excluding teacher self-management). The views of teachers and learners established during these two phases were compared. (For details see Baumann et al., 2008; Murphy et al., 2010; Murphy et al., 2011; Shelley et al., 2006; White, Murphy, Shelley & Baumann, 2005.)

This exploration of distance language learner views took place in 2008 and involved a cohort of learners who had opted for *either* a programme with face-to-face tutorials, *or* one with synchronous online tutorials. Subsequently, this choice was removed and all programmes now include a blend of *both* face-to-face *and* online tuition alongside the other elements of the blend, that is, print and audio-visual material and asynchronous online activities. Accordingly, all teachers and learners are expected to engage in both face-to-face and online tutorials rather than opting for one or the other. In 2011, the third phase of the research was undertaken in which the learner survey was repeated to investigate the impact of increased online tuition on students' views of teacher expertise compared with the 2008 study. The 2011 survey was based on the same taxonomy, but the defining features for IT skills had been up-dated by teachers to take account of the technological changes, such as increased use of synchronous audio-conferencing.

## Methods of investigation

In both 2008 and 2011, following ethical approval, a questionnaire based on the taxonomy of teacher skills and qualities was sent to a random sample of distance learners of French, German and Spanish at beginner, intermediate, upper-intermediate and advanced levels (see Tables 4.1–4.3). Learners were asked to rank up to five of the attributes and the skills in the taxonomy in order of perceived importance, and then to rank the defining features for each skill. Open questions invited them to identify and explain differences perceived between the skills required for classroom and distance teaching in 2008 or classroom and distance blended teaching (which is a mix of face-to-face and online tuition) in 2011 (see Appendix to this chapter). Interviews were conducted with a sample of volunteer respondents including male and female representatives from each level, language and qualification background. In 2008, interviews invited respondents to say more about the skills they thought were important for distance teaching. In 2011, interviewees were invited to talk about the skills and qualities of their ideal 'blended' language teacher. Interviews were recorded with consent and transcribed in full.

Quantitative survey data was initially analysed by frequency of response using SPSS. Frequencies of combined first and second choices for each question were submitted to chi-square tests. Those with positive residuals were accepted as the preferred skills and qualities. Analysis of qualitative survey and interview responses was supported by computer assisted qualitative data analysis software and combined concept- and data-driven approaches. Responses were coded to categories reflecting the attributes and the skills and their defining features listed in the questionnaire as well as further themes which emerged from the data, before being explored within Garrison and colleagues' CoI framework.

## Sample profile

The learners were adults, studying part-time in distance mode. The random sample was selected to be representative of the cohorts studying at the time. A profile of the respondents is presented in Tables 4.1–4.3 and is also broadly representative, apart from the higher number of female respondents. Just over half of language learners were female at the time. There are no formal entry qualifications for undergraduate courses.

*Table 4.1*  Survey sample and responses in 2008 and 2011

|  | Sample size | Responses | Response rate | Male | Female | Interview |
|---|---|---|---|---|---|---|
| 2008 | 500 | 144 | 29% | 48 (33%) | 96 (67%) | 12 (8%) |
| 2011 | 350 | 112 | 32% | 35 (31%) | 77 (69%) | 11 (10%) |

*Table 4.2*   Age profile of respondents in 2008 and 2011

| Age groups | 2008 | 2011 |
|---|---|---|
| 20 and under | 0 (0%) | 0 (0%) |
| 21–30 | 16 (11%) | 7 (6%) |
| 31–40 | 21 (15%) | 14 (12%) |
| 41–50 | 38 (25%) | 25 (22%) |
| 51–60 | 40 (28%) | 32 (28%) |
| 61–70 | 21 (15%) | 27 (24%) |
| 71–80 | 8 (6%) | 9 (8%) |

*Table 4.3*   Highest previous educational level of respondents in 2008 and 2011

| Qualifications | 2008 | 2011 |
|---|---|---|
| No formal qualifications | 4 (3%) | 4 (3%) |
| Less than 2 A levels | 29 (20%) | 22 (20%) |
| 2+ A levels or equivalent | 31 (21%) | 12 (11%) |
| HE qualifications | 57 (40%) | 35 (31%) |
| Postgraduate qualifications | 17 (12%) | 22 (20%) |
| Not known | 6 (4%) | 17 (15%) |

## Findings and discussion

### Quantitative data

Comparison of the survey data from both years gave a broad picture of the teacher qualities and skills that learners perceive as essential for blended/online teaching compared with traditional distance/face-to-face teaching. Unsurprisingly, in both years, subject matter expertise and teaching expertise were the most highly ranked taxonomy items (Table 4.4). It was notable that in 2008, no-one ranked IT skills as one of their five most important categories, compared to almost 20% who did in 2011, although rarely in the highest positions. Ranking of the defining features for individual taxonomy items was very similar in each year (Table 4.4 shows the highest ranked features in 2011. See Murphy and colleagues (2011) for 2008 rankings and discussion). Quantitative survey data alone, therefore, indicated some increase in the importance attached to IT skills as might be expected with the increase in online tuition, but otherwise indicated little difference between what learners see as the essential teacher qualities and skills in traditional distance/face-to-face learning contexts compared with blended/online learning contexts.

*Table 4.4* Taxonomy category ranking in 2011 and highest ranked features within each category where 1 = highest and 5 = lowest rank

| | Teacher skills and qualities: Overall taxonomy category ranking in 2011 | Highest ranking features in each category |
|---|---|---|
| **Teacher qualities** (ranked separately from skills) | Affective qualities and orientation | Approachable (2.4) Committed (2.8) |
| **Teacher skills with ranking** | | |
| 1 (1.9) | Subject matter expertise | Native speaker competence (2.0) Understanding of grammar (2.0) and provide appropriate help with this (2.4) |
| 2 (2.0) | Pedagogical expertise | Give examples (2.5) and models (2.6) Assist with pronunciation (2.7) Take account of different learning styles (2.9) |
| 3 (3.5) | Interactive support skills | Establish a friendly atmosphere (2.1) Provide prompt, unambiguous, individualized feedback (2.7) Understand learner strengths and provide appropriate support (2.9) Adapt to learners' levels (2.9) |
| 4 (3.6) | Knowledge of OU systems and distance learning | Know course materials well (1.7) Know what is expected in assignments and advise learners (2.7) |
| 5 (3.8) | Group management and support skills | Establish a friendly atmosphere (1.7) Explain mistakes in a non-threatening manner (2.9) |
| 5 (3.8) | IT skills | Use audio-conferencing tools with confidence (2.2) Keep in touch with learners via e-mail and forums (2.3) Plan mix of plenary/small group activities for online tutorials (2.4) |
| 6 (3.9) | Organization | Be well-organized with records and materials (2.3) Respond promptly (2.3) Sort out problems quickly (2.7) |

As in 2008, with respect to cognitive functions (Tait, 2000), the features of expertise which learners particularly valued were native or near-native speaker competence (often explained by the greater cultural input this signified for them), teaching expertise (particularly ability to explain and support development of grammar and pronunciation) and a good knowledge of the course concerned. These items rely on the exploration and integration, the connection and application of ideas, which are features of cognitive presence. Importance was attached to the affective aspects of the teacher role. Learners looked for teachers who were approachable, committed, supportive, enthusiastic and encouraging, who created a group atmosphere where learners could participate with confidence and who responded positively to diverse learning needs and styles. These priorities reflect the categories of open communication, group cohesion and affective expression which characterize social presence. Learners expected teachers to plan carefully and be well-organized and focused in order to make good use of limited contact time. They should be competent users of the available IT tools and keep in touch. In other words, learners also looked for the structure and leadership of teaching presence.

## Qualitative data

Qualitative data from the open survey questions and interview data provided a more detailed picture of learner perspectives in relation to the research questions at the core of this chapter. In 2008, learners perceived little difference between the skills required for classroom and distance teaching, but felt that the latter required more attention to interpersonal skills and relationships due to the absence of non-verbal communication channels. They also felt it required better organization and focus, especially during limited teaching contact time, and a greater degree of empathy and understanding of the learner's individual circumstances and the difficulties of studying alongside work and other commitments. In 2011, the importance of these skills and qualities was again stressed, but learners obviously viewed them all through the lens of online activity and attached more significance to skilful use of online tools. These are perspectives explored in more detail in the next sections within Garrison and colleagues' CoI framework, and with reference to Tait's learner support functions.

### Teaching presence and the systemic function

As mentioned earlier, research studies, such as Shea and colleagues (2006), suggest that teaching presence directly influences the creation and sustainability of social and cognitive presence. The data from the present study demonstrate its significance in creating a positive learning climate. The importance of the design and organization of online teaching to facilitate participation and provide instruction was frequently mentioned in responses. For example, awareness of learner ability and circumstance should translate into organization of differentiated activity or learner grouping. The range of levels and experience among a group of adult distance language learners on an open entry programme necessarily demands this, but this theme also emerged strongly in 2011 in relation to online tuition in the open question on the questionnaire:

> The main problem for the tutor is to cater for the different skills and it is more difficult online.

> They should be perceptive of learning techniques and strengths and weaknesses ... when we have our online tutorial and we're all put into separate rooms, I always feel that my tutor ... knows our abilities and again our strengths and weaknesses and she'll pair us up for that reason ... you know to do the various tasks ... to actually benefit from them.

This issue was raised again in interviews. Interviewee E noted:

> The level of language competence is absolutely massive within the group ... when you go online you see loads of people contributing in er, brilliant Spanish ... you do feel so demoralised ... then you're on Elluminate[1] and you can't see them ... you go into massive panic mode.

Interviewee K backed up this point:

> There are people who are much more confident than me, there are people doing my module that already speak French ... And I can't possibly go into an Elluminate room with these people because I come out feeling awful ... but ... a separate session for students who put their hands up and say look, I just am not in the least bit confident, I don't want to speak in front of these people, maybe a smaller group of less confident people every now and then would be great ...

These comments could be said to reflect the importance of the affective function – the quality of interaction and inclusion which is the essence of social presence. However, they also clearly illustrate the learners' desire for teaching presence, that is, leadership in creating a structured, non-threatening atmosphere within which learners can successfully contribute, develop and expand their language skills. Respondents in 2011 emphasized this structure and leadership in connection with use of online tools, group organization and management, but it had to be based on knowledge of learner capabilities or interests and inclusion. Many commented on the questionnaire on the greater need for active group management online, for example:

> Online tutorials perhaps require more people management as chat doesn't happen naturally.

> I think she's got to have a lot of skills in group management so that she can involve the students that are more silent.

> I feel the tutor needs to take more control of online sessions and explain the way they want it to work. When group-work is taking place, explain who is to start etc.

> The need for good planning and a flexible approach seems to be more critical online ... there is no 'thinking time' for a tutor when only a few tutees of very mixed ability log on – my tutor is flexible and obviously has alternatives ... differentiated tasks with clear instructions are also important to avoid long silences with tutees you have never previously met.

These points highlight the importance of aspects of teaching expertise (such as differentiation), and organizational and group management skills. They also illustrate the significance of teaching presence in facilitating the inclusion and group cohesion of social presence as well as features of cognitive presence: exploration, information exchange and application of new ideas or language concepts.

### Social presence and the affective function

Responses to open survey questions and views expressed by interviewees indicated the importance of social presence and the teacher's role in facilitating this, as suggested by Shea and colleagues (2006). It was expressed in various ways, such as in the need for good interpersonal communication which conveyed the teachers' personality and the need to fulfil the affective function of the teacher role. Both were felt to be exceptionally important online, as shown in the following comments:

> Stronger personality needed to come through online.

> Interpersonal skills of tutor are paramount ... e.g. tutor needs to communicate online in a way recognisable to students as being friendly and encouraging.

> Interpersonal skills are almost more important online, not less.

The impact of teacher social presence on learners was summed up by interviewee J:

> This tutor is more laid back, so more confident. You often find that the more skills a person has, the more relaxed they can be ... It makes us really more relaxed.

The role of the teacher in enabling learners to establish social presence was evident from the importance attached to teacher awareness of learner circumstances, strengths and needs, as explained by interviewee A, whose comments reflect what Tait (2000) expresses as how teachers can create 'an environment which supports students, creates commitment, and enhances self-esteem' (p. 289):

> You really do need to try and get to know your student ... in terms of what else is going on in their life, what their ultimate aim might be in order to then move a step forward to help them a little bit more. The tutor I've got at the moment will go out of her way to make conversation ... actually make contact with you as a person and try and find out a little bit about you ... that certainly instilled a lot of confidence in what I feel I can do and how I can approach that tutor for help when and if I need it.

The importance of responding to individual differences was emphasized in open question responses such as:

> They have to be aware of student strengths etc. and be prepared to manage more dominant students which is harder online.

> They need to be able to ... cater for different learning styles and preferences.

Such teacher awareness and skill in responding to varied strengths and needs appeared to be crucial to underpinning the structure and leadership of teaching presence, discussed above, and crucial to the relationship between learner and teacher in this environment.

### Cognitive presence and the cognitive function

As noted earlier, survey responses emphasized the importance attached to cognitive presence through the high ranking of specific domains and features of subject and teaching expertise together with a good knowledge of the course concerned. Qualitative responses further illustrate the influence of teaching presence in enabling learners to explore, exchange information, connect and apply ideas.

> They've got to be organised and have tutorials planned in advance and have those sent in advance so you know what you'll be discussing, then you can have a quick look, if you have the time ... and make sure ... so that when you're being fired questions at, you've got an idea.

> I feel that you're excluded if you don't actually know anything about the topic which is why I think they should actually be talking about something that we will all have looked at.

It could be argued that these comments would apply equally in a traditional distance/face-to-face context, but respondents noted that teachers needed to adapt to the online environment in order to deploy this expertise effectively in that context; for example:

> Tutor needs to be able to adapt their teaching style as without a face-to-face connection, they cannot really know how well received the tuition is.

Discussion of subject and teaching expertise was dominated by the specific IT tools used. Learners' comments indicated awareness of the need for adaptation to online teaching underpinned by significant levels of IT competence in order to support the features of cognitive presence. Many expressed opinions about online tutorials and the Elluminate tools used for online synchronous tutorials. Their comments point to the importance of the higher levels of Hampel and Stickler's skills pyramid, and confirm that learners in 2011 had strong views about teachers' technical competence in using the software (pyramid levels one and two; see introductory chapter), while recognising that learners themselves have a responsibility to develop their own IT skills too. Interviewee J explains why teachers need to have basic IT skills, but to have moved to the higher levels of the pyramid in order to facilitate cognitive presence:

> The ability to use Elluminate really efficiently is really important and therefore you've got to be good at Powerpoint, good at Word. I've noticed that the ones who get the message across have got significantly above-average IT skills, you know, really clever use of material. Because a hell of a lot of what we take in goes in through our eyes ...

if the screen is engaging you ... as opposed to just there as a filler, then you are capturing your students' attention. That takes effort, but it also takes skill to upload the stuff, and the ability to teach and knowledge of the subject, but it also depends on how you put it across.

A few simple slides can be more effective.

These comments highlight the importance of specific technical competence combined with creativity to engender a 'sense of puzzlement' or inquiry, information exchange, connection between ideas or new ways of applying language.

Beyond the need for specific competence (pyramid level two), and creativity in use of tools (pyramid level six), respondents wanted teachers to be able to 'deal with constraints and possibilities of the medium' (pyramid level three). Apart from the ever-present possibility of technical breakdown, there was recognition that teachers had to be prepared to deal with different IT skills and levels of familiarity with the tools. For example:

Since online communication is often difficult – students come unprepared to use Elluminate and can't hear/be heard – tutor needs to be very well prepared and flexible with regard to student needs.

I think Elluminate is great, but a fair amount of time is always lost at the beginning of tutorials whilst people overcome various IT or sound problems. This then impacts on the rest of the group and reduces this valuable learning time.

Learners noted the need to adapt expertise to an environment where absence of many kinds of non-verbal cues meant teachers could not easily establish learners' reactions.

In face-to-face tutorials, the tutor has the advantage of being able to read body-language and facial expressions of students and can respond to non-verbal communication.

Face to face the tutor can pick up learner difficulties better just by watching and involve the 'quiet' more actively.

Many of the earlier comments related to teacher awareness of individual learners' needs and interests, group management, differentiation and boosting learner confidence in participating online. They illustrate the importance of teaching presence in relation to cognitive and social presence and the links between them. They also point to the significance of online socialization and community building (pyramid level four). Teachers can feel under pressure to cover a lot in the relatively short online sessions. Learners feel that structure and planning is vital, but also want that structure to include opportunities for less intensive activity. Several respondents pointed to the consequences of not devoting sufficient time or having appropriate skills and qualities to achieve this.

> In previous times ... we always had warm up sessions ... I think that talking about things that are nothing to do with the course for a little bit to get you into speaking Spanish ... 'cos if you haven't spoken Spanish to anyone for a month, it makes you actually feel better.

Some respondents felt that Elluminate did not allow the sort of spontaneity that face-to-face interaction permits, whether because absence of usual non-verbal cues meant they did not know when to come into a conversation, or because of the way the Elluminate tools were used by the teacher, making participants 'raise their hand' to speak and controlling turn-taking, for example:

> The Elluminate tutorials are very stilted and unnatural ... we never seem to cover much material and we are always waiting for our turn to speak.

These concerns point to the importance of specific IT competence in facilitating communicative competence (i.e. facilitating communication, interaction and collaboration through task design, pyramid level five) through mastery of the tools in order to promote more spontaneous interaction between learners and indicate a need for teachers to enhance their existing skills and expertise in recognition of the online environment.

## Conclusions

Analysis of the 2011 survey and interview data in comparison with the 2008 data indicates that learners prioritize similar skills and qualities for both face-to-face and online teaching, but increasingly view them through the lens of online teaching now that it is part of all programmes rather than a matter of choice. Learner responses show that although the preferred skills and qualities are largely unchanged in blended learning, all need to be transformed in the online context. The significance of teaching presence in creating and sustaining social and cognitive presence, encouraging an open and constructive learner–teacher relationship and helping to boost learner satisfaction is evident from this study. This may be no different from other teaching contexts, but learners have a clear view of the need to adapt practice and transform existing skills to create effective relationships in online teaching. Learner responses underline the 'interconnectedness [of these presences] at the heart of the online experience' (Woods & Ebersole, 2003, p. 2). Furthermore, they suggest that the 'pyramid' skills do indeed have to be acquired concurrently, as argued by Compton, since it appears they are equally essential for effective online teaching from a learner perspective, or at least that teachers need to progress as quickly as possible to higher levels and to be aware of the importance of acquiring those skills (see Chapter 5 for further discussion and suggestions). However, as Edwards and colleagues (2011, p. 114) suggest, effective teaching in any medium appears to depend on more than possessing a list of required attributes or a list of necessary skills. This study clearly shows that teachers have to transform existing teaching skills in order to create the kind of structured, non-threatening, inclusive online learning space which learners need in order to explore, exchange information, connect and apply ideas and successfully develop their language skills.

## Reflective task

Look at the sample IT skills identified in the questionnaire excerpt in the Appendix to this chapter. Which ones can you confidently say you have? Which ones do you feel you need to acquire?

In a second step:
Whether you are already teaching online or only starting to prepare for it, imagine teaching situations (in class, in a blended context or online) where you would need to employ these IT skills and consider the following questions. Which skills would help you:

- to establish your teaching presence online?
- to establish social presence in an online forum?
- to establish social presence in an online synchronous tutorial via video conferencing?

How would you go about employing these skills and how would you evaluate your own performance?
How might you enhance these presences in future sessions? What sort of development would help you do this?

## Appendix

### Excerpt from student questionnaire distributed in 2008 and 2011, showing changes in the IT skills question

[...] Please select up to five qualities or skills which you feel are most important and rank them in the order of importance to you, where 1 = Most important, 2 = Second most important and so on. Add any others that you feel are missing in the space provided and include them in your ranking.

**IT skills**

(2008) Tutors should:

Have computer literacy skills
Use web resources for communication and information between individual, institution and learner
Use e-mail (First Class) for communication with learners and institution
Use text/audio conferencing
Optimise/integrate online learning with other support
Be aware of relevant online resources
Other (please specify in the box below)

(2011) Tutors should:

Use e-mail and forums for communication with learners
Use audiographic conferencing (Elluminate) tools with confidence
Plan online tutorials including plenary and small group activities
Make connections between forums, on-line tuition and other study activities including face-to-face tutorials
Use relevant online resources such as websites in their teaching
Encourage students to exchange information about relevant online resources
Use other online tools such as blogs and wikis in their tutoring

## Note

1. Elluminate *Live!* was the name of the synchronous audio-conferencing software in use at the time.

# 5

# Transforming Teaching: New Skills for Online Language Learning Spaces

*Ursula Stickler and Regine Hampel*

## Introduction

The use of digital technologies has transformed language learning and teaching, and today a multitude of online spaces are available that have a potential for learning. These spaces are multimodal, multicultural and multilingual, and they serve a number of purposes, from providing factual, reliable information and allowing learners to create individual or collaborative texts, to opening up fictional worlds and making available games for education. As they offer an almost unmanageable choice (Stockwell, 2012), teachers and course designers need a number of new skills to understand and select from what is available and subsequently to be able to transform these online spaces into coherent and usable learning spaces. Most language teaching is not conducted purely online or in only one medium, and this poses additional challenges, not just for teachers, but also for course and syllabus designers. These include integrating different communication channels (for example online and face-to-face teaching), choosing between asynchronous and synchronous tools, combining core teaching and optional 'fun' activities, or working with the 'flipped classroom' concept. In addition, although young learners in particular are often quite literate when it comes to the use of new technologies, they are not necessarily able to exploit these effectively in the context of the language classroom (Parry, 2011; Pegrum, 2011).

The previous chapter, 'Online language teaching: the learner's perspective', focuses on the skills, knowledge and attributes that online language learners feel their teachers should have. Based on questionnaires and interviews of students at The Open University UK, Linda Murphy and her colleagues found that teacher presence is important for students in the online environment (in terms of the systemic, affective and cognitive functions of the teacher's role) and that it helps to create a constructive learner–teacher relationship. Following this, the current chapter focuses on the skills that online teachers need in order to generate such favourable conditions for online learning, as well as other skills that they need to realize the possibilities and to deal with the challenges that are an integral part of using new learning spaces for language learning. These skills can be summarized as follows:

- Awareness of the affordances of different media and the intercultural dimensions of online materials in order to transform online spaces into online learning spaces;
- Teachers' ability to exploit new tools for specific pedagogic purposes, evaluate and select available online materials and tools, adapt materials – if necessary – to the appropriate level and format, and exploit the offered materials and tasks for language learning;
- Teachers' skill in encouraging their learners to take responsibility for their selection of learning spaces and activities and engage in the negotiation of suitable spaces and their appropriate use for online language learning.

With the help of the reflective task at the end of this chapter, readers can analyse their own online teaching skills using a pyramid model based on Hampel and Stickler (2005) and consider how to further develop their own skills.

## Background

Ten years ago we argued that language teachers needed to develop specific online teaching skills to become successful online teachers (Hampel & Stickler, 2005). Today this is no longer disputed. Various models and frameworks have arisen and ICT is increasingly being integrated into teacher training programmes. In this section we will sketch out some of these models to show the developments that have taken place over the past ten years.

Our own work was grounded in a sociocultural understanding of learning and therefore emphasized the higher skills of facilitating online socialization, creativity and developing a teaching style that could be 'owned' by an individual teacher. These higher skills are supported by a set of lower skills based on more technical or procedural knowledge that are shared with other approaches to teaching and learning, for example the Technological Pedagogical Content Knowledge (TPACK) framework (Koehler & Mishra, 2009). In our view of learning, however, 'know[ing] how to facilitate L2 [second language] acquisition rather than online socialisation' (Compton, 2009, pp. 81–82) is not enough.

As we argued in the introductory chapter to this book, language teaching online is a socio-constructivist endeavour. However, despite a clear theoretical trend toward socio-constructivism in online language teaching and learning (Felix, 2002; Johnson, 2006; Kern et al., 2004), many teachers still use the technology in predominantly 'old' ways, adapting new tools to their traditional teaching style (Cutrim Schmid & Whyte, 2012) rather than acquiring new skills to use the pedagogical affordances of the tools (Dougiamas, 1998; Wang, 2014).

Hampel and Stickler (2005, p. 316) demonstrated that previous literature about training teachers to teach languages online had focused mainly on technical aspects, that is, 'dealing with ICT problems and limitations'. An exception, albeit not in the context of language education, was Bennett and Marsh (2002) who pointed to two other skills, namely to 'identify the significant differences and similarities between face-to-face and online learning and teaching contexts' and to 'identify strategies and techniques to facilitate online learning and help students exploit the advantages in relation to both independent and collaborative learning' (p.16). In contrast to this somewhat generic approach, Hampel and Stickler (2005) developed a model that reflects the particular skill-set that language teachers need when teaching online (see Figure 1.1 in Chapter 1). This model consists of seven skills levels, including basic ICT competence, specific technical knowledge, and the skill to make pedagogic use of technologies, socialization and fostering communicative competence, and it culminates in teachers being able to be creative and develop their own online teaching style.

The pyramid model indicates that skills build on each other, not in a successive time sequence of training events but as increasing competence, with the lower levels forming a solid, reliable foundation. It is difficult for a teacher to show creative use of a medium for language learning and teaching that s/he is not very familiar with. These more basic skills are frequently neglected by trainers once it is assumed that they have been achieved by teachers, so the pyramid shape is also a reminder that sometimes more basic levels will need to be re-visited, particularly if technology changes. We have adapted our pyramid slightly for this chapter (see Figure 5.1), focusing more on the levels beyond the basic ICT competence which today tends to be taken for granted (at least in technologically advanced countries),

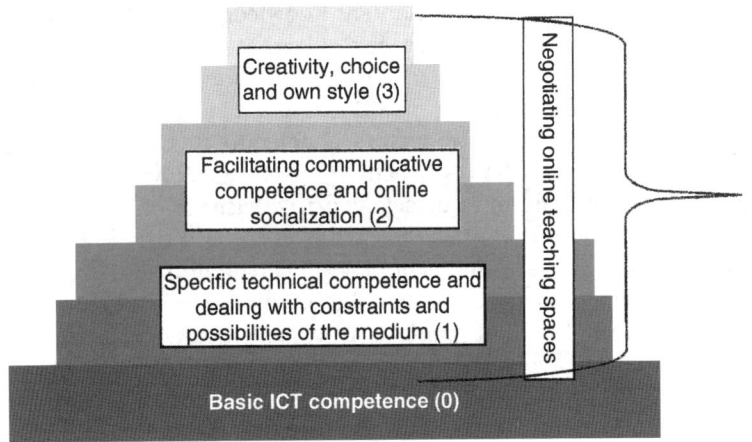

*Figure 5.1*  Skills pyramid (adapted)
*Source*: Hampel & Stickler, 2005.

regardless of whether teachers work in blended or purely face-to-face environments. The element 'negotiation of online teaching spaces' has been introduced as an accompanying skills measure that permeates all levels.

The importance of socialization and collaboration is echoed by Jones and Youngs (2006) who highlight three areas that have been identified as being 'keys to success in online teaching and learning: socialization to the online environment to build both student-teacher and student-student relationships, stimulation of active participation, and collaboration' (p. 266). Creating the conditions that allow for such outcomes is part of the skills that online teachers have to develop. However, in Jones and Youngs' (2006) instructor training checklist of preparatory steps and necessary skills (http://ml.hss.cmu.edu/facpages/cjones/TrainingChecklist.pdf), teacher preparation seems to have been reduced to technical and practical checks and advice.

Hubbard and Levy (2006b, p. 10) argue that both technical and pedagogical knowledge and skills are crucial for computer-assisted language learning (CALL): '*technical* knowledge and skills that are necessary for the competent operation of the computer technology, and *pedagogical* knowledge and skills involving the computer technology's impact on a learning environment and its appropriate and effective integration into the teaching and learning process'. They describe the knowledge and skills that teachers need for CALL in more detail (see Table 5.1).

*Table 5.1*  Technical and pedagogical knowledge and skills for CALL

|  | Technical | Pedagogical |
|---|---|---|
| CALL Knowledge | Systematic and incidental understanding of the computer system, including peripheral devices, in terms of hardware, software and networking. | Systematic and incidental understanding of effectively using the computer in language teaching. |
| CALL Skill | Ability to use technical knowledge and experience both for the operation of the computer system and relevant applications and in dealing with various problems. | Ability to use knowledge and experience to determine effective materials, content and tasks, and to monitor and assess results appropriately. |

*Source*: Hubbard and Levy (2006b, p. 16).

Compton (2009) has developed a more sophisticated model, consisting of three skills sets which are then organized into three levels of expertise, namely novice, proficient and expert.

> The first set, technological skills, relates to knowledge and ability to handle hardware and software issues. Next, the pedagogical skills refer to knowledge and ability to conduct and facilitate teaching and learning activities. Lastly, the evaluative skills refer to the analytical ability to assess the tasks and overall course and make necessary modifications to ensure language learning objectives are met. (p. 81)

Rather than designing models and frameworks, Levy and colleagues (2009) take a complementary approach and investigate 'the processes of learning that the trainee online tutors must undergo to acquire the requisite skills' (p. 18). In order to find out more about the micro skills that online tutors need to acquire, the authors set up a training programme which combined online practice teaching with self-reflection and monitoring reports, and allowed the teachers to develop their technological skills alongside their pedagogical skills. Similarly, Ernest and colleagues (2013) trialled an online training programme for teachers, which used an experiential, hands-on approach to develop their skills (focusing specifically on fostering learner collaboration). Gallardo and colleagues (2011) also point out that in a blended context the 'variety of skills and knowledge required of teachers will need to be addressed, as will the accrual of technological, pedagogical and research expertise which will help teachers to develop them, together with their motivation to do so' (2011, pp. 230–231).

This change in the research literature from a focus on technology to an acknowledgement that the use of technology must be pedagogy-driven is reflected in the changes that associations such as ISTE (International Society for Technology in Education) have undergone, moving from a focus on technology competence (see ISTE, 2000) to standards that focus for example on facilitating learning and creativity and fostering citizenship (see ISTE, 2008).

The following sections examine in more detail the skills framework proposed in Hampel and Stickler (2005) as amended above (see Figure 5.1).

## Matching pedagogies and technologies (Level 1)

When implementing a language learning curriculum which includes digital technologies, teachers need to base their choice of tools on pedagogical criteria. However, these decisions can only be effective if teachers possess both the specific technical competence for using different tools and also an awareness of their affordances for language learning – that is, knowing about their potential as well as their constraints (see the lower level of the pyramid in Figure 5.1). This will help teachers to evaluate and select electronic tools for specific language learning purposes (for example providing learners with language input, giving them the opportunity to provide output, or allowing them to interact with other learners or speakers of the language) and to tailor the tools to learner needs. Teachers will also need to be able to adapt existing materials and design activities that will make the most of the online environments used.

These environments might be public ones, such as online forums, wikis, or social networking sites, or they may be spaces that have specifically been developed for educational purposes, such as Moodle (an open-source learning platform) or Blackboard Collaborate (which offers web conferencing). Hanna and de Nooy (2009) argue for teachers to include authentic online spaces such as Internet forums in their curriculum as part of a genre-based approach to writing. They point out that this has the potential to foster students' language learning and develop their intercultural communicative competence (see also Furstenberg et al., 2001). Other teachers and researchers have produced authentic Wikipedia entries with their students (McDonald, 2007), whereas a group of EFL teachers at a Chinese university chose Twitter as a communication tool to encourage active learning using very short written utterances (Borau et al., 2009). In all cases, teachers need to be mindful of the dangers of using public forums, prepare students carefully and mitigate any possible negative feedback that students might get.

Teachers might consider it preferable not to use sites that are open to the public but still take advantage of tools with which students are familiar in personal, leisure contexts. Tools such as Facebook, for example, allow for closed groups to be set up. For this to be successful, teachers need to check which online tools their students use, reflect on the affordances of these tools for language learning, and consider whether and how these might be used for teaching purposes. In the context of the DOTS project (http://moodle.dots.ecml.at/; for a full project description see Chapter 10), user familiarity was taken into account in the selection of tools that form part of the resources recommended. Thus they include YouTube, a publicly available site for sharing videos that many teachers and learners use, and Skype, a tool that offers video and voice calls. The educational use of popular tools such as Facebook and Skype is also attracting research (for example Androutsopoulos, 2013; Aydin, 2014), and such publications provide additional information for teachers.

However, even if some tools seem appropriate for certain language learning purposes, there may be other conflicts. Online behaviour that learners have developed while interacting via social networking sites, instant messaging or online games may not be appropriate in a classroom context. Thorne's (2003) concept of cultures-of-use highlights the fact that groups of people using a particular environment to communicate develop certain cultural practices, that is, ways of interacting with each other that are governed by certain norms and forms of activities. This can cause clashes between different cultures-of-use, with students either unable or unwilling to use a communication tool that is deemed private, for learning purposes. A recent study of undergraduate students in the US concluded the following:

> Even when safeguards are promised, students resist the integration into education of technologies that they perceive to be primarily personal, clearly indicating that because some technology is used widely by students does not mean that it should be leveraged for academic use. (Dahlstrom et al., 2013, p. 6)

Skilled teachers know that the perspectives of teachers or course designers and learners can clash in other ways too. A teacher may see

FlashMeeting (http://flashmeeting.open.ac.uk/home.html) as an ideal language learning setting for synchronous spoken group interaction, while there may be individual learners who are too shy to participate and who prefer just to listen to the recording of the conversation, or participate using the text chat rather than the audio channel (Stickler & Hampel, 2010). In his study, Montoro Sanjosé (2012) showed that while a teacher may consider YouTube to be an ideal medium for students of English to upload a short video in which they introduce themselves, learners might lack confidence in disclosing information about themselves publicly. Even today's young learners, who have grown up with digital technologies, need to be socialized into using online tools for learning purposes.

Teachers who have developed expertise in using online technologies in their teaching will also be aware that students tend to use additional tools outside the 'designated' learning environment. Thus, language students are likely to have an online dictionary open or be using Google Translate when interacting synchronously or asynchronously in a virtual learning environment.

Even those environments specifically designed for learning usually need to be customized to suit the particular needs of the course or the learners. This may relate to the overall learning design (Conole, 2013), to the combination of tools that are chosen (for example in Moodle where a range of tools is available which, if used in their entirety, may overwhelm students), or to the tasks that need to be designed (Hampel & Pleines, 2013).

## Developing social cohesion and fostering communication (Level 2)

This section relates to the middle level of the skills pyramid (Figure 5.1), that is, facilitating communicative competence and online socialization. As argued in the introductory chapter, interaction and communication allow learners to co-construct knowledge (Mercer, 1995) and contribute to successful language development. Online environments offer great potential for socializing, communicating and collaborating, both within a class but also with the wider world. Students can work with their peers (in pairs or in larger groups); they can interact with their teacher; learners of an L2 can communicate with L1 speakers of the language in their own or another country; and students can join an authentic online community (for example Massive Multiplayer Online Games (MMOGs) or Wikipedia). However, they need guidance in doing so.

Although the teachers' role in facilitating such interaction is crucial, their training often takes place in face-to-face settings, where they facilitate the development of collaboration and social cohesion in a physical classroom, thus creating opportunities for interaction at close proximity. In contrast, digital environments provide very different sites for interaction, with potentially very different spatial and temporal characteristics and different rules of engagement. Although they allow for an almost unlimited geographical reach (provided that the interlocutors are online too), the tools used often 'reduce' communication in terms of modes (for example forums with a focus on written language, social networking tools with an emphasis on visuals, or audio-conferencing, such as Skype, with a focus on spoken language). In addition, interaction does not necessarily happen in real time. Asynchronous tools, such as forums or blogs, would be examples here. The absence of body language can cause miscommunication – silences, for example, can be interpreted wrongly (Stickler et al., 2007). As a result, social presence has to be created in different ways compared with face-to-face encounters (Satar, 2010), and users have to become familiar with new patterns of communication (Hampel, 2014). As Ware (2005) points out, learners in asynchronous online environments in particular are also more likely to miss opportunities for communication because of the delayed response time or the lack of social consequences of not engaging in a topic.

Successful communication is easier to achieve when students share common goals. However, this can be particularly problematic in telecollaborative settings where two possibly quite different groups are tasked with communicating with each other, with the aim of contributing to each other's second language development (O'Dowd & Ritter, 2006). Developing communicative competence for learner-led communication with L1 (first language) speakers requires a high level of online intercultural literacy in order to be able to interpret humour, to understand the need for being explicit (for example regarding time management) and to negotiate status and boundaries.

Online teachers can support their learners at various levels and in different forms, ensuring that learners find safe and unthreatening spaces for interaction and know how to communicate in them. A way to ensure that learners meet with interlocutors who are not overly critical and will not give up easily, is by replacing real dialogue partners with 'chatbots'. These provide machine-derived answers that allow L2 learners to practise quasi-dialogues online (in written or spoken format) with a machine designed to comprehend an utterance and respond in a suitable form (Fryer & Carpenter, 2006). For beginner learners this mock conversation might help to overcome the shyness and anxiety involved in trying out a new language (Horwitz et al., 1986). See http://www.abenteuermedien. de/jabberwock/ for an example of a Jabberwock chatbot.

Dialogues with well-meaning interlocutors can be supported by integrating a cycle of recording, reflecting, improving and re-recording messages before they are posted to an asynchronous forum for written or spoken communication (González & St. Louis, 2008). The time delay and additional loop allow learners to stretch their language further while still maintaining an element of real – albeit delayed – two-way communication. The interlocutors in such a forum can be peers or sympathetic native speakers. See Voxopop (http://www.voxopop.com/) for an example of a voicethread forum.

The teacher's role is thus crucial in helping language learners develop not only linguistic expertise but also social and interactive skills so they can succeed in communicating and developing group cohesion. Possible ways of supporting students in this include the following (Ernest et al., 2013):

- Careful planning and management
- A training phase for exploring the tool to be used (see also Heiser et al., 2013)
- Appropriate activity design (which could include warm-up activities to support the development of group cohesion, and tasks that focus on the use of particular modes of communication to facilitate interaction)
- Ground rules for participation (including an online netiquette)
- Close monitoring of interaction (particularly in the early stages)
- Moderation of online communication
- Regular feedback, encouraging learners to reflect on the experience

## Enhancing creativity online (Level 3)

This section links to the higher level of the pyramid (see Figure 5.1), dealing with creativity (for both teacher and learner) and the teacher's own style of teaching. Creativity plays a role across different methods of language teaching, making language practice varied and interesting (Richards, 2013). This is important as L2 learning comprises skills related to both learning and practice as well as content learning and learning about a language and culture. Irrespective of whether language teachers adhere to constructivist theories of learning in their strongest form (Glasersfeld, 2007) or favour a different teaching style, their role in the language classroom will entail supporting their learners' tentative utterances, encouraging the use of language beyond their current ability, and mediating between interlocutors to facilitate comprehension.

In a CALL context, creativity is still a relatively under-researched area and skills needed to enhance online creativity in language learning are emerging slowly in practice and research. As a creative user of the L2 and in order to support creative language use in learners, the language teacher needs to develop the following skills:

- Selecting creativity-enhancing (online) tools
- Introducing and supporting the use of these tools without over-emphasizing the technological aspect
- Ensuring that creativity is a necessary element of all learning
- Explaining the pedagogical value of creativity in language learning
- Providing supportive evaluation and positive feedback
- Clearly demonstrating the delineation between re-use and plagiarism
- Furthering critical self-evaluative skills in learners

The first two skills areas are located at tool level and might be associated with the more technical side of online teaching; points three and four relate to a more conceptual level, ensuring that creativity is valued and understood in online learning and teaching; and the last three skills areas can be associated with digital literacies more generally, emphasising the critical and evaluative skills necessary to make sense of a complex online world, which may be even more difficult to understand when it is mediated through the L2.

Online teachers can enhance the creativity of their learners at various levels and in different forms. Modelling creativity by playing with language or using multimodal representations (for example animated slide shows and text combined with images and recorded sound) can help beginners as well as more advanced learners to find new ways of expressing their meaning and to overcome obstacles to communication caused by their limited range of language. Tools recommended for this purpose include Animoto (http://animoto.com/) or Voki (http://www.voki.com/).

Learners might already have the skills for expressing meaning in creative ways, and the teachers' role may go no further than enabling and supporting the transfer of skills from one area (digital, computing) to another (language learning). Learners can create videos, mash-ups and links, use social bookmarking, and re-mix different elements, for example text, music and video, using tools such as Vimeo (https://vimeo.com/), YouTube, or Diigo (https://www.diigo.com/).

Teachers can and should encourage critical awareness and evaluative skills if students are to use spaces and tools online effectively. Dealing with more or less trustworthy and reliable sources, being careful about what information to share with whom, and being prepared to give critical and supportive feedback to others are all elements of digital literacy and important skills that the online learner needs to develop. Language teachers often have to deal with situations of uncertainty or ambiguity where their learners are not entirely confident about understanding the subtext of utterances in the L2 and might need help in choosing appropriate behaviours. Skills of evaluation and critical awareness will be crucial in social bookmarking, awarding symbolic feedback (for example thumbs up, star-rating) or in promoting published utterances (for example re-tweeting).

Teachers can also help their learners to become more aware of creativity as a tool (Davies et al., 2013) which can enhance their language learning, by encouraging reflection on creative energy or on dialogues surrounding their creative efforts. Ambitious learners might strive to become authors in the L2 in their own right, able to manipulate the new language in a way that is appreciated by L1 users and recognized as adding to the repertoire of the language by producing creative texts. In developing an identity as L2 creative writers or producers, students can evolve from being L2 learners to being L2 users, supported by their peers and teachers. They can participate in authentic online authoring and editing and thus use online publications and feedback on their writing as learning tools (for example by creating Wikipedia entries and tracking changes to their entries (McDonald, 2007), or by writing fanfiction and giving feedback to other authors (Black, 2005; Thorne et al., 2009)). To support their students successfully, teachers will need to understand the pedagogical implications of creativity (Craft et al., 2014).

Possible challenges and misunderstandings that need to be addressed in the development of creative language use online include the misinterpretation of re-mix or mash-up creativity as plagiarism. The differences between a creative use of translation engines and 'cheating' for a language exam need to be clarified, and the boundaries between evaluating others' work (feedback) and negative use of feedback functions, in extreme cases 'flaming', need to be discussed.

## Negotiating online learning spaces

Across all the skills levels and linking them together runs the need to negotiate what is a learning or teaching space and what remains private or social. The suitability of tools needs to be considered both on a technical level and on a social, intercultural and communicative level (Pasfield-Neofitou, 2011). As pointed out above, what teachers see as an ideal online teaching space may not always coincide with the learners' perspective. And, conversely, students might use online spaces for their own, private communication and social purposes, which could be re-defined as learning spaces. Which spaces are used and how is a matter of negotiation in a socio-constructivist learning environment. Clearly defining a space as a 'learning space' is important in order to avoid misunderstandings, confusion of purpose and unacceptable behaviours. This starts at a purely technical level in arranging access to agreed learn-ing spaces, and reaches up to the level of creativity, where acceptable use and re-use of 'found' and re-mixed content could be negotiated between teacher and learners.

At all levels, students and teachers need to be clear about the rules of acceptable online language use, particularly if learners are to be assessed, and they also need to work together to identify guidelines for the correct usage of online tools and activities. With an explicit and negotiated netiquette, learners will also be encouraged to develop a sense of responsibility in online environments and a clear under-standing of 'safe' and 'open' spaces. Teachers have a responsibility to ensure that their learners' work is not made publicly available without their permission and they should be aware of privacy and copyright issues. For more information see Chapter 7 on open edu-cational resources and the DOTS project website (http://moodle.dots.ecml.at/).

Teacher training programmes for language teachers need to include considerations of online teaching so the teachers learn how to enhance their online teaching skills, to implement and support the creative dialogue and collaborative creativity with their students, and to nego-tiate the use of online spaces for learning in collaboration with their students. If teacher trainers can highlight the benefits of a collaborative construction of knowledge, link collaborative creativity to constructiv-ist pedagogy, and show clearly how to fully exploit the benefits of digi-tal technology, this truly has the potential to advance online language pedagogy.

The next chapter will consider ways of finding free online training spaces where teachers can work on enhancing their professional skills related to online teaching. The reflective task below will help readers select an appropriate level of training, and evaluate the level of their current skills.

## Reflective task

Use the pyramid in Figure 5.2 as guidance to reflect on your own skills regarding the use of new technologies in your teaching. In which areas do you feel especially confident or experienced, and where do you think you need more training, support or peer advice?

Do the task in two steps:

First, reflect on your strengths, giving concrete examples. For example, you could say:

> *'As our class forum does not allow voice threads, I have encouraged students to use a wiki to share their speaking tasks. This means I have to support two different types of tools, but it is worth it because of the benefits of developing students' speaking skills.'*

Now link your skills to different skills levels. For example:

> *'As our class forum does not allow voice threads, I have encouraged students to use a wiki to upload their speaking tasks.'* = Skills levels: Specific technical competence and dealing with constraints and possibilities of the medium.

> *'This means I have to support two different types of tools, but it is worth it because of the benefits of developing students' speaking skills.'* = Skills levels: Facilitating communicative competence and online socialization.

You have also shown that you can evaluate and weigh up the benefits and drawbacks of different media and give reasons for selecting a particular tool.

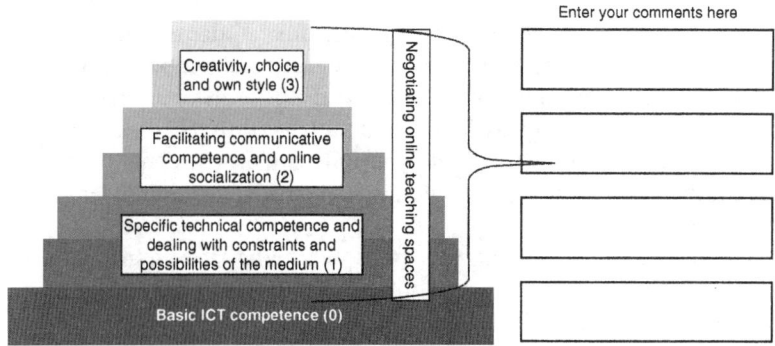

*Figure 5.2*   Skills pyramid for reflection

If you are not very experienced in using ICT for your teaching, you might tend to focus predominantly on deficits. Try to take a more positive outlook by selecting some features of your face-to-face classroom experience and your generic ICT skills and considering how you might use them to develop ideas for online teaching in the future.

For example, you could say: *'My strength in classroom teaching is creating a really lively and chatty atmosphere.'*

This strength can be linked to facilitating online communicative competence and online socialization. Your next step might be to identify suitable tools that support informal online communication (for example choose a synchronous text chat rather than a more deliberate and slow-paced forum).

To prepare for the next steps, identify areas where you need more training, support or peer advice.

For example: *'I know how to get students to talk to each other in class but I need to learn more about suitable online behaviour in a social networking site. Before letting my students use it on their own, I would like to try out an online chatroom, or maybe ask other teachers which rooms are safe for young learners to use.'*

Don't forget that to feel confident and creative in the higher skills levels, your foundation levels need to be solid, and you need to have basic ICT skills and be able to cope with constraints and affordances of commonly used tools.

# 6
# Free Online Training Spaces for Language Teachers

*Joseph Hopkins*

## Introduction

Starting in the 1980s, teacher educators began to recognize that in addition to formal training courses, informal learning (or learning resulting from everyday work-related, family or leisure activities (see OECD, 2007)) plays a key role in teachers' professional development. Various authors, such as Touriñán (1983), Trilla (1997) and Sarramona and colleagues (1998), have stressed the need for integrating informal elements into formal teacher development. Attwell (2010), taking a more critical stance, views the lack of attention given to informal learning as a fatal flaw in traditional training models. According to this author:

> ... the present training course driven, schooling paradigm, fails to recognise the intrinsic curiosity, creativity of human beings to learn from the environment around them. such learning does take place through informal learning. But it is largely discounted by our present systems. (n.p.)

The notion that traditional training is insufficient is not new to the field of language teaching. Indeed, beginning in the 1990s, various authors have argued that the main goal of language teacher development should be to foster autonomy, or rather, to encourage trainees to become self-directed practitioners (Nunan & Lamb, 1996; Richards & Lockhart, 1994; Wajnryb, 1992). According to this non-prescriptive approach, language teacher training should equip teachers with the necessary strategies, such as keeping a teaching journal, conducting structured observation or using self-assessment forms, so that they may discover for themselves teaching and learning problems in their classrooms. Once a problem has been identified, the self-directed practitioner is encouraged to adopt an action research approach by incorporating a change in his/her teaching practice and, subsequently, evaluating the outcome (Wallace, 1998) (see also Chapter 9 in this book).

With the advent of the Internet, opportunities for such self-directed development have increased dramatically. As we shall see in this chapter, teachers now have easy access to a wealth of freely available resources, such as websites, blogs, tutorials and online courses aimed specifically at language teachers wishing to develop their online teaching skills (for more information on open educational resources for language teachers see Chapter 7). Furthermore, the World Wide Web allows teachers to come into contact with peers in online teacher communities, or communities of practice (Lave & Wenger, 1991) (see also Chapter 8). Various authors (for example, Cross, 2010; Downes, 2007; Siemens, 2005) stress that such networks greatly expand the possibilities for informal or self-directed learning by allowing practitioners who do not coincide in the same physical location to share ideas and experiences related to their teaching. Thus, members of these online communities are not solely recipients but may also be creators and disseminators of new knowledge, both within the online community and amongst their colleagues at their face-to-face institutions. Indeed, a study conducted by Petrides and colleagues (2010) found that an online training network supported 'conversations and practices that may not traditionally be available through professional development' (p. 5). Specifically, the community observed promoted sharing of resources, practices and teaching challenges, thereby increasing the likelihood that members would become actively involved in implementing innovation in their teaching.

Online resources, therefore, hold great potential for the professional development of language teachers, especially with regard to the integration of information and communication technology (ICT) into teaching. However, with the vast number of resources available, locating appropriate websites that meet the needs of specific individuals in specific teaching contexts can be an extremely daunting task that could result in information overload if teachers do not know where to begin. With this in mind, we conducted a search for free online resources currently available that could be used by self-directed teachers, teacher trainees, or teacher trainers. For this, the following criteria were utilized:

• The online resources should provide language teachers with tutorials, guidelines, self-study modules or other information specifically related to the use of ICT for language teaching. Sites containing only ready-made online exercises or tasks were not included.

- Teachers should not be required to pay a fee or make a purchase to access the sites.

We began by compiling a list of websites already known to us that met these criteria. The initial list was then expanded by conducting a web search and through consultation with various experts in teacher training and computer-assisted language learning (CALL).

In the following sections we will present a critical review of selected websites, along with a categorization scheme, or typology, which emerged from our search. The aim of this typology is above all practical and is meant to aid language teachers in understanding and selecting appropriate resources for self-directed development. Underpinning this scheme is the notion that knowledge is socially constructed (Vygotsky, 1978) and that communities of practice (Lave, 1991; Lave & Wenger, 1991; Wenger, 1998) play a key role in teachers' professional development. Using some of the criteria that have been suggested for evaluating open educational resources (see for example http://www.open.edu/openlearn/education/creating-open-educational-resources/content-section-4.2), the review focused on whether the site in question offered the following:

1. Content:
   - Relevant topics
   - Well-designed materials
2. Pedagogy:
   - Pedagogical approach, indicating why a particular technology might be of use to teachers
   - Clear indications or concrete examples of how the tools can be used for teaching
   - Added value of the use of technology for teaching and learning
   - Theoretical underpinnings of using ICT applications in language teaching
   - Interaction with peers (for example, through an online discussion forum)
3. Usability:
   - Indication for the novice user of where to begin
   - Search tool
   - Regular updating

At the end of this chapter, recommendations for developing a self-training plan will also be provided. This will concentrate on resources of specific relevance to language teacher development. For a consideration of how freely available teaching/learning tasks can be utilized by language teachers, please see Chapter 7.

## Typology of free online training resources

From the list of training resources identified, a typology consisting of five main categories emerged (see Table 6.1). In the sections that follow, representative sites will be critically reviewed for each of the types identified. It should be stressed, however, that given the ever-changing nature

*Table 6.1* Typology of freely available training resources

| Resource type | Best suited for | Examples |
| --- | --- | --- |
| Self-training modules and online workshops | Initial training, linking pedagogy with use of technology | • Developing Online Teacher Skills (DOTS) http://dots.ecml.at/ <br>• CARLA Technology Integration Modules http://www.carla.umn.edu/technology/modules/index.html <br>• Electronic Village Online http://evosessions.pbworks.com |
| Massive open online courses (MOOCs) | Initial training, linking pedagogy with use of technology | • Task-Based Language Teaching with Digital Tools https://www.canvas.net/courses/task-based-language-teaching-with-digital-tools-1 |
| Directories of online tools | Identification of suitable tools | • Directory of Learning & Performance Tools http://c4lpt.co.uk/directory-of-learning-performance-tools/ <br>• Son's Online Tools for Language Teaching http://www.tesl-ej.org/wordpress/issues/volume15/ej57/ej57int/ |
| Tools training by language teacher trainers | Identification of suitable tools | • Nik Peachey's Learning Technology Blog http://nikpeachey.blogspot.com.es/ <br>• Russell Stannard's Teacher Training Videos http://www.teachertrainingvideos.com/ <br>• Thomas Strasser's New Learning Technologies Blog http://learningreloaded1.wordpress.com/ |
| Online communities of practice | Interaction with other teachers, sharing best practice, identification of suitable tools | • Dave's ESL Café's Discussion Forum on Computer-Assisted Language Learning http://forums.eslcafe.com/teacher/ <br>• Classroom 2.0 http://www.classroom20.com/forum <br>• Webheads in Action http://webheadsinaction.org/ <br>• DaF-Community (German as a Foreign Language) http://dafnet.web2.0campus.net/ |

of online tools and resources, it is likely that the proposed typology will change over time. Indeed, only a few years ago massive open online courses (MOOCs) would not have been included, and it is probable that new types of free training sites will continue to appear.

In addition to these training resources, some university teachers give access to their course materials online. Philip Hubbard at Stanford University, for example, offers a course entitled 'An Invitation to CALL' which he describes as 'Foundations of Computer-Assisted Language Learning' (http://web.stanford.edu/~efs/callcourse2/)'. Mark Pegrum, who is based at the University of Western Australia, hosts a wiki which contains e-learning resources, e-learning references and e-learning training. The section 'E-learning courses' includes useful material from various courses that he teaches (http://e-language.wikispaces.com/courses).

## Self-training modules and online workshops

While somewhat uncommon, there are a few free sites offering self-training modules and workshops focusing on general pedagogical considerations regarding the use of technology in the language classroom and/or on the use of specific online tools. One example is the Developing Online Teaching Skills (DOTS) website, the focus of Chapter 10, along with the two sites reviewed below. These resources are particularly useful for teachers who have little or no experience using ICT in their teaching.

### CARLA Technology Integration Modules

http://www.carla.umn.edu/technology/modules/index.html

These freely available training modules have been developed by the Center for Advanced Research on Language Acquisition (CARLA) at the University of Minnesota as a part of the CoBaLLT Project (http://www.carla.umn.edu/cobaltt/index.html). Unlike more technological approaches of other language teacher training sites, CARLA highlights first and foremost why teachers should use ICT in their classes and for what purpose. Reflecting this pedagogical approach, in the introductory module, the authors state that, generally,

> workshops and tutorials consist of generic content aimed at teaching 'how to's' or the 'button-pushing' skills of particular computer tools. What those generic workshops are missing is the 'application' piece: in our case, the application of technology specifically for language teaching and learning. (CARLA, n.d., n.p.)

The topics of the various modules are as follows:

- Introduction
- National Technology Standards
- Generic Software
- Find Web Resources
- Use Web Resources
- Create Web Resources
- WebQuests
- Telecollaboration
- Using Digital Images
- Web Tools for Digital Storytelling
- Brain-Based Multimedia: Principles for Using Multimedia

Each of these modules begins with suggested readings, followed by specific examples of how the technology can be used. Subsequently, participants are invited to create a language-learning task based on the topic of the module and to participate in online forum discussions with other users on a NiceNet platform.

The topics in the Technology Integration Modules are interesting and the materials are very well designed, thus providing users with a very sound pedagogical basis for the implementation of ICT in their teaching. In addition, the fact that users can interact with peers online is a potentially powerful tool for the exchange of ideas and knowledge. However, in an examination of the NiceNet platform at the time of writing this chapter, only ten people had joined and only four messages had been posted. This is most likely due to the absence of a 'core group' of frequently participating members, something which Probst and Borzillo (2008) point out as essential for the success of an online community of practice.

*Electronic Village Online*

http://evosessions.pbworks.com
The Electronic Village Online (EVO) is a project that was initiated by TESOL's Computer-Mediated Language Learning Interest Section aimed at language teachers from around the world. Since its inception in 2001, every year for five weeks during the months of January and February, EVO offers free online workshops focusing on various aspects of language teaching and learning. Many of these events, which are moderated by experts in the field who donate their time to EVO, are directly related to the use of technology in the classroom and provide participants with

the opportunity not only to develop their teaching skills, but also to interact with fellow practitioners from all over the globe. To illustrate the type of workshops on offer, in the 2014 edition of EVO, those specifically devoted to the use of technology for language learning included the following:

- Information and communication technology for English language teachers
- Moodle for teachers
- Podcasting for the ESL-EFL classroom
- Use of mobile applications in language classrooms
- CLIL: Using technology for content and language integrated learning

## Massive open online courses

A relatively recent phenomenon, massive open online courses (MOOCs) are freely available courses open to an unlimited number of participants. These courses typically consist of a set of texts, videos or multimedia materials, along with dedicated discussion forums for learners to interact with one another and sometimes with instructors. MOOCs are generally hosted on online platforms, such as edX, Coursera, or Udacity, which offer numerous free courses on various topics. Increasingly, governments are considering using MOOCs to support mainstream education (see http://www.wired.co.uk/news/archive/2014-01/22/gove-moocs).

Despite the fact that they provide learning opportunities to millions worldwide, MOOCs have generated a great deal of controversy within academia. Critics point to issues such as high dropout rates and a general lack of sound pedagogy in course design (see for instance Vardi, 2012). Nevertheless, MOOCs are a potentially powerful resource for teachers, especially for those with little or no experience in the use of technology in their teaching, as can be seen in the following example.

### Task-based Language Teaching with Digital Tools

https://www.mooc-list.com/course/task-based-language-teaching-digital-tools-canvasnet

This six-week course, held on the Canvas Network, is led by Brian Hutchinson. Participants first receive an introduction to task-based learning before they explore web-based and non web-based technology and begin designing digital tasks. They then consider other aspects such as assessment, lesson plans, and designing a digital task-based syllabus (see Table 6.2). In order to receive a course certificate, participants need to participate in the weekly discussions held throughout the course.

*Table 6.2* Syllabus for task-based language teaching with digital tools

---

Week 1: An Introduction to Task-Based Language Teaching
Week 2: An Introduction to Digital Tools for Task-Based Language Teaching
Week 3: An Introduction to Authentic Assessments
Week 4: An Introduction to Task-Based Lesson Planning
Week 5: More Digital Resources for Task-Based Language Teaching
Week 6: An introduction to the Task-Based Syllabus

---

As there are to date very few MOOCs specifically for language teachers, this course is a welcome addition to the freely available training opportunities currently on the Web. Similar to the CARLA Technology Integration Modules, this course also puts pedagogy, in this case a focus on a task-based approach to language teaching, ahead of technology, with the added value of frequent contributions from participants in the online discussions.

## Directories of online tools

Once teachers have received initial training in the use of ICT for language learning, directories of online tools can be an invaluable resource for locating applications that are best suited for a particular teaching/ learning situation. Two examples of such sites are reviewed below.

### Directory of Learning & Performance Tools

http://c4lpt.co.uk/directory-of-learning-performance-tools/
This online directory is owned and maintained by Jane Hart, an independent educational consultant. It provides a comprehensive list of, along with links to, online learning tools that are mostly free, although there are some that require payment. While the site is not specifically aimed at language teachers, it includes relevant information such as social and collaborative spaces; document, video and audio handling tools; and communication and sharing tools. The directory is regularly updated and includes a useful list of the top 100 tools, based on feedback obtained from over 500 users, who may also suggest new tools to be included in the directory by means of an online form.

One drawback of this site, however, is that it does not provide indications or specific examples of how the tools in the list could be used for teaching. In addition, Son (2011) asserts that because of its exhaustive nature, this directory is of limited use to language teachers. According to him, '[w]hile the directory itself is an excellent database of learning tools, its extra wide coverage makes it difficult for language teachers to

*Table 6.3*   Son's (2011) tool categories

**Online Tools for Language Teaching**

- Learning/content management systems
- Live and virtual worlds
- Blogs and wikis
- Resource sharing
- Web exercise creation
- Dictionaries and concordancers
- Communication
- Social networking and bookmarking
- Presentation
- Website creation
- Web search engines
- Utilities

use their online time effectively in choosing particular tools with direct relevance for language teaching' (n.p.).

### Online Tools for Language Learning

http://www.apacall.org/member/sonjb/projects/tools/

In response to what he sees as the limitations of Jane Hart's directory, Son has developed this non-exhaustive list in order to provide language professionals with a more succinct directory of online tools available specifically with language teaching in mind. He also proposes a categorization scheme for online tools that could be used for language teaching (see Table 6.3). Son's directory is especially useful for teachers who are new to ICT and who might be overwhelmed by the extensive nature of some of the other inventories of online tools. However, like Jane Hart's directory, it does not provide users with specific examples of how online applications could be used for teaching.

### Tools training by language teacher trainers

There are a number of websites run by teacher trainers devoted to showing language teachers how to use specific online applications that they could use with their students. Below we will review three such resources that are currently available. These sites provide an invaluable training resource for language teachers. Users should be aware, however, that in the case of the first two, one of their main purposes is to promote the authors' for-profit consultancy activities. This, together with the fact that these sites rely on funding from sponsors, such as publishers, language schools, teacher training institutions, and other stakeholders, calls into question their truly open nature and the impartiality of the information presented.

*Nik Peachey's Learning Technology Blog*

http://nikpeachey.blogspot.com
Nik Peachey describes himself as a 'freelance technology consultant, writer, and trainer' (http://about.me/technogogy). His Learning Technology Blog is aimed specifically at English language teachers, although most of the information available is relevant for teachers of other languages as well. The site features regular blog posts from Peachey himself, which focus on tutorials on how to use particular online tools or pedagogical issues related to the use of ICT in language teaching (see Figure 6.1). Users can consult past posts by using the search feature, by browsing by year or by going to a list of the ten 'most popular posts'. There is also a form for visitors to sign up for a newsletter. In the section 'Free Downloads', users can access a number of free resources, such as a manual authored by Peachey entitled 'Web 2.0 for language teachers', as well as 12 short training tasks on specific online tools designed for teachers new to ICT.

The site contains a wealth of extremely useful resources, especially for teachers who are already using online tools in their teaching and who

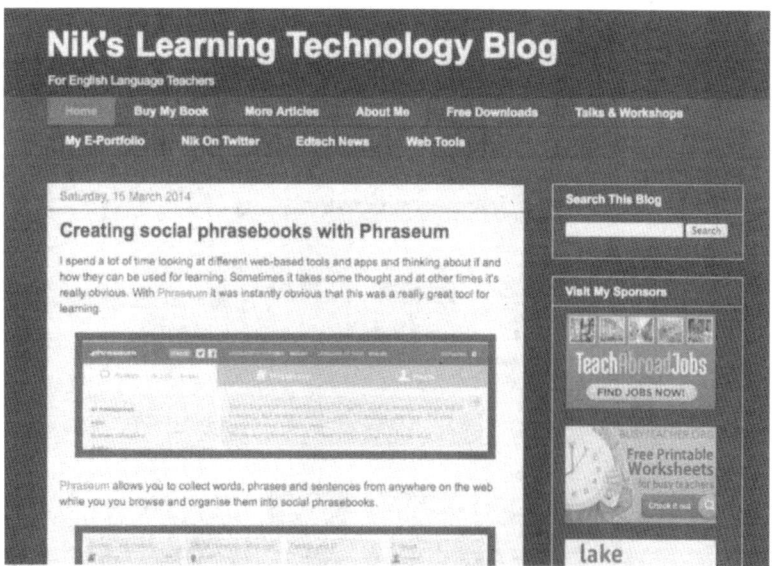

*Figure 6.1* Nik Peachey's Learning Technology Blog

are looking for new ideas. For the novice ICT user, however, the sheer volume of information could be overwhelming. In addition, reflecting the challenge of keeping technology-related sites up to date, some of the tools in the short training tasks included on the site when this chapter was being written were no longer available, such as the blog tool Posterous.

### Russell Stannard's Teacher Training Videos

http://www.teachertrainingvideos.com/

Russell Stannard is also a freelance language teacher trainer. His site features step-by-step training video tutorials on the use of specific online tools. Each tutorial is divided into several short video clips focusing on a different aspect of a tool (see Figure 6.2). The site has no search option, although the tutorials are organized by category (for example, words and vocabulary, images, dialogues, writing, and sharing and collaboration), which allows resources to be located fairly easily. There is also a link to the most popular 20 videos on the site. Users may sign up for a monthly newsletter to keep abreast of developments.

While Stannard's video tutorials provide useful tips on the set up and use of a particular tool, as with Nik Peachey's blog, the amount of information, along with the fact that there is little indication of where to begin, could be daunting to a newcomer to technology. In addition,

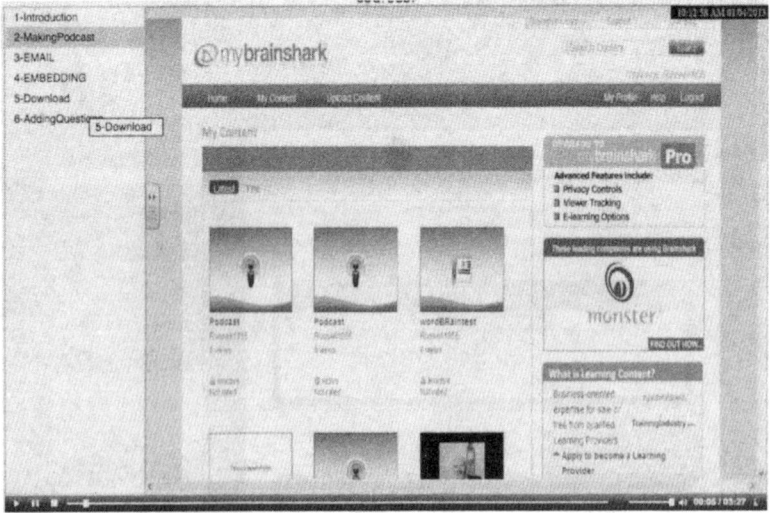

*Figure 6.2*   Russell Stannard's video tutorial on creating podcasts

although there is some mention in the tutorials of why a teacher would use a tool in his or her teaching, there are few concrete examples of tasks that could be designed with them and little consideration of the added value that the use of technology would afford for teaching and learning.

*Thomas Strasser's New Learning Technologies Blog*

http://learningreloaded1.wordpress.com/

This blog is owned and maintained by Thomas Strasser, an educational technologist and teacher and teacher trainer of English as a Foreign Language at the Vienna University of Teacher Education. The site contains various resources, such as slides from some of his presentations available for download, as well as recordings of online seminars (or 'webinars') he has led. In addition to this, included in the 'Online publications' section are articles written by him, most available in both English and German, that focus on the use of online tools in language teaching, such as Edupad for collaborative writing or Mahara for creating digital learning portfolios. Unlike Nik Peachey's or Russell Stannard's websites, Strasser does not provide an extensive selection of the tools available. What his online publications do offer, however, are a consideration of the theoretical underpinnings and pedagogical affordances of using ICT applications in language teaching, along with concrete examples of how specific tools could be used to enhance learning. Therefore, the strength of this blog is not so much related to the breadth of information on online applications, but rather in terms of the depth with which they can be exploited for pedagogical gains. It should also be noted that this site, as opposed to the previous two tools training resources reviewed, does not rely on advertising from third-party sources for funding.

## Online communities of practice

Communities of practice (Lave, 1991; Lave & Wenger, 1991; Wenger, 1998) can be defined as 'groups of people who share a concern, a set of problems, or a passion about a topic, who deepen their knowledge and expertise in this area by interacting on an ongoing basis' (Wenger et al., 2002, p. 4). While originally conceived of in face-to-face contexts, it is widely recognized today that communities of practice can also occur in online settings (see for instance Murillo, 2008), and indeed numerous online communities of practice devoted to language teaching currently exist (see Chapter 8). Two such communities are reviewed below that are of particular interest to language teachers wishing to obtain examples of best practice and to share their experiences of ICT in their teaching.

*Dave's ESL Café's Discussion Forum on Computer-Assisted Language Learning*

http://forums.eslcafe.com/teacher/

Founded by Dave Sperling in 1995, Dave's ESL Café was one of the first online sites aimed at language teachers and remains very popular today. Amongst the many resources are various discussion forums, of which there is one devoted specifically to computer-assisted language learning (CALL). Participants use this forum to discuss technology, exchange information on tools, share ideas and receive feedback from peers, as can be seen in the list of recent discussion topics in Figure 6.3. It is worth noting that whereas organizations such as IATEFL and ACTFL have online discussion forums devoted to technology and language teaching, these are open to paying members only. Dave's ESL Café's CALL forum is one of the few active online communities specifically for language teachers that can be accessed for free.

*Classroom 2.0*

http://www.classroom20.com/forum

This very active community currently has over 79,000 members. Although not specifically aimed at language teachers, the online

| Topics | Replies |
| --- | --- |
| Announcement: Call for Participation: Project We Say Tomato | 1 |
| e.readers - do you want them? | 5 |
| Toys for teachers | 3 |
| I think teachers need this website... | 6 |
| Contributors wanted | 0 |
| Opinions on my dictation exercises | 8 |
| Uploaded Seven New Learn English Videos | 0 |
| Podcasting sites | 12 |
| Ideas for teaching classes via Skype | 8 |
| Getting Flashy with Moodle | 0 |
| Are all computer learning solutions really so bad? | 1 |
| Audio added to Learn English with Pictures | 1 |

*Figure 6.3*   Dave's ESL Café's Computer-Assisted Language Learning Forum

discussion forum allows for a rich exchange of information and ideas amongst educators in all fields. A useful search tool allows users to easily locate topics of interest. Users may order the discussions by most recent and most popular, or browse them by category, such as 'Reviews of Software, Tools, and Services', 'Philosophy/Pedagogy' and 'Success Stories'.

*Webheads in Action*

http://webheadsinaction.org/
Webheads in Action (WiA) was initiated in 2002 by Vance Stevens as a five-week training event within the framework of TESOL's Electronic Village Online. Since then it has evolved into a very active online community of practice, bringing together practitioners from all over the world. Members meet online each Sunday at 12:00 GMT, usually via video conferencing tools such as Blackboard Collaborate or Google+ Hangouts, to have informal discussions and to help one another learn about online tools that can be used in language teaching. Details on how to join these meetings are available on WiA's Learning2gether wiki (http://learning2gether.pbworks.com/). In addition, information about upcoming events, such as free online webinars, can be found on the group's Google+ Community site (https://plus.google.com/communities/114550321376936920900).

WiA is an online community specific for language teachers and soundly based on a collaborative effort.

*DaF-Community (German as a Foreign Language)*

*http://dafnet.web2.0campus.net/*
Some online communities are specific to languages, as for example this online community of German teachers. The site provides regular online meetings and new members are encouraged to introduce themselves to the community. The organizers regularly invite guest speakers to present topics of interest to teachers of German. These presentations are live but are also recorded for members to view later. In addition, the site offers a calendar of events, a comment function and links to recommended online resources and other communities.

## Discussion and conclusion

In the previous sections, we have seen that there is a wealth of freely available resources on the Web that language teachers could use to support the implementation of ICT into their teaching. Without a doubt, these could be of great value for the self-directed practitioner identified at the beginning of this chapter. The sheer quantity of information, however, could be overwhelming and could make it difficult to know where to begin. Thus, teachers need specific advice to guide them in their autonomous learning.

Firstly, it is important to be aware of the limitations of these online resources. In the case of tool directories, for example, the tendency noted is for administrators to continue adding online tools to an ever-growing list, often without critical information regarding the affordances and challenges of their use. Likewise, tools training sites tend to focus on the installation and set-up of computer applications, although often with scant attention paid to how they could be implemented most effectively in teaching. It is interesting to note that whereas many of these sites continue to focus on 'how-to' tutorials, many applications now offer their own training through their help pages. Good examples of these are the 'Wiki Tours' offered by Wikispaces (http://www.wikispaces.com/content/wiki-tour) or the 'Learn Wordpress' site for WordPress blogs (http://learn.wordpress.com/). What teachers really need, therefore, are more examples of best practice of technology being used for language teaching and learning.

With regard to sites with self-training modules, these provide an excellent way for teachers, especially for those new to technology, to receive a general overview of ICT for language teaching, along with the pedagogical principles underpinning their use. The ephemeral nature of technology, however, means that there is the danger of such modules becoming obsolete shortly after they have been developed. Unlike directories and tool training sites, which are generally administered by teacher training consultants, self-training modules tend to be produced as part of a funded project. The natural consequence of this is that once the project has reached its end, it is unlikely that the modules will be updated. MOOCs, on the other hand, could provide teachers with training similar to that of self-training modules, with the advantage of up-to-date content and the possibility of interaction with fellow participants. However, the MOOC described earlier, on technology and task-based language teaching, was the only one of its kind we were able to locate at the time this chapter was being written. It remains to be seen whether more such courses will be developed in the future.

Despite the limitations of freely available online training sites, used wisely and combined appropriately, they can play an invaluable role in teachers' professional development. With this in mind, specific recommendations for a development plan incorporating free online resources for self-directed, reflective practitioners who would like to incorporate technology into their teaching are provided in Table 6.4.

*Table 6.4*  Recommendations for a teacher self-development plan

| Action | Useful online resources |
| --- | --- |
| **1. Make time**<br>As you would do if attending a formal training course, you should set aside a few hours a week to devote to self-training. Make a realistic timetable for yourself, for example, 90 minutes a week. | — |
| **2. Seek out initial training** | Self-training modules and online workshops<br>MOOCs |
| **3. Reflect**<br>Think about your own teaching situation. What teaching and/or learning problems can you identify? Problems could include aspects such as how to practice specific skills, encourage collaboration, increase motivation etc. Which issues do you think technology might help you to overcome? | — |
| **4. Research**<br>Find an appropriate tool, or tools, to address one of the problems you identified in step 3. | Directories of online tools<br>Tools training sites<br>Online communities of practice |
| **5. Implement**<br>Define the learning objectives and design a task using the tool or tools you selected in step 4. Think of any challenges you might face and try to pre-empt these in your task design. Carry out the task with your students. Note: Technology does not always work as expected. You should have an alternative to your online task in case there are technical problems. | — |
| **6. Evaluate**<br>Take note of what is happening when students are doing the task. Afterwards, get feedback from them. | — |
| **7. Reflect**<br>Ask yourself the following questions: To what extent were the learning objectives fulfilled? What things went well? What things did not go well? Would you use the same tool(s) again? Would you use the same task? How could you change the task design in order to better meet the learning objectives? | — |
| **8. Share**<br>Let the others know about your experience. Seek advice for improving your learning task. | Online communities of practice |

## Reflective task

Social bookmarking tools, such as Diigo (https://www.diigo.com/) or Delicious (https://delicious.com/), allow users to save links to websites (or 'bookmark' them) so they can easily refer back to them later from any computer or Internet-enabled device. These tools also enable users to organize links by tagging them with relevant keywords, by writing notes or short descriptions of the webpage content, or by categorizing related sites into lists. Users can create groups based on a specific topic so that they, along with others, can contribute to a collaborative library of bookmarked sites. When links are saved, individuals can keep them private, share them with members of groups they may belong to, or make them public so all users can see them. Similarly to other social networking applications, social bookmarking tools also allow users to find and 'follow' other individuals or groups, thus allowing them to receive notifications when new links have been saved publicly. In this way, people with similar interests can pool their resources.

In the steps below, we provide suggestions of how teachers could select an appropriate social bookmarking tool and set up their own library of free online training spaces.

> Step 1: Learn about the basic features of Diigo, Delicious and any other social bookmarking tools you are able to find. A good way to do this is to locate video tutorials on these tools by using Google or another search engine. For example, to find tutorials on Diigo, simply enter 'Diigo tutorials' in the search box.
> Step 2: Once you have found out about the features of different tools and how they work, select one that seems most suitable for your needs.
> Step 3: Go to the website of your chosen tool and create an account.
> Step 4: To start your library, add the training resources that appear in Table 6.1. Organize these entries into lists, for example, by using the following categories described earlier in this chapter:
>
> - Websites with self-training modules
> - MOOCs
> - Directories of online tools
> - Tools training by freelance language teaching consultants
> - Online communities of practice
>
> Step 5: Using appropriate keywords, search the web and add more training resources to your library. With Google, try using the **'related:'**

search operator to locate resources similar to those you have already bookmarked. For instance, to try to locate more sites like Russell Stannard's Teacher Training Videos (www.teachertrainingvideos.com), enter the following into the search box: related:www.teachertraining videos.com

Step 6: Browse your social bookmarking site to find individuals and/ or groups with similar interests. Use the 'follow' feature to receive updates on their bookmarking activity.

# 7
# Sharing: Open Educational Resources for Language Teachers

*Anna Comas-Quinn and Kate Borthwick*

## Introduction

The last decade has seen an increase in the number of open online spaces through which users can share their educational content. These may be institutional websites, national initiatives (such as Jorum in the UK or COERLL in the US), online communities of practice (see Chapter 8), or commercial websites. At the same time, the notion that using and creating Open Educational Resources (OER) is a positive, beneficial activity has gathered momentum across the world at political and strategic levels with the establishment of a range of initiatives aimed at promoting engagement with OER. In 2012, UNESCO adopted the 'Paris OER Declaration', which affirmed support and encouragement for the development of governmental policies integrating OER into education, and in 2013, the European Commission launched the 'Open Education Initiative' which aims to enhance the digital skills of European Union residents through 'the development and availability of OER' (European Commission, 2013). Since then many European projects have been funded to expand the integration of OER into teachers' practices (such as LangOER, which aims to harness open practice to support minority, regional and less used languages).

A discipline-based approach to creating, sharing and reusing open content has yielded fruitful results for languages in the UK context, both in the provision of resources for learning, teaching and/or research (LORO, OpenLIVES), and as a catalyst to pedagogical reflection and professional development (Community Café, On-Stream). This chapter will introduce the concepts of Open Educational Resources (OER) and Open Educational Practices (OEP), explore the benefits of sharing and reusing open content in relation to teacher professional development and provide practitioners with practical guidance to get started on the road to embracing 'openness'.

## Open Educational Resources

The philosophy of Open Education is largely based on the concepts of social responsibility and widening participation (Conole, 2012) and is inspired by 'the simple and powerful idea that the world's knowledge is a public good, and that technology in general and the World Wide Web in particular provide an extraordinary opportunity for everyone to share, use and reuse it' (Smith & Casserly, 2006). Open Educational Resources are 'materials used to support education that may be freely accessed, reused, modified and shared by anyone' (Downes, 2011). They are normally, though not necessarily, digital, since the online medium facilitates access and distribution to a much greater extent than is possible for traditional paper-based or physical resources.

Besides the right of access, adaptation and distribution, many other definitions[1] of OER include a reference to open copyright licensing that allows everyone everywhere to use the resource. For some this licence should be completely open and not limited to specific uses – for example, in commercial settings – whereas for others not even the licence is a requirement as long as the intention of the resource owner is to allow free access and adaptation. There is an ongoing discussion around the semantics of the term 'free' (the *'gratis'* vs *'libre'* debate, see Reed, 2012; Suber, 2008), with some proponents maintaining that 'free' should be understood in the broadest sense of the word, to include 'without payment' but also 'with freedom to use, modify and distribute'.

Through open licensing, resource owners indicate how others can use their work ('some rights' as opposed to the default 'all rights reserved'). The most popular licensing system in open education is Creative Commons, a set of licences articulated around four conditions:

- Attribution (BY) so that the author is acknowledged
- NoDerivatives (ND) so that changes made are not distributed
- NonCommercial (NC) so that resources are not used for commercial purposes
- ShareAlike (SA) so that any works derived from a resource are shared under the same type of licence

Licence choice is down to the resource owner, and it is important to point out that less restrictive licences enable wider dissemination of a resource and increase reusability.

In a blog post, Wiley (2009) proposed a list of conditions to measure how open content was. The 4Rs Framework included the rights to: Reuse, Revision, Remix and Redistribution, and an open licence would enable the resource owner to indicate this. Concerned by the ways in which publishers are exercising control over educational content by, for example, moving from selling to time-restricted leasing and subscription to digital content, Wiley (2014) has recently revised his framework to include ownership (Retain) as a fifth right:

The 5Rs of Openness (Wiley, 2014)

- Retain – the right to make, own and control copies of the content.
- Reuse – the right to use the content in a wide range of ways (e.g., in a class, in a study group, on a website, in a video).
- Revise – the right to adapt, adjust, modify or alter the content itself (e.g., translate the content into another language).
- Remix – the right to combine the original or revised content with other open content to create something new (e.g., incorporate the content into a mashup).
- Redistribute – the right to share copies of the original content, your revisions or your remixes with others (e.g., give a copy of the content to a friend).

The size and complexity of the resource, often referred to as granularity, is another important aspect when discussing open content. Weller (2010) uses 'big' and 'little' OER to distinguish between whole courses or units of learning with 'explicit teaching aims', such as the open courses in the P2P (Peer to Peer) University's School of Open or some of the Massive Open Online Courses (MOOCs) in FutureLearn, and individual items, such as the photographs, handouts and presentations found in the LORO or HumBox repositories. Individual items may not have explicit teaching aims or be part of a course, but can nevertheless be shared and reused by teachers. Weller (2011) refers to a 'pedagogy of abundance' in which the creation of complex, high-value educational content (courses) takes place alongside the production of a myriad of smaller, less polished but also useful resources, which, if shared, can also have value for teachers and learners. Thomas (2014) makes an important distinction between 'use value' – that is, the utility or usefulness of an educational resource – and 'exchange value' – that is, whether it can be monetized: 'most teaching resources can have a high use value both for primary use and secondary reuse, without that ever translating into an exchange value. They might be valuable but you can't sell them' (Thomas, 2014).

The concept of 'use value' is also pertinent when discussing quality in relation to OER. One of the claims of open education is that OER can enhance the quality of teaching and learning. For some, this could be achieved by providing highly sophisticated open resources, perhaps including high levels of multimedia and interactivity. For many, quality might be evidenced in brand, author or institutional reputation, ratings, reviews or provenance from quality-controlled repositories, amongst other things (Pegler, 2012). However, Wiley and Gurrell (2009) reject these static conceptions of quality and instead suggest that 'utility', understood as how useful a resource is for a specific user in a specific context, is a better construct with which to approach an OER. Ultimately, the quality of OER should be measured in relation to how well it enables learning (Wiley, 2013).

## Benefits and barriers to using OER

Some of the benefits of OER are obvious and readily understood: making a wider range of content available to students, extending the use of resources to realize a greater return on an initial investment, and being able to save time by not having to create content from scratch. OER have also been claimed to support lifelong learning (Joyce, 2006); provide savings for students through decreased reliance on commercially published textbooks (Hilton et al., 2012); improve teachers' pedagogical and digital skills (Conole, 2012; Joyce, 2006; Petrides & Jimes, 2008); and facilitate translation to reduce language barriers to access (Beaven et al., 2013; Hilton et al., 2012). However, benefits are not equal to motivators, and whilst learners and institutions clearly benefit from the process, for teachers additional time and effort is required to learn the new skills and knowledge that will enable them to search, evaluate, create, adapt and repurpose OER (Pegler, 2012). Additionally, research has shown that awareness and use of OER are still low amongst language professionals (Thoms & Thoms, 2014).

Several studies have identified what teachers perceive as the advantages and disadvantages of engaging with OER (Beggan, 2010; Browne et al., 2010; McGill et al., 2008; OER Synthesis and Evaluation Project, 2012). The following two exemplify the types of issues that are raised.

Prior to the creation of the LORO repository in 2009, sharing was not widespread amongst teachers at the Department of Languages at the Open University, UK, and happened mostly on demand and with a small number of colleagues. However, attitudes towards sharing were generally positive, although for some teachers certain conditions had to be met (remuneration, reciprocity, requiring user feedback), and a small minority were overtly negative towards the idea, citing issues around trust, remuneration and time investment. Asked about the benefits of sharing, these teachers listed the following: finding inspiration and ideas; learning from others; benefiting the students; saving time by adapting rather than reinventing; and usefulness for teaching specific points that the teacher might not be an expert on. The challenges identified related to questionable quality and usefulness of the resources; time investment; and lack of remuneration, reciprocity and recognition (Tomás, 2011).

In another qualitative study on how best to foster teachers' reuse of OER (Masterman et al., 2011) the following benefits were reported as being associated with OER:

- the license for reuse, which reduces fear around copyright infringement;
- having additional material to match students' interests and preferences;
- enabling teachers to provide content they would lack the skills, resources or time to create;
- benchmarking teachers' own practice in terms of content, approach and quality;
- allowing them to teach topics beyond their areas of expertise;
- stimulating networking and collaboration.

Time saving was not recognized specifically as a benefit in the short-term and OER use was seen as limited, mainly because of the teachers' need to maintain 'their own teaching voice' (Masterman et al., 2011, p. 139) and the learning they derived themselves from preparing their material. Enabling factors that could lead to increased and sustained use of OER were identified and classified as: attitudinal (disposition towards reuse, sharing and collaboration); pedagogic (relevance of content and fit with teachers' purpose); logistical ('critical mass' of content and easy to find); and strategic (institutional policies, embedding in professional development).

These two studies show that teachers are generally well disposed towards sharing. They also reveal that engagement with OER is complex and involves a variety of different activities, some of which have the potential to challenge teachers' practice and identity. These activities have been termed 'open educational practices' (OEP). In the next section, we look at how OEP may be defined, six core activities which constitute OEP, and the impact OEP can have on professional development and innovative teaching.

## Open educational practices

In this chapter, we take a broad view of open educational practice, in line with the 2008 Cape Town Open Education Declaration:

> [O]pen education is not limited to just open educational resources. It also draws upon open technologies that facilitate collaborative, flexible learning and the open sharing of teaching practices that empower educators to benefit from the best ideas of their colleagues. It may also grow to include new approaches to assessment, accreditation and collaborative learning.
>
> (Open Society, n.d., n.p.)

Providing a simple definition of Open Educational Practices is not easy, but the authors of the synthesis and evaluation report on the UK government's multi-million pound UKOER programme (2008–2012) suggest that the following six activities can be considered part of adopting open practices in education (see Beetham et al., 2012):

- the production, management, use and reuse of OER;
- developing and applying open pedagogies in teaching practice;
- open learning and access to open learning opportunities;
- open scholarship and open research;
- the open sharing of teaching ideas and knowledge;
- the use of open technologies for education.

In the context of language teaching it is easy to understand what is meant by production and management of OER, and use, reuse and adaptation of OER. Some examples are provided below to illustrate what each of the other activities in the list means in relation to the work of language teachers.

*Open pedagogies* are characterized by a high level of learner input into course structure, learning outcomes, review and assessment. They might include asking students to blog about their learning experiences, or contribute to open websites that crowd-source their content, such as YouTube or Wikipedia. Beasley-Murray (2008) describes how he asked his students of Spanish to contribute to Wikipedia by writing and editing featured articles about Spanish or Latin American authors they were studying as part of their course. His students embraced the task and became involved in writing, reviewing and rewriting for a wide public audience, with their Wikipedia pages receiving thousands of hits. Assessment of the task was based on the standing of their articles within Wikipedia and, therefore, was decided by an external audience. Beasley-Murray found that the task encouraged good writing practice, critical thinking and self-reflection/review, and offered students a real-world project with demonstrable impact.

The notion of *open learning* encompasses learners participating in open courses, and practitioners creating and coordinating programmes of study that are freely available to all. Open learning may also include informal learning through collaborative working in an open, online space, such as contributing to an open wiki or crowd-sourcing project (for example, contributing to the translation of open content through a volunteer translation community such as the TED Open Translation Project).

*Open scholarship and research* involves the open, free publication of research data and outputs for others to access and use for educational and research purposes. As part of the OpenLIVES project (2011–2013) interview data recounting the experiences of Spanish exiles was published as open educational content, licensed for reuse, which language teachers could then use in different ways (Nelson & Pozo-Gutiérrez, 2013). Open publication also enabled the wider public to connect with the data, and gave it a longevity and visibility that was never envisaged by its original collectors.

*Open sharing of experience and knowledge* can take place online through wikis, comment-sharing sites, blogs, micro-blogs (such as Twitter), open mail lists and other social networking sites. There are also online community repositories of OER, which enable users linked by a common discipline or interest to share resources and comment on the work of others.

Finally, *open technologies* refers to the plentiful online spaces for sharing content, many of which are well-know and well-used, such as Flickr, Facebook, YouTube and Google, and to the many open source or free services which can be used in language education, for example, for delivering course content (Moodle), voice recording (Audacity, Voki), creating 'talking' pictures (blabberize), or enabling social interaction focused on language learning (busuu). Services like these both enable and encourage open educational practices, and teachers can find examples of how to train themselves in their use in Chapter 10.

Open practice, as highlighted above, comfortably accommodates differing levels of engagement: an individual may choose to browse the work of others; another may choose to download and adapt OER but not share their own work; yet others may choose to use open tools and encourage their students to publish OER as part of their studies. Choosing whether and how far to engage with OEP inevitably entails a range of reflective and evaluative activities that are a key part of ongoing teacher professional development, and so engagement with OEP has the potential to offer significant professional development opportunities.

## Open practice as catalyst for professional development

A reflection on aspects of teaching or professional practice is part of all the activities mentioned above; for example, searching for resources for classroom use involves the consideration of student needs, level, and context, as well as the constant evaluation of each OER against this knowledge. Once an OER is selected, consideration must also be given to whether, and how far, it needs adaptation for a new context. Browsing, evaluating and adapting OER reveals others' teaching practices, approaches and techniques, and allows practitioners in a community to learn from each other in a neutral environment. Likewise, being part of knowledge-sharing communities offers a potentially low-cost, accessible response to the ICT-training needs of language teachers highlighted in Chapters 2 and 3.

Preparing resources for open sharing online involves a high level of reflection and self-evaluation, as the creator considers the quality and content of the resource, refines and reviews it, chooses appropriate open licensing and then constructs relevant descriptive information to catch the attention of a wider public audience beyond their own classroom. OER are open for public comment and feedback, which may be in the form of download or viewing statistics, via public contributions in comment boxes, or as direct feedback to the resource creator. Tutors involved in a study by Borthwick and Gallagher-Brett (2014) noted how surprising and pleasing it was to receive feedback from an unknown audience: 'My resource has got a high number of views … I was surprised … it made me think I could upload my whole lecture series' (p. 175).

## Open practice and innovation

Collaboration, knowledge-sharing and reflection in OEP can lead to innovation in teaching practice and curriculum design which can be motivating for teachers and offer students real-world experiences through the use of open tools. Two interesting examples of such activities are described in this section.

Language students at Oberlin College, USA, created their own blogs and sought out related blogs with which to interact and post comments in the target language. The students found that by leaving comments on other blogs, they often captured the attention of the blog creators, who then followed the students' own blogs and left their own comments. An authentic exchange of information and ideas began to take place which was spontaneous, student-directed and in the target language (Sawhill, 2013).

Martínez-Arboleda (2013) used open research published by the OpenLIVES project as the basis of a final-year course where students engaged with the research data (interviews with Spanish exiles) and then carried out their own research with local Spanish economic migrants. Innovative assessment (student-created audio documentaries) replaced the customary essays, and all teaching and assessment materials were published as OER. The course enabled students to define their own project and to learn a range of new technical, ethical and research skills in the knowledge that the resources they generated would make a tangible contribution to academic knowledge about Spanish immigration in the UK. Many students reported that they valued the opportunity to conduct primary research and to have some academic and creative control over their education. The open nature of the activities undertaken on this course offered an opportunity to establish new approaches to teaching and learning, which led to professional development opportunities for both students and staff involved.

With their social and collaborative nature, open educational practices have the potential to transform teaching practice, and as open sharing websites and tools proliferate, it is becoming increasingly important to know how and where resources can be discovered and shared. This is the subject of the next section.

## Repositories and online sharing communities

OER can be found and shared online in many ways but repositories which are dedicated hosting sites for OER are a good starting place for teachers, since they have been designed specifically to facilitate use and re-use of educational resources by educators. Such repositories are examples of negotiated, trusted online spaces as outlined in Chapter 6.

The OER found in dedicated repositories are usually accompanied by descriptive information (metadata) which is likely to include the resource's title, author details, date of creation or publication online, open licensing information and permissions for reuse, and keywords (tags) associated with the resource. Some repositories also include space for user comments or a preview of the resource itself. The descriptive information accompanying an OER is designed to assist users in discovering the resource and in understanding how they might use it in their own learning and teaching.

OER repositories can either contain the actual resources for download and reuse, and/or metadata for other OER and a link to where that OER can be found. For example, Xpert, managed by the UK's University of Nottingham, contains both resources and metadata/links; while the US open repositories MERLOT and OERCommons explicitly state that they only contain metadata and links to OER held elsewhere. The role of repositories that contain aggregations of links is to curate and manage open content to help educators navigate their way through the large amount of freely available information on the web.

OER can be found in different types of repositories and online spaces:

- Institutional OER repositories;
- Community repositories;
- National/international repository initiatives;
- Open courses;
- Open sharing websites.

### Institutional OER repositories

These websites are primarily created to house and archive OER produced by staff working within a particular educational institution. There is a strong promotional ethos behind the establishment of such repositories, which aim to 'showcase' the excellent teaching resources of the institution concerned. Some institutional OER repositories are an integral part of an institution's standard webpages (for example OTTER at the University of Leicester, or UNED Abierta for Spain's National Distance University, UNED) while others exist on a separate, standalone basis (for example OpenSpires, at the University of Oxford). Some institutional repositories might have different levels of sharing so that some resources can be shared internally amongst staff at the institution, whilst others are completely open allowing the wider public to view and download them (for example EdShare at the University of Southampton). Different institutions have different policies on how their OER are managed and published: some allow free, un-moderated publication by staff and others conduct a quality-check and moderation process prior to publication.

## Community repositories

These online websites are designed to serve an identified group with a shared topic of interest and are characterized by their openness and inclusivity: anyone can register and join the site to share their work. Community repositories can be discipline-specific or specific to a particular educational sector. TesConnect, for example, is an online community which has grown out of the website of the *Times Education Supplement* newspaper in the UK and has over 3,000,000 registered users from all disciplines predominantly in the primary and secondary education sector. There are also small-scale community repositories which are solely devoted to sharing OER, such as LanguageBox, which contains OER related to language learning and teaching, and HumBox, which features OER of interest to humanities practitioners in higher education. Although community repositories are hosted and maintained by particular educational institutions or organizations, the community they serve typically extends beyond the institution. These repositories do not usually have a moderation process prior to publication, which means that the OER published on these sites may be less polished than those found on moderated institutional sites. Some studies have shown that a key strength of these types of repositories is that OER sharing is taking place within an identified community of practice. For example, users of the HumBox repository reported a high level of trust in the site because they began to associate it with its community of users, who were humanities practitioners in UK higher education (Millard et al., 2013, p. 299). Equally, language teachers taking part in the JISC-funded FAVOR (Finding a Voice through Open Resources) project reported that being part of a community repository gave them encouragement and a sense of security in sharing their own work (Borthwick, 2012). Further discussion of the advantages and challenges of online communities of practice for professional development are dealt with in Chapter 8.

## National/international repository initiatives

These OER repositories are often generic, include a large number of OER on a wide range of disciplines and topics, and feature larger numbers of contributors. Connexions is a good example of this type of repository. Established in 1999, it is managed by Rice University in the USA and has evolved with funding from charitable organizations. It houses 'chunks' of open content which can be fitted together to form bigger courses of learning and typically includes open textbooks or groups of related OER. National governments have also supported the creation of repositories which can house OER and offer a platform for sharing, for example, the Netherlands' Wikiwijs, Ireland's NDLR, Belgium's KlasCement, and the UK's Jorum. At a European level, the Learning Resource Exchange is a federation of repositories housing OER for schools and has grown to become the largest website of its kind in Europe, with more than 200,000 resources. The EU has also funded the creation of the Open Education Europa portal, which aims to bring together open resources and other open educational initiatives in one gateway portal.

### Open courses

Open content can also be found within open learning spaces offering free, open courses, for example, on the UK Open University's OpenLearn website. The OER on this site are embedded and presented within a coherent course structure and are mostly licensed to allow adaptation and reuse. Other websites offering open courses contain resources which can be freely accessed, but which are usually not licensed for re-use. This is the case for the many sites offering Massive Open Online Courses (MOOCs) such as EdX, Coursera, Miríada X, FutureLearn or the Khan Academy.

### Open sharing websites

Many widely used websites also offer the possibility of finding open resources which are licensed for educational use, adaptation and sharing. Google Images and Flickr, for example, both allow users to filter search results by whether an image is labelled for reuse, adaptation etc.

The range of places where OER can be found makes discoverability (how easy it is to find something online) both important and problematic. How can users find the content they are seeking without spending hours trawling the web? How can OER authors get their resources noticed? Discoverability is an issue that preoccupies repository managers as the range of open content increases on the web, and curation/OER management websites are part of the response to this issue. However, it is the creators of OER themselves who play a key role in aiding the discoverability of resources, for example, by ensuring their OER are published in online spaces frequented by teachers and learners or by writing useful resource descriptions and adding keywords. In this respect, creators of OER, while acting as individuals, can have an impact beyond their own students and peers on a wider global community.

### Conclusion

In this chapter, we have described how the terms 'Open Educational Resources' and 'Open Educational Practices' are commonly understood, and given some examples of how open practices might be incorporated into teaching and benefit the professional development of teachers. We have indicated why engaging with OER can benefit teachers and learners and outlined some of the online spaces in which OER can be found and shared. Practitioners wishing to take their first steps into open practice may find the following suggestions helpful to get started:

- Explore whether your educational institution has an OER repository which you can use.
- Join a community repository which suits your interests/discipline area.
- Think about how you might get one of your own resources ready for sharing. Imagine how your resource could be used in other contexts and think of keyword tags to illustrate some of these possibilities. Ensure the title and descriptive information for your resource is sufficient for others to know what it contains and how it could be used for learning.
- 'Dip your toe in' first: start by sharing small, exemplar pieces of your work and see what the reaction is, and how you feel about doing this.
- When you publish an OER, promote it via Twitter and other social media sites, e.g. the #MFLTwitterati on Twitter are an active group of language teachers sharing tips and knowledge.

## Reflective task

In this task you will explore and analyse three different repositories of OER:

- LanguageBox (www.languagebox.ac.uk)
- MERLOT (www.merlot.org/merlot/index.htm)
- OpenLearn (www.open.edu/openlearn/)

The aim of the task is to raise awareness of how different repositories of OER might relate to your personal teaching context and professional situation.

Consider these sites from the perspective of the user (someone wishing to discover and download a resource to use in teaching).

- What kinds of resources can you find here: big OER or small OER; courses or materials?
- Could you use them in your own teaching or learning? How might you use them?
- Is it easy to browse and search for appropriate resources?
- Is it clear whether you can adapt and reuse the resources?

- Is it possible to review resources or leave comments about resources on the site? What kinds of comments have been added?
- Are there other kinds of feedback available on the site, such as ratings?

Now consider these sites from the perspective of the contributor (someone wishing to share resources on the site).

- Can anyone register to share resources on the site?
- Do you feel you could share some of your resources on the site? Why? Why not?
- Is it possible to review resources or leave comments about resources on the site? How do you feel about this?
- Is there a sense of community associated with the repository?

## List of sites

### COERLL

http://www.coerll.utexas.edu/coerll/
Centre for Open Educational Resources and Language Learning, one of 15 National Foreign Language Resource Centers funded by the US Department of Education.

### Community Café

https://www.llas.ac.uk/projects/6192
A project to create and share online materials to support the teaching of community languages in the UK.

### Connexions

http://cnx.org/
A repository and a content management system optimized for the delivery of educational content.

### Creative Commons

http://creativecommons.org/
A 'nonprofit organization that enables the sharing and use of creativity and knowledge through free legal tools'.

### EdShare

www.edshare.soton.ac.uk
The UK University of Southampton's repository of teaching and learning materials.

## FutureLearn

www.futurelearn.com
A provider of free online courses, owned by The Open University, UK.

## HumBox

www.humbox.ac.uk
A repository to store, manage and publish humanities resources.

## Jorum

http://www.jorum.ac.uk/
A repository of OER for Further and Higher Education in the UK.

## KlasCement

http://www.klascement.net/
A digital educational resources network for teachers, supported by the Flemish government in Belgium.

## LangOER

http://langoer.eun.org
A European project to enhance the teaching and learning of less used languages through OER/OEP.

## LanguageBox

www.languagebox.ac.uk
A 'repository to help you store, manage and publish your resources on the web'.

## Learning Resource Exchange

http://www.eun.org/teaching/resources
A 'service that enables schools to find educational content from many different countries and providers'.

## LORO

http://loro.open.ac.uk/
Languages Open Resources Online is a collection of freely available resources for language teaching and learning, based at the Department of Languages at The Open University, UK.

## Merlot

http://www.merlot.org/merlot/index.htm

A 'free and open peer reviewed collection of online teaching and learning materials'.

### OER Commons

www.oercommons.org
A 'worldwide learning network of teaching and learning materials freely available online'.

### OnStream

http://www.linksintolanguages.ac.uk/resources/2589
A project designed to link teachers of Russian in secondary, university and complementary schools in London, UK, to share resources and ideas on teaching.

### Open Education Initiative

http://openeducationeuropa.eu
A portal to access all European OER for learners, teachers and researchers.

### OpenLearn

www.open.edu/openlearn
A portal that gives free access to learning materials from The Open University, UK.

### OpenLives

http://openlives.wordpress.com/
A project to digitize and publish as OER materials documenting the experiences of Spanish migrants to the UK and returning migrants to Spain.

### OpenSpires

http://podcasts.ox.ac.uk/
A site where the University of Oxford, UK, shares 'audio recordings of public lectures, teaching material, interviews with leading academics, and information about applying to the university'.

### OTTER

http://www2.le.ac.uk/departments/beyond-distance-research-alliance/projects/otter
A project to enable the production and release of high-quality open educational resources drawn from teaching materials delivered at the University of Leicester, UK.

## School of Open

https://p2pu.org/en/schools/school-of-open/
A 'global community of volunteers providing free online courses, face-to-face workshops, and innovative training programs on the meaning, application, and impact of "openness" in the digital age'.

## TED Open Translation Project

https://www.ted.com/about/programs-initiatives/ted-open-translation-project
A global volunteer effort to subtitle TED Talks in different languages.

## TESConnect

www.tes.co.uk
A UK-based site hosting a large collection of free teaching resources shared by a network of teachers.

## UNED Abierta

www.uned.es/unedabierta
A portal to OER created by the UNED, Spain's National Distance University.

## Wikiwijs

http://www.wikiwijsleermiddelenplein.nl/start/
A platform where teachers can publish and download teaching materials, commissioned by the Ministry of Education in the Netherlands.

## Xpert

http://www.nottingham.ac.uk/xpert/
A distributed repository of elearning resources developed by the University of Nottingham, UK.

## Note

1.  https://wiki.creativecommons.org/What_is_OER.

# 8
# Online Communities of Practice: A Professional Development Tool for Language Educators

*Aline Germain-Rutherford*

## Introduction

*'A place for shared materials'*, *'accessing common and current resources'*, *'possibilities for dialogue with other educators'* and *'a place of trust and honesty'* were the key elements that language teachers and trainers who were surveyed during two professional development workshops in the context of using ICT for teaching[1] identified when asked about the three main elements that were essential in a community of practice. One participant at the workshop organized in the context of a European Centre for Modern Languages project wrote:

> Your question has made me think about what I really appreciate and why I find some communities more useful to my needs as a teacher than others. I believe that three main elements that are essential in a community of practice are:
>
> - It represents a group of people coming from various backgrounds, with various levels of expertise in teaching, both mentors and mentees – *the variety* is important because it makes it possible to see every problem from different angles and get different perspectives, every discussion is more fruitful.
> - There is the atmosphere of *collaboration and sharing* – the willingness to help and ask for help.
> - The teachers are active, *they care about the community* and believe in *the power of the community* to improve the work of individual teachers – projects are started, surveys done, papers read and discussed, members comment on one another's blogs, it is easy to get feedback, etc. (my own italics)

113

The focus of this chapter is to define and explore three different communities of practice for language teachers, and to examine how these notions of 'variety', 'collaboration and sharing' and 'power of the community', as well as other important characteristics of these communities impact on the success of a community of practice.

## What are communities of practice?

'They are groups of people informally bound together by shared expertise and passion for a joint enterprise' (Wenger & Snyder, 2000, p. 139); or, as described slightly more comprehensively by Wenger (2006): 'Communities of practice are groups of people who share a concern or a passion for something they do and learn how to do it better as they interact regularly' (p. 1).

First introduced by Jean Lave and Etienne Wenger in the late 1980s, the term refers to the ancient concept of a 'guild' or 'corporations' of craftsmen where apprentices would learn their craft and trade by associating themselves and working for a certain period of time with experienced, skilled workers (Wenger & Snyder, 2000). *Les Compagnons du tour de France* in the Middle Ages (Les Compagnons du tour de France, n.d.), for instance, would execute their *'Tour de France'* to work with and learn from experienced artisans to develop a mastery of their craft that would then be evidenced by their *'Chef d'oeuvre'* (masterpiece). Still in existence today,[2] the *Compagnonage* enables a young apprentice to learn a trade from competent masters as well as from experiencing the community of a profession while living in a *Compagnon* house. The process of learning in these 'associations' of professionals that we call today communities of practice is based on a social theory of learning (Wenger, 2006, 2010):

> learning is recognized as a social phenomenon constituted in the experienced, lived-in world, through legitimate peripheral participation in ongoing social practice; the process of changing knowledgeable skill is subsumed in processes of changing identity in and through membership in a community of practitioners (Lave, 1991, p. 64)

For the *Compagnons* in France, or young professionals in other parts of the world, learning in these situations of apprenticeship occurs mainly outside of a didactic structure and through an ongoing mediated experience of observation, guided practice and informal conversations. Learning is nourished in the relationship with the practitioners of the community, engendering an evolving and deepening sense of professional identity and membership in that community. 'Learning is a social becoming' (Wenger, 2010, p. 179).

Rooted in Vygotsky's sociocultural theory of learning (1978), a community of practice 'engages people in mutual sense-making' (Eckert, 2006, p. 683) in a fluid and organic way.

Although communities of practice can often appear unstructured and without clear purposes and/or outcomes because of their informal and evolving nature, they are defined by three important characteristics: a shared domain of interest between all members; a network of members who by mutually engaging in sharing knowledge and experiences form a community; and a growing repertoire of resources that defines over time a shared practice among the practitioners of this community (Lave 1991; Wenger, 2006; Wenger et al., 2002). It is the ongoing flow of activity between these three interconnected constituents (domain, community and practice) that generates improved understanding and practice within the domain (Byington, 2011).

Communities of practice have been known by different names at various times, such as 'learning communities', 'thematic groups', 'peer groups' and 'knowledge networks'. But even if these communities or groups have different purposes, they remain similar in general intent: to develop and expand one's knowledge and expertise by engaging in meaningful interactions with fellow professionals. By contrast, work groups or project teams, focusing on and defined by the product or the task to deliver, do not fit the definition of a community of practice that exists through the cooperative process itself and the commitment of its self-selected members (Wenger & Snyder, 2000). In an opinion piece on effective professional development (PD) for educators, Blake-Plock highlights the importance of social networks and social media in helping teachers connect and interact with their peers to 'develop the profession themselves' (2013, n.p.), in contrast to the disempowering and disengaging practice of using online videos or other ready-to-use and static professional development tools and materials.

> The paradigm of what constitutes engaging and quality PD has shifted in favor of those who are actively involved, through the informal and social media-driven opportunities that educators are now creating for themselves. (Blake-Plock, 2013, n.p.)

## Virtual communities of practice: advantages and challenges

Web 2.0 technology and social media have expanded the possibilities for online communities of practice by allowing and generating greater and richer collaboration among professionals, easier access to resources and larger, diverse membership (Byington, 2011; Guldberg & Mackness, 2009; Yang, 2009). To echo the participant, quoted above, from an ICT-REV professional development workshop,[3] the variety of perspectives and of levels of expertise in a community of practice that has a very diverse membership broadens and strengthens the collective expertise and professional knowledge that is progressively built and owned by the group.

However, Internet and social media technology can also bring the challenges of distance and time differences to online communities of practice. Maintaining empathy and a strong sense of belonging to a 'virtual' group is difficult and demands a strong commitment from its participants (Preece, 2004; Wenger at al., 2002). Examining factors that would foster or hinder participation and engagement in a virtual community of practice, Guldberg and Mackness (2009) have identified five key dimensions to monitor while designing and maintaining a live, active community of practice: 'Emotion; Technology; Connectivity; Understanding Norms; and Learning Tensions' (p. 532).

The level of emotion participants feel while engaged in the different activities of the community of practice is an important factor. Wenger, in his definition of a community of practice mentioned at the beginning of this chapter, uses the word 'passion' to describe the type of commitment members bring to a community of practice (Wenger, 1998, 2006). However, the experience can also be challenging and might inhibit members' willingness to participate further: 'I became so frustrated I simply stopped participating' (Guldberg & Mackness, 2009, p. 532).

The type of technology used and the level of expertise members have using this technology also represents a challenge. Although today's free access to many synchronous and asynchronous communication tools broadens the possibilities to communicate and collaborate online, lack of training and different time zones can deter participation.

Feeling connected to the group also influences greatly the level of participation and of learning, with a sense that working together on a common project strengthens the relationships and raises the level of 'connectedness'.

Sharing the same understanding of the cultural norms of the virtual community and being familiar with the community's netiquette when collaborating and discussing online encourages a strong commitment to the group: 'Participants needed to understand the rhythms of posting and receiving responses to their posts and how people are "listened" to online' (Guldberg & Mackness, 2009, p. 533). These social norms develop over time and help create a trustful and empathic learning environment for explicit and tacit knowledge to be shared (Preece, 2004).

Finally, acknowledging and working with the inherent learning tensions of a community of practice can only enrich the learning experiences of its members. The constant back and forth between theoretical knowledge and practitioners' experiences, between novices in the field and seasoned professionals, and between acting on this knowledge and experience and reflecting on it all create exceptional learning environments 'if kept in balance' (Guldberg & Mackness, 2009, p. 533).

## Communities of practices for language teachers

The concept of communities of practice, virtual or offline, is now used in many different professional contexts, and is seen as a transformative way to approach both professional development and learning as a process. This has been particularly true in the last two decades in education and more specifically for world languages, where communities of practice are widely used for language educators' professional development and to provide language learning environments for students.

> [B]uilding COPs for foreign language and second-language teachers is a way to prepare the next generation of foreign language teachers while embracing learning. (Fraga-Cañadas, 2011, p. 297)

This is where the social theory of learning on which the dynamic of a community of practice is based meets with the socio-constructivist framework of second language development. Contrary to other professions, a community of practice for language teachers not only is a place to collaboratively develop professional expertise in the practice of language teaching, but can also be a learning community for non-native language teachers to achieve higher language proficiency and to gain deeper intercultural awareness, through negotiation of meaning and social interactions in the target language.

The challenge, however, is to develop a supportive and empathic enough environment that enables non-native language teachers to go beyond the inhibiting barrier of feeling inadequate or less competent as a teacher because of their non-native mastery of the language (Cook, 2005;

Fraga-Cañadas, 2011). Having, in the target language, both a safe and trusted place to share values and knowledge about language education, and to discuss personal experiences, stories, and opinions about teaching practices can raise social capital (Daniel et al., 2003; Preece, 2004) and strengthen the community. It can also help non-native language teachers to develop confidence and to consolidate their identity as fully legitimate language professionals (Fraga-Cañadas, 2011). Feeling part of and supported by the community has a positive impact on teacher retention (Ruggles Gere, 2010).

Another noted benefit of virtual or offline communities of practice for professional development when contrasted with more traditional and prescriptive teacher training workshops, and when focused on student outcomes, is the potential increase in the quality of teaching and improved student achievement (Vescio et al., 2008). Within the diverse community of language professionals, language educators are able to discuss, explore, and research many different answers to language teaching and student learning issues (Levine & Marcus, 2010; Vescio et al., 2008).

A diversity of experiences and perspectives in the development of a broader and richer knowledge and practice in the profession can also mean belonging to multiple communities of practices. Interestingly, a study examining professional development needs in Communicative Language Teaching (CLT) for ESL teachers in Japan[4] shows how a teacher developed a 'context-appropriate methodology' by participating, even from the periphery, in multiple offline and virtual professional communities of practice presenting different cultural perspectives on the communicative approach (Nishino, 2012). A more prescriptive approach of western views on CLT discussed in one community of practice was balanced by observations and imitations of more local and culturally relevant practices by colleagues in other communities of practice; this helped the teacher of this case study to develop a very personal and context-appropriate communicative teaching approach for his ESL students. This personal approach supported communicative activities in which students could interact in the target language, while accommodating a more teacher-centred approach rooted in the 'particularity' (Kumaravadivelu, 2008) of the tradition of the Japanese education system.

> The idea of pedagogic particularity is consistent with the hermeneutic perspective of *situational understanding*, which claims that a meaningful pedagogy cannot be constructed without a holistic interpretation of particular situations. (Kumaravadivelu, 2008, p. 171)

## Designing communities of practice

The longevity of a community of practice, virtual or offline, is dependent on its design and although it may seem that the fluidity of the social space, the informality and unpredictability of interactions are due to the spontaneous nature of exchanges, careful planning in the design of the community is key to explain its success and 'aliveness' (Wenger et al., 2002).

A shared focus and a clear purpose help define the social architecture and communication patterns of the community of practice. One community's goal might be to develop a network of colleagues and generate certain types of activities and levels of engagement that can differ greatly from those of another community whose learning purpose is to acquire deeper expertise in the profession. Cambridge and colleagues (2005) identify four categories of purposes. Communities of practice can indeed focus on developing a relationship with other professionals, on learning and improving a practice, on collaborating on a project, and on innovating and creating new knowledge (Cambridge et al., 2005, p. 2).

However, clarity of domain and purpose are not enough to bring a community of practice to life and 'cultivate' it. Wenger and colleagues (2002) have identified several essential principles to consider in the design of a community, such as the need to nourish and support the very 'human' and 'evolving' nature of a community. Therefore the structure of the social space should be designed to optimize organic growth and accommodate flexibility.

Multiple views from a diverse membership, as mentioned earlier by one workshop participant, are seen as another important principle to take into account. Tension between divergent and convergent thinking enriches the dialogue and brings new knowledge and innovative practices. Opening the community to specialists but also non-specialists in the domain is a way to invite different perspectives and ways to look at problems (Wenger et al., 2002).

However, not all participants are fully engaged in a community's activities and discussions. Often a large majority are silent participants who occasionally read the posts and sporadically browse or use the resources shared by others, but usually do not contribute. Speaking more generally about online interactive groups, Nielsen refers to the 90–9–1 rule to describe the unequal members' participation 'in most online communities, [where] 90% of users are lurkers who never contribute, 9% of users contribute a little, and 1% of users account for almost all the action' (Nielsen, 2006, p. 1).

These peripheral members nonetheless learn and disseminate content through their passive participation (Gotto et al., 2008; Nishino, 2012; Wenger et al., 2002). Designing an inclusive community structure, which offers equal opportunities for active and peripheral participants to learn from others, is another essential element to consider in the design:

> The key to good community participation and a healthy degree of movement between levels is to design community activities that allow participants at all levels to feel like full members ... [S]uccessful communities 'build benches' for those on the sidelines. (Wenger et al., 2002, p. 57)

A communication structure that allows fluidity for private conversations and smaller group networking is also seen as an important design concept to strengthen and stimulate the larger network of the community of practice; so too is the notion of rhythm of contributions and community events to create a predictable and reasonable pace in the interactions, especially when combined with special events that re-invigorate the community. However, all these design principles add up to one important notion: that the members see, as they evolve in the community, the true value for them in being part of it.

> Rather than attempting to determine their expected value in advance, communities need to create events, activities, and relationships that help their potential value emerge and enable them to discover new ways to harvest it. (Wenger et al., 2002, p. 60)

In the light of these design principles we will now observe and analyze three active communities of practice for language teachers in terms of membership behaviours, types of activities and levels of vitality.

## Three case studies

These three examples of online communities of practice, though created for slightly different purposes, share the same domain of language education. The first example is the Language Educators Community created in 2010 by the American Council on the Teaching of Foreign Languages (ACTFL). The goal of this community is described as follows:

> An open forum for language educators at all levels and assignments, and of all languages to come together to share and discuss topics of general interest. (Language Educators Community, 2010, n.p.)

The second example describes a community of practice created in the autumn of 2013 by Middlebury Interactive Languages,[5] to address professional development needs of a group of teachers in Vermont, USA, using for the first time online language course materials in fully online or blended learning implementations. The purpose of the Middlebury Interactive Teachers Community is described as:

> a place where you can ask questions, share experiences and information and learn from others in the Middlebury Interactive Community. (Middlebury Interactive Teachers Community, 2013, n.p.)

The third example is a regional community within the larger online community of practice that was developed by the Developing Online Teaching Skills (DOTS) project team (Stickler et al., 2010a; see Chapter 10 for a detailed description of the DOTS project). Coupled with on-site professional development workshops this online community enables participants

> to join a larger community of language professionals and online teaching experts [to pursue discussions started during the on-site workshops], to watch video clips of experts explaining their use of tools, and to discuss different experiences and needs. They can also create their own training activities, upload materials for others to use, and translate the existing activities into various languages. (European Centre for Modern Languages, 2008, n.p.)

### The ACTFL Language Educators Community

A very open community for ACTFL members, former members and non-members, the Language Educators Community offers a space to share ideas, questions and information related to language education and teaching practices. The technical architecture is a simple forum where its members can post threaded messages to share resources with or without attachments.

This community has been in existence for four years, and shows strong vitality by the growing number of its members (18,000 members with an average of two new members per week joining the community) and the regularity of its membership's contributions to the forum (an average of two postings daily). The open access to this community allows for a large and diverse membership and questions or requests for information on the forum are rarely left without an answer because of the high number of its active participants. The annual ACTFL Congress attracts new members every year and helps to maintain the daily flow of contributions to the forum.

Yet the design of the community, in accordance with its purpose, does not facilitate in-depth discussion or collaboration with smaller groups of participants. This explains why most of the 3,000 contributions are forum postings which generate usually only one or two answers, and no deeper threaded conversations. In four years only 56 items were shared in the community's library (eight items this year, 15 items a year ago, six items two years ago and 27 items three years ago), with a large majority of them being Word or Portable Document Format (pdf) files, and four slide shows. However, none of the 56 documents has been commented upon, which shows that sharing is mostly unidirectional and does not lead to a deeper dialogue between the resources' authors. Nevertheless, these resources are widely viewed and downloaded (see Table 8.1).

With an average of 188 downloads per slide show and 91 per document, for example, this provides evidence for the view that peripheral members participate in the life of the community by actively downloading the resources that are offered by the other members.

Based on Wenger's categorization of activities in a community of practice (Wenger, 2006), an analysis of the questions posted by participants which generated a thread of five or more answers (less than 1% of the postings) shows that the two most frequent requests concern information on available resources, and questions seeking experience about specific teaching strategies, or ways of using particular types of material. Questions related to problem-solving and seeking permission to reuse existing materials are two other categories that generated multiple answers by participants. One last question which generated nine threaded answers (a high level of interaction if we consider that 99% of postings generate less than five answers) related to the definition of the domain and the purpose of the Language Educators Community, specifically in reaction against postings by language materials vendors. This posting and the answers sent by other participants show that the shared value to be found in this community is about dialogue and exchanges

*Table 8.1*  Participants' activity in the library of the ACTFL Language Educators Community

|  | 56 Word or pdf documents | 4 Slide shows |
| --- | --- | --- |
| Total Views | 6,104 | 1,152 |
| Total Downloads | 5,096 | 752 |

of experiences with colleagues, and not as a space to be distorted by commercial perspectives. (See Table 8.2 for examples of each type of question asked by members of the community.) Activities related to 'coordination and synergy' of efforts to achieve a goal, to 'invitations for site observations' and to 'knowledge mapping' to identify gaps and follow up actions, which are also part of Wenger's typology of activities

*Table 8.2*  Activity types in the ACTFL Language Educators Community

| Activity type | # of postings | # of threaded answers (average) | Sample messages |
|---|---|---|---|
| Request for information/ resources | 40 | 7 to 8 | Subject: Thanksgiving activity Message: I would love to have ideas on a fun Thanksgiving activity for Spanish III or IV students where they will be learning. Gracias. |
| Seeking experience | 34 | 6 to 7 | Subject: Second year – high school – curriculum Message: Just curious, but would any French teachers at the secondary level please let me know if you teach the subjunctive and/ or the passé simple? We are revising our district's curriculum and are in a heated debate on which levels are most appropriate for these topics. Thanks! |
| Problem solving | 9 | 5 to 6 | Subject: Managing multi-levels in FL classroom Message: I'm requesting ideas as to how to deal with students taking a foreign language for the first time in the class with students who may be on their third or forth year. This seems to particularly happen in elementary. Inevitably, the class is split in their degree of exposure to the target language, and we end up teaching to the lowest common denominator. This means that more advanced students barely get past the basics and have copious review each year. Due to vast age differences and schedules, we cannot teach by mastery level. How can we utilize the more advanced students' expertise and challenge them, while teaching the less experienced or novice student? |

*(continued)*

*Table 8.2*   Continued

| Reusing assets | 3 | 8 | Subject: Animated Spanish Videos with Interactive Activities Message: Hello All, I created two Spanish videos a while ago, and decided to add interactive activities to them. They are basic, but different. Watch Azul, a wrestler from Spain talk about himself, and watch him with his best friend, Flama Caliente, a female wrestler from Mexico. If you want to know how I made the videos so that you can create your own with your students, let me know and I can blog about it when I get a chance. Have fun with them! (click on the links below) 1. Azul el luchador: Introductions, Greetings, etc. 2. Azul y Flama Caliente: Hobbies and pastimes. |
|---|---|---|---|
| Defining the goal of the community | 1 | 9 | Subject: postings from vendors Message: Perhaps others feel differently, but I would prefer that this group be off-limits to postings from commercial vendors, and dedicated only to suggestions and resources from my teaching colleagues. |

in a community of practice (Wenger, 2006, p. 3), were absent from the questions shared in this community of practice.

It seems from this analysis that the shared value to be found in this community is more about dialogue and exchanges of experiences with colleagues, than collaborative planning and action to achieve specific goals.

### The Middlebury Interactive Teachers Community

Relatively new and with a small membership of approximately 100 language teachers, the community is designed to facilitate growth in terms of membership, diversity and purposes. Its technical architecture facilitates the creation, by its members, of subgroups per languages, per topics, or per projects, and therefore encourages a combination of private and public conversations to allow more focused interactions or more general discussions. The space allows for threaded discussion via its different forums, and for new members to introduce themselves more extensively and creatively than by just a profile form.

The goal of developing among peers an understanding and an expertise in online and blended learning methodology is also facilitated by the access to the Resource Library, an organized space to share research articles, best practices, lesson plans, media files for project collaborations, teaching tips and teaching materials.

The home page of the community's website keeps members informed by offering an overview of all the latest activities in the community, and a moderator oversees the site to regularly add information and resources that could benefit the professional development of these teachers (see Figure 8.1).

However, the degree of value members find in this community is still in its infancy, with sporadic contributions of research articles, teaching tips and shared practices. Social bonding and professional networking was encouraged during a full-day face-to-face professional development workshop where all the teachers involved in the Vermont Initiative were invited to work collaboratively in different groups to better know each other, and to share the products of their collaborations in the

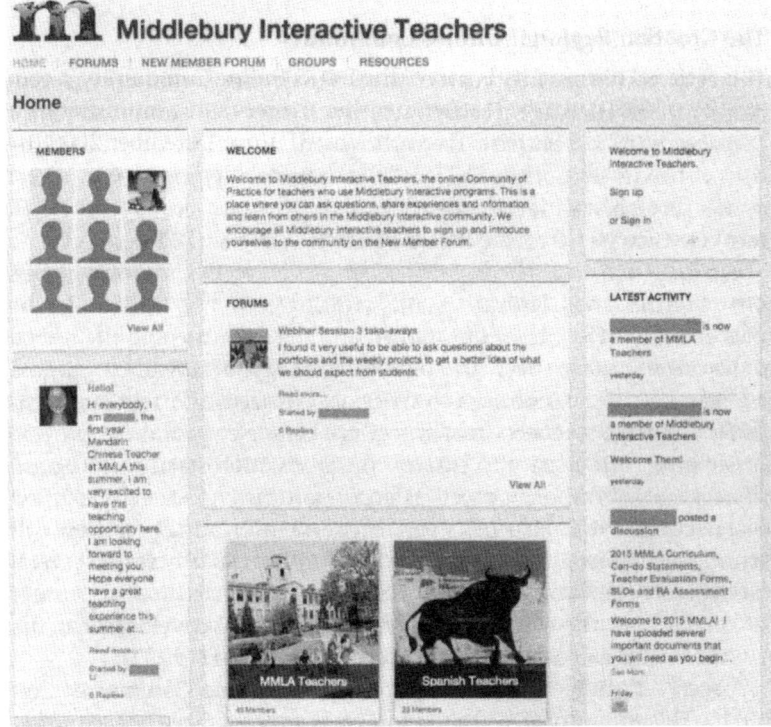

*Figure 8.1*  Home page of the Middlebury Interactive Teachers Community
*Source*: Courtesy of Middlebury Interactive Languages. Copyright © 2014 by Middlebury Interactive Languages. All rights reserved.

community of practice to familiarize themselves with the concept of the community and its website.

Wenger and colleagues (2002) and Cambridge and colleagues (2005) identify several stages in a community's life cycle. Wenger and colleagues (2002) define these phases as Potential (a loose network of people recognizing common interests around a key issue); Coalescing (the community establishing the value of sharing knowledge and developing relationships and sufficient trust); Maturing (the community clarifying its focus, role and boundaries, and shifting from sharing tips to developing a body of knowledge); Stewardship (the community maintaining its relevance and its voice, keeping the tone and focus lively and engaging, and keeping itself on the cutting edge); and Transformation (communities naturally transforming or dying). Based on these five stages, it seems that Middlebury Interactive Teachers Community has not yet reached the maturing stage and is still in the process of defining its boundaries and values.

### The Croatian Regional Online Community

This regional community is part of the DOTS Online Community, a community of 358 language teachers, teacher trainers and administrators of language programmes that have participated, since December 2008 (the date of the creation of the DOTS online community), in one or several on-site professional development workshops organized by the DOTS team (see Chapter 10 for a detailed description of the DOTS project).

Learning from and sharing with other professionals, improving one's own practices and innovating and creating new knowledge are the goals of the DOTS online community, and the structure and the design of the online space reflect the complexity and flexibility of its purpose and membership. In addition to series of bite-sized ICT training activities for language teachers, smaller regional online communities provide participants with a space to extend communication started during on-site regional workshops as well as an opportunity to strengthen their local networks while sharing experiences and innovating practices with technology. Indeed, these regional communities, usually created several weeks before the two-day on-site workshops, help participants to meet before and after the event, reinforcing social capital development, 'the glue that holds a community together' (Preece, 2004, p. 297).

A recent example is the Croatian Regional Online Community created in the autumn of 2013 to support and expand a face-to-face professional development workshop organized by the DOTS team in Zagreb in December 2013.

A rapid statistical analysis of the DOTS online community for a period of three months shows how the level of activity of its participants (views and posts in the forums and in the ICT training activities) follows the rhythm of the on-site regional workshops (see Figure 8.2). Indeed, the DOTS team offered a workshop in Croatia on 13–14 December 2013, which explains the increase of activities in mid-December; a workshop in Finland on 6–7 February 2014, hence the second jump in activities for the first two weeks of February, and a third workshop in Hungary on 21–22 February 2014, which again explains the third rise in activities just after these dates. What this statistical report shows, however, is the lack of activity in between the professional development workshops, and therefore the difficulty in maintaining participation in and relevance of the DOTS online community and its smaller regional online communities.

In the case of the Croatian Regional Online Community, 29 members signed in. This community was created on 15 November 2013, four weeks before the two-day on-site workshop. The first increase in activity started on that day with one of the workshop organizers inviting participants who would come to the workshop in Zagreb in December to introduce themselves and get to know each other on the Croatian Regional Online Community. The purpose of this early 'social bonding' activity, reinforced during the on-site workshop, was to help create a trusting and welcoming online community for Croatian language professionals to use after the two-day meeting. 22 members answered this invitation to share information on their professional activities and goals in 59 postings spread throughout the month of November until the first day of the workshop.

A second rise in activity appeared just after the workshop and was caused by the posting of photos taken by participants during the workshop. 28 posts by 16 participants relate to the positive impact that the face-to-face workshop and now the online community were having on strengthening the relationship and sharing of this group of Croatian teachers and teacher trainers. This was then demonstrated by 40 posts in the two months following the workshop where two thirds of the participants shared links to online software, best practices for implementing these tools in language classrooms, and information about existing communities of practice or networks for Croatian language teachers. In just four months, 20 members had posted 158 messages, viewed 1,378 times by all the members of the Croatian Regional Online Community. However, this activity diminished rapidly the further away the participants were from the date of the on-site workshop, in both the core group of participants and among the more peripheral members. Figure 8.3

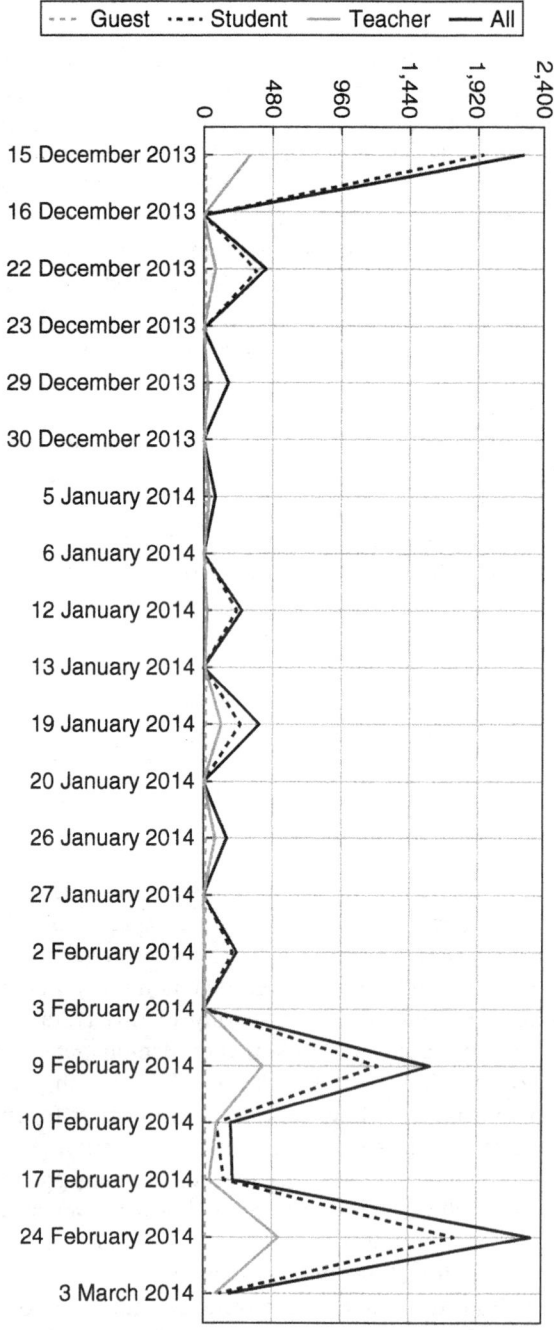

*Figure 8.2* Level of activity (views and posts) by participants in the DOTS Online Community

*Figure 8.3* Level of activity (views and posts) per member of the Regional Croatian Online Community

shows a regular decrease in the number of posts contributed and viewed by the 29 members of the community from 9 December 2013 (two days before the on-site workshop) to the week of 3 February 2014 (two months after the workshop).

## Discussion

'Facilitation is the most important factor in determining CoP success' (Gotto et al., 2008, p. 17). Both the Middlebury Interactive Teachers Community and the Croatian Regional Online Community have facilitators who initiated members' participation by asking them to introduce themselves and by encouraging them, before and after the on-site professional workshops, to share resources and experiences, to ask questions and to learn from others. To model the type of interactions members could have in the community, the moderator of the Middlebury Interactive Teachers Community regularly shares documents related to research and best practices in second language teaching strategies, and actively invites colleagues to share similar resources and start discussions in the forum of the community. But the art of facilitation is difficult and demands frequent communication with the members. A certain number of strategies, such as using notification alerts via email each time a post has been contributed by a participant, or tracking and making visible changes, most recent activities or new members, as well as providing the option of a photo gallery for members and the possibility to rate posts and resources, are ways to increase participation and enhance facilitation (Tarmizi et al., 2007).

It seems, however, that the role of the moderator is even more important when the membership of a community is relatively small, as in the case of the Middlebury Interactive Teachers Community and the Croatian Regional Online Community. Indeed, although the relationship between the members can be very tight and intimate, as in the case of the participants of the Croatian Regional Online Community, who know each other quite well professionally and enjoy keeping in touch, a network may be too small to ensure prompt and multiple answers to a question. In contrast, the ACTFL Language Educators Community has no moderator, but its very large membership, however loose and impersonal, ensures the regularity of contributions and multiple perspectives in responses. The 'scale' of membership might be an additional factor to consider in determining the success of an online community of practice.

## Conclusion

> Professional development is viewed as a career-long, context-specific, continuous endeavor that is guided by standards, grounded in the teacher's own work, focused on student learning, and tailored to the teacher's stage of career development. It is ... more than a series of training workshops, institutes, meetings, and in-service days. It is a process of learning how to put knowledge into practice through engagement in practice within a community of practitioners. (Schlager & Fusco, 2004, p. 124)

Designing effective and successful offline or online communities of practice to support and nurture this organic process of mutual transformation demands, however, careful planning and specific sets of principles. As observed in the three communities of practice presented above, a sense of shared values and relevance, a mutual commitment to engage in a meaningful dialogue around shared practices, and a plurality of perspectives are key elements to allow participants to evolve in their professional identity and knowledge.

An effective community of practice, with active members from diverse perspectives, experiences and locations engaging, supporting, stimulating and encouraging one another (assisted by but not dependent on facilitators), can be a catalyst for an unexpected and even surprising communal re-thinking and re-imagining of practices.

## Reflective task

1. Several language educators, already members or future members of communities of practice for language professionals, were asked the following question during a professional development workshop:
   - What three main elements would you consider most useful in an online community of practice?

The results, visualized in this Wordle (see Figure 8.4) highlight the notion of shared resources ('sharing', 'lesson' and 'materials'), of diversity ('various', 'different' and 'perspectives'), and of practitioners ('teachers'). How would you answer this question? What type of relevance are you looking for in a community of practice related to your profession?

2. The following list combines the characteristics and principles considered as essential in the design and cultivation of an active and

*Figure 8.4* A visual representation of participants' answers generated by the software 'Wordle'

successful community of practice. Use this checklist to assess the design and the strength of the community of practice you have developed or in which you are actively engaged:

A Characteristics (Wenger et al., 2002, p. 45)
- A shared domain
- A community of engaged members
- A shared repertoire of practices

B Design principles (Wenger et al., 2002, p. 51)
- Design for evolution
- Open a dialogue between inside and outside perspectives
- Invite different levels of participation
- Develop both public and private community spaces
- Focus on value
- Combine familiarity and excitement
- Create a rhythm for the community

C Typical activities (Wenger, 2006, pp. 2–3)
- Problem solving
- Requests for information
- Seeking experience
- Reusing assets
- Coordination and synergy (combining resource or expertise for a project)
- Discussing developments
- Documentation projects
- Visits
- Mapping knowledge and identifying gaps

D Liveliness and relevance (Gotto et al., 2008, p. 21)
- High participation level
- Shared history
- Solidarity and support
- Conflict resolution
- Group identity and self-awareness
- Roles and governance

This list can also serve as a survey outline to collect feedback from community members.

## Notes

1. Language teachers and teacher trainers who participated in two professional development workshops, one in Europe (European Centre for Modern Languages, 2013: ICT-REV Initiative) and one in The United States (Middlebury Interactive Languages (MIL), 2013: The MIL Vermont Initiative), were surveyed.
2. In 2010 The French *Compagnonage* was registered on the Representative List of the Intangible Cultural Heritage of Humanity of UNESCO under the title *Compagnonage, network for on-the-job transmission of knowledge and identities.*
3. ICT-REV is an initiative carried out within the framework of a cooperation agreement between the European Centre for Modern Languages and the European Commission, focusing on providing training and awareness-raising workshops for teachers, education stakeholders and multipliers in the context of self-training in the use of ICT.
4. The Communicative Language Teaching (CLT) approach focuses on learning to communicate through interaction in the target language. For the last two decades, the Ministry of Education, Culture, Sports, Science, and Technology (MEXT) of Japan has supported initiatives to promote the CLT approach in ESL.
5. Middlebury Interactive Languages is a for profit company created in partnership by Middlebury College, Vermont and K12 Inc., an online course provider to develop and offer online language courses for students from kindergarten through high school.

# 9
# Theoretical Approaches and Research-Based Pedagogies for Online Teaching

*Regine Hampel*

## Introduction

> [A]s computers have become more a part of our everyday lives – and permeated other areas of education – the question is no longer whether to use computers but how. CALL researchers, developers and practitioners have a critical role in helping the overall field of second language learning come to grips with this domain. (Hubbard, 2009, p. 1)

This observation by Philip Hubbard – a long-standing scholar in the area of computer-assisted language learning (CALL) – underlines how the position of CALL has been strengthened within the field of second language learning research and it highlights the role of the teacher in enabling CALL.

This book is grounded on the premise that online teaching needs to be based on theoretical foundations and in the recognition that teaching is an iterative process of choosing pedagogical approaches, applying them in one's practice, and critically reflecting on how successful this process has been in terms of teaching and learning. This allows developers and teachers as well as researchers to find out about the *how* of using computers and improve online teaching in the process. As all pedagogy is based on an assumption about how people learn, this chapter starts off with a brief overview of relevant learning theories and how these have influenced language learning theories. Then the focus moves to pedagogical approaches that have been shaped by these theories, and the chapter concludes with selected methodological approaches that are suitable for research in the area of online language education. The theories presented are rooted in sociocultural frameworks of language learning and teaching; the methodologies are qualitative and interpretivist, and they include participatory research, action research, ethnography, and discourse analysis. These conceptual foundations are illustrated with the help of different studies that have used these different approaches. The chapter concludes by suggesting areas of practitioner research that might be useful for the reader in his or her own context.

In terms of audience, this chapter should be of interest both to teachers involved in language education who are keen to research their own practice and to researchers who want to find out about online language teaching, particularly in relation to the various theoretical and methodological approaches that have been used by researchers. Rather than encompassing all possible uses of CALL, the spotlight is on online communication and interaction (which is also referred to as computer-mediated communication or CMC) between language learners or between learners and speakers of the target language (L2).

## Sociocultural theory

In order to explore online communication and interaction in this chapter, approaches that see learning as a social activity and that stress the importance of the context of learning seem more appropriate than more traditional transmission approaches or approaches that are based on psycholinguistic principles, such as Krashen's (1985) input hypothesis or Long and Robinson's (1998) interaction hypothesis. Although psycholinguistic approaches recognize the importance of interaction, they see teaching in terms of providing input and tend to focus on cognitive processes and on the acquisition of particular linguistic features rather than understanding second language development as learning a social practice by using the language in communication with other speakers. This chapter therefore takes sociocultural theory as its starting point. Sociocultural theory links individual mental processes with the cultural, institutional and historical context and emphasises the role of cultural mediation in the development of higher psychological functions (for example thinking, reasoning, self-awareness, or the use of signs such as language). According to Lantolf (2006), three cultural factors play a fundamental role in this mediating process, namely activities (e.g. play, education, work), artifacts (including language and technology) and concepts.

These cultural factors mediate the relationships between people, between people and the physical world, and between people and their inner mental worlds. Humans in all of their manifestations are organized in accordance with the various activities, artifacts, and concepts that they jointly construct through history. (p. 69)

Although sociocultural theory was initially developed in Russia in the 1920s and was not introduced into Western thinking until the late 1970s it has since become enormously influential and has generated various sub-theories, all of which centre on the social nature of learning. Socio-constructivism, for example, sees knowledge as socially constructed (Vygotsky, 1978) and cognition as socially shared (Wertsch, 1991a); situated learning understands learning as 'an integral part of generative social practice in the lived-in world' (Lave & Wenger, 1991, p. 35). Lave and Wenger (1991) also introduced the notion of communities of practice: 'In contrast with learning as internalization, learning as increasing participation in communities of practice concerns the whole person acting in the world' (Lave & Wenger, 1991, p. 49; see also Chapter 8).

Johnson (2006, pp. 240–241) summarizes the impact of sociocultural theory on how we see knowledge as follows:

From the epistemological stance of the sociocultural turn, knowledge that informs activity is not just abstracted from theory, codified in textbooks, and constructed through principled ways of examining phenomena, but also emerges out of a dialogic and transformative process of reconsidering and reorganizing lived experiences through the theoretical constructs and discourses that are publicly recognized and valued within the communities of practice that hold power.

However, these are general educational theories and concepts. So how has sociocultural theory been received by researchers interested in language learning, and what has its impact been on teaching? It has affected a change in language learning theory, going beyond the computational view of learners processing input and producing output to focusing on ecological approaches with a greater focus on the language learner in his or her context, through notions like motivation, identity or L2 self, and concepts such as learner autonomy, empowerment of the learner, and agency alongside more general sociocultural notions such as collaboration and the co-construction of knowledge. Hand-in-hand with this goes the notion that the teacher is a facilitator and a mediator rather than an instructor. As a result, sociocultural theory has also had an impact on teacher education, which has shifted from a sole focus on content and appropriate teaching practices 'to position[ing] L2 teachers as knowers and to position[ing] their ways of knowing that lead to praxis alongside the disciplinary knowledge that has dominated the traditional knowledge base of L2 teacher education' (Johnson, 2006, p. 243).

Sociocultural theory has also been influential in terms of theorizing online learning and teaching. As mentioned above, it sees learning as a social phenomenon that is mediated by a number of tools – including digital environments. When we interact through information and communication technology (ICT), the communication and meaning-making that takes place is mediated by the language used as well as by these tools which have certain affordances (that is, possibilities as well as constraints), allowing learners to interact in certain ways but not in others. Online environments also have the potential to facilitate the move from perceiving teachers as instructors to valuing their mediating role in the learning process. When using new technologies, teachers thus need to be aware that these form part of the social context in which learning takes place, and they need to be able to realise their potential as well as deal with the challenges (see also Chapter 5 in this volume). Sociocultural theory places learning firmly in a socio-historical context; when the environment shifts, so does the interaction that learners engage in and – by extension – the learning that takes place. As we claim throughout this book, using digital environments in the language classroom has an impact on how students learn and should also influence our understanding of how we teach.

## Pedagogical approaches

Sociocultural theory has been influential in shaping pedagogical approaches to second language development in the context of CMC. Cummins (2000, p. 546) describes the power of information technology in the context of a transformative pedagogy which can develop students' academic language and critical literacy as well as challenge social inequities. The approaches discussed here are task-based language teaching and CALL (Ellis, 2003; Thomas & Reinders, 2010), telecollaboration with its emphasis on intercultural learning (O'Dowd, 2006) and mobile language learning allowing for learning anytime anywhere. These three approaches bring together a focus on the process of language learning rather than on the product with communicative and intercultural approaches, thus foregrounding different but complementary aspects of online language learning and teaching. These are the role of the teacher who designs tasks and of the learners who engage with these activities and change them in the process; the role of communication and how interactants can develop intercultural skills in the process of communication; and the digital literacy that learners need to develop when learning online.

## Task-based language teaching

Task-based language teaching (TBLT) places the activity as well as the learners at the centre and includes both the planning stage that involves the teacher preparing a workplan and the implementation stage that sees learners engage with the task – often in ways that differ from what the teacher had planned (Ellis, 2000, 2003). Thomas and Reinders (2010) point out the synergies between computer-assisted language learning (CALL) and task-based approaches to language learning and teaching in the way that both 'deconstruct the traditional roles typically ascribed to teachers and learners in the language learning process' (p. 3).

TBLT has been embraced in computer-enhanced language learning contexts to allow learners access to a wider range of resources (including 'authentic' language), give them greater control over their learning, and develop their autonomy. However, it also poses certain challenges, some of which are outlined in Lai and Li's (2011) review of technology and TBLT, including various demands on learners and teachers, and the need for developing new knowledge and skills. Various researchers have proposed principles and models for the use of TBLT by teachers in a context that includes the use of digital media. Thus Doughty and Long (2003) bring together psycholinguistic principles and sociocultural theory to guide the use of technology in distance language learning. They advocate the following ten methodological principles for task-based language teaching:

1. Use tasks, not texts, as the unit of analysis
2. Promote learning by doing
3. Elaborate input (do not simplify; do not rely solely on 'authentic' texts)
4. Provide rich (not impoverished) input
5. Encourage inductive ('chunk') learning
6. Focus on form
7. Provide negative feedback
8. Respect 'learner syllabuses'/developmental processes
9. Promote cooperative/collaborative learning
10. Individualize instruction (according to communicative needs, and psycholinguistically)

The observation that a task-as-plan and the implementation of the task can substantially differ, inspired Dooly (2011) to compare a task-as-workplan, i.e. 'the intended task plan (as understood by the teacher)' (p. 76), with the-task-as-process, i.e. 'the way in which the students are negotiating and interpreting the task' (p. 79) in a detailed study. Her research shows

> that the students are making use of dialogic opportunities provided by 'digital learning objects' (Meskill & Anthony, 2007, p. 81). Different from the way it is planned by the teacher, the 'public; malleable; unstable and anarchic' (p. 81) dimensions of technologies provided the students with possibilities that the teacher was not (at least at first) able to integrate into the task-as-process. (p. 86)

Hampel (2006) uses the idea of the difference between the task-as-work-plan and the task-as-process to help teachers and developers improve task development in online environments. She suggests a three-level model which brings together the notion of the task as a plan with the implementation in the classroom and consists of approach, design and procedure. In the context of computer-assisted language learning, the approach refers to theories about the nature of language and language learning as well as the possibilities (and constraints) that the technology in question affords; design considerations comprise the syllabus, functions and types of tasks, and learner and teacher roles; and procedure refers to the actual implementation of the tasks and their use by the learners. In applying this model to the development of online activities in a distance language learning course, Hampel (2010) and Hampel and Pleines (2013) have shown how it can inform an iterative process of planning, implementation and evaluation.

There is plenty of scope for research on online task-based language learning and teaching. Here are a number of areas that merit further research:

- What types of tasks are suitable for what kind of purpose?
- How is a task-as-workplan implemented in the online classroom?
- How do teachers create the conditions that allow for learning in a task-based setting?
- How can teachers step back while still supporting learners where needed?

### Telecollaboration and intercultural learning

Whereas task-based language learning and teaching focuses on the authenticity of the task, in telecollaborative learning authentic communication is at the centre. Telecollaborative approaches to language teaching thus foreground the interactants and the skills that learners need in order to communicate successfully in a technologically-mediated environment and to develop intercultural competence. Belz (2003, p. 68) describes telecollaborative projects as involving 'the use of Internet communication tools by internationally dispersed students of language in institutionalized settings in order to promote the development of (a) foreign language (FL) linguistic competence and (b) intercultural competence'. Communication in such projects usually takes place either between two individual learners or between two groups of learners, with only indirect teacher input (e.g. through tasks or pre- and post-activities). The benefit of telecollaboration, as Kern and colleagues (2004, p. 254) point out, is that it allows teachers 'to help students enter into a new realm of collaborative inquiry and construction of knowledge, viewing their expanding repertoire of identities and communication strategies as resources in the process'.

However, there are also a number of challenges that are associated with telecollaborative projects of which teachers need to be aware. These challenges are often related to mismatches and tensions between the two groups involved (O'Dowd & Ritter, 2006). According to Ware (2005), these can arise from differences in expectations, in interactional purpose, and in using linguistic conventions, from social and institutional differences, and from individual differences in motivation and use of time. An early and influential project that used a telecollaborative approach was the Cultura Project. Furstenberg and colleagues (2001) summarize the success factors, which highlight the important role that the teacher plays (and which – if heeded – can prevent the kind of challenges that Ware (2005) encountered in her project).

- There needs to be an equal degree of commitment between the partners. One of the reasons our own experiments have worked so well, in our opinion, is that all instructors on both sides of the Atlantic have demonstrated an equal degree of commitment and involvement. It is, in fact, a crucial requirement in our opinion. It is not a given, but we are convinced that anything short of that will fail.
- Both parties need to agree to make culture the focus point of the language course they are teaching.
- Logistics need to be solved, such as what days and times a week and how often classes on both sides of the Atlantic meet.
- Finally – and that is of the utmost importance – the Web site requires steady and close maintenance.

(Furstenberg et al., 2001, p. 95)

As with task-based language learning and teaching, there is a range of areas that merit research. These include:

- How do teachers create the conditions that allow for learning in a telecollaborative and intercultural setting?
- What kinds of tasks are suitable?
- How do learners need to be supported so they can collaboratively construct cultural knowledge, build intercultural competence and develop their language skills?
- What are the impacts of engaging in a telecollaborative and intercultural project on learners' identity?
- How do groups/dyads interact online?

## Mobile-assisted language learning

Another recent pedagogy is mobile-assisted language learning (MALL) with its focus on learning anytime anywhere. The hardware used includes devices that learners can carry around easily, that is, MP3 players, tablets and smart-phones. These not only allow for learning in real-world settings but can also make use of geolocation services, thus offering learners access to information about their immediate context. Mobile learning is particularly useful to provide informal, incidental learning opportunities (Kukulska-Hulme, 2012), thus complementing classroom-based learning, or giving people language learning opportunities who do not have access to institutional contexts (e.g. migrants or travellers).

According to Scanlon and colleagues (2014), places, tasks, tools, social support, outcomes and the learner's journey are the key learning elements in mobile learning. However, these are also the areas that are likely to pose challenges, for example around the 'noise' (acoustic and other distractions) that can occur when mobile learning takes place in public places such as cafés, buses or in the street. Effective task design and appropriate tool choice are further aspects that teachers need to engage with. As mobile learning usually takes place outside a conventional classroom and as an individual activity, teachers also need to devise new ways of supporting students without restricting their creativity and building interaction into the tasks. Furthermore, there is a potential conflict between the personal and the academic space.

Comas-Quinn and Mardomingo (2012) have examined mobile blogging through the lens of tasks that help language learning 'on the move'. They point to similar challenges as Scanlon and colleagues (2014), including the need for renegotiating the roles of teachers and learners and for careful training and support, as well as personal and cultural factors that may play a role in determining whether such tasks are successful.

MALL has not been widely investigated yet and research is needed to explore these challenges. Possible questions are as follows:

- What kind of support do learners need and how can this be provided?
- How do tasks have to be designed to foster successful learning?
- What role does the context where learning takes place play?
- How can social interaction and communication be built into a mobile language learning project?
- In what ways can informal mobile learning activities be integrated into a more conventional classroom setting?

## Methodologies

After examining a number of pedagogical approaches to online teaching, this section introduces various methodologies – or forms of inquiry – that lend themselves to exploring online language teaching and learning, particularly by practitioners themselves. The methodologies presented here are mainly qualitative and interpretative, that is, they deal with non-numerical data such as written texts and images as well as audio and video recordings, and use interpretative methods for analysis rather than statistical ones. They also tend to be used for research 'in the field' rather than in connection with experimental research that uses controlled testing to determine cause and effect.

Four methodologies have been chosen for the purposes of this chapter. They only represent a selection and fall into two more general categories. Participatory research and action research are research practices or broader frameworks for conducting research, whereas ethnography and discourse analysis stipulate what the focus of the research is, namely a certain community or culture (which in the context of this chapter would be online) and language, respectively.

### Participatory research

While in the past the people who were the focus of research were seen as passive 'subjects' or even 'objects', in social sciences today they tend to be recognized as active participants. Central to this shift have been educationalists such as Paulo Freire with his principles of critical pedagogy and the notion of dialogue, which is applied not just to education but also to research (Freire, 1982). Participatory research thus acknowledges the value of the knowledge of ordinary people, and it has been called 'people's research' (Park, 2006, p. 83). By being given a voice and contributing to the research process, research participants are able to assume some agency.

Based on Cornwall (1996, p. 96), Truman and Raine (2001) have developed a typology of six different modes of participation (co-option, compliance, consultation, cooperation, co-learning and collective action) which correspond to varying degrees of user involvement (from token representation, to users working with researchers, to users setting their own agenda and mobilizing to carry it out without the input of outside researchers), and a move in the relationship between research and users from research *on* users to research *for* users to research *with* users to research *by* users. (For more information, see Participatory Research at http://www.lancaster.ac.uk/researchethics/5-2-outlook.html.)

There are various ways of involving participants in a study – beyond questionnaires and interviews. Narrative methods include learner diaries (written or audio-recorded) or video documentation collected by research participants. Pellerin (2014, p. 15) summarizes the results of her study with young children as follows:

> The use of mobile technologies renders language learning visible through digital documentation (audio and video recordings), providing the learners with new means to self-assess and monitor their own language learning. By revising their own 'traces' of the use of the oral language, learners engage in a metacognitive process through self-reflection about their oral competencies in the target language, and self-regulate their own language development.

Another method that is increasingly used in language learning contexts is stimulated recall (Gass & Mackey, 2000), which involves recording participants to document how they carry out a task and then presenting the video footage to them afterwards and discussing what they did and why. Examples are Montoro Sanjosé (2012) who used stimulated recall within an activity theoretical approach to find out about the contradictions between teacher expectations and actual learner activity in the context of an online task, or Cutrim Schmid (2011) who used video-stimulated reflection in the context of teacher professional development.

Another participatory approach that has been used in teacher training is to get trainee teachers to research their own practice – for example using an action research approach (Cabaroglu, 2014).

## Action research

Action research connects research with the practice in the classroom (face-to-face and online) and has great appeal for practitioners who want to research their own practice. Kurt Lewin, who coined the term action research, saw it as research that leads to social action and brings about change. As he explains: 'The research needed for social practice ... is a type of action-research, a comparative research on the conditions and effects of various forms of social action, and research leading to social action. Research that produces nothing but books will not suffice' (Lewin, 1946, p. 35). Lewin describes action research as 'a spiral of steps each of which is composed of a circle of planning, executing, and reconnaissance or fact-finding for the purpose of evaluating the results of the [next] step' (Lewin, 1946, p. 38).

As Figure 9.1 shows, action research is both a cyclical and a spiral movement, leading to greater understanding of a phenomenon and to change. It is made up of an initial cycle of planning an action, implementing the action, observing it and reflecting on the result, which then leads to further such cycles (see also Kemmis and McTaggart's (2000, p. 595) action research spiral).

In education, action research tends to be located in the realm of the practitioner and is tied to self-reflection and the notion of reflective

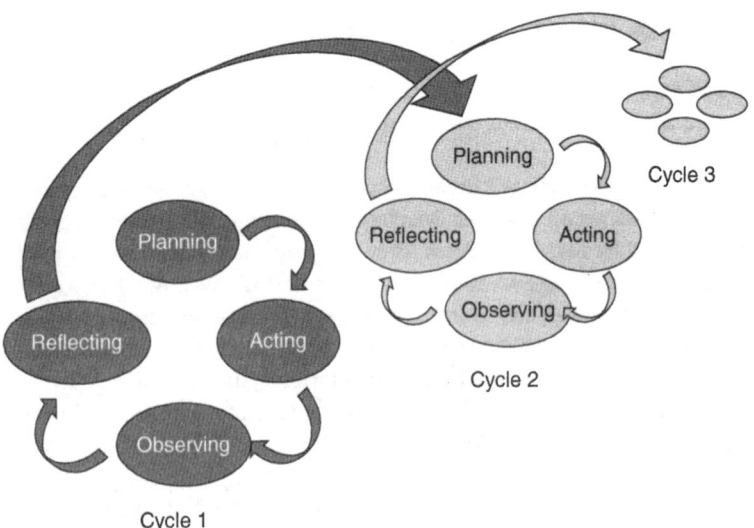

*Figure 9.1*   Action research spiral

practice (Schön, 1983). Action research thus constitutes a critical enquiry into our practice with the ultimate aim of improving this practice. The journal *Educational Action Research* describes its aims and scope as being 'concerned with exploring the dialogue between research and practice in educational settings', and describes a range of approaches, 'for example, to promote reflective practice; professional development; empowerment; understanding of tacit professional knowledge; curriculum development; individual, institutional and community change; and development of democratic management and administration' (http://www.tandfonline.com/action/journalInformation?show=aimsScope&journalCode=reac 20#.UvN-USidD8s).

Pellerin (2013, p. 48) shows how participation of teachers in a collaborative action research project empowers them to adopt new inclusive instructional strategies through the use of digital technologies in early French Immersion classrooms.

Hinkelman and Gruba (2012) provide an illuminating account of a study of implementing a blended language learning programme at two Japanese universities, combining an action research approach at one of the universities with ethnographic research at the other. The aim was to investigate innovation in institutional programmes and how power and hegemony were exercised, but the results also highlight the difficulties that action researchers can face. Although the action research approach resulted in small changes being made, bigger ideas were abandoned because of a lack of cooperation and commitment in the action research team and the institutional constraints on teachers.

Action research has much in common with participatory research, involving research participants in the research process itself (see above) and often blurring the distinction between researchers and research participants. Although an action researcher might use quantitative methods, qualitative methods such as interviews, focus groups (for a greater diversity of opinions), participant observation and document review tend to be more common.

## Ethnography

As Hammersley and Atkinson (2007, p. 1) explain, in 19th century anthropology 'an ethnography was a descriptive account of a community or culture, usually one located outside the west'. The late 20th century and postcolonial theories brought about a turnaround in the field by shifting the ethnographic lens to include the investigation of Western culture. Although ethnography has its roots in cultural anthropology, it is an approach to research that is being used across the social sciences today. It is centred on a researcher who observes and often participates in the life of a group to find out more about it – for example, in terms of their social practices. The researcher thus attempts to understand the world from the perspective of the people observed by taking an insider's view rather than that of the outside researcher.

Today the focus of ethnographic research has widened from remote tribes to social groups more generally – including users of a particular online forum or language learners engaged in multiplayer video games (MMOGs or massively multiplayer online games). Thorne and colleagues (2009, p. 804), for example, examine such 'Internet interest communities', which can 'provide rich empirical grounds for exploring the varied forms of L2 engagement, development, and socialization that are taking place via new information and communication technologies'. Their examples of ethnographic research into such communities include Lam's (2000) work on how immigrant youths in the US improve their language and literacy practices by participating in fan communities, and Zheng and colleagues' (2008) study which, as Thorne and colleagues (2009, p. 809) summarize, 'examined the role that *Second Life* can play in teaching Chinese language and culture. Their study utilized ethnographic observation, participant mapping, and interview data to assess levels of engagement within *Second Life* and the potential benefit to learners of avatar-embodied participation in virtual space'.

In terms of methods used, observation plays a central role in ethnography – alongside field notes, charts, audio and video recordings etc. to record these observations. In ethnographic studies interviews are often used to access people's experience, and the analysis of documents that are gathered as secondary data can help to provide a fuller picture of the group that is studied. Androutsopoulos (2008) engages in what he calls 'discourse-centred online ethnography', bringing together ethnographic observation and interviews with linguistic log data to help contextualize the data, interpret findings and shaping the research questions, thus making use of the 'power of ethnography to uncover the unexpected' (n.p.). One difficulty of ethnographic research is that studies tend to be long-term and time-consuming, and a particular challenge for online ethnographers is the delineation of the field (Parker Webster & Marques da Silva, 2013). On the other hand, language teachers observing their own classrooms as an ethnographic 'field' are in an ideal position for long-term research.

## Discourse analysis

In language learning, verbal interaction is crucial. Rather than focusing on the behaviour of a group and its culture, discourse analysis is a more micro-level endeavour that concentrates on the language used. In online contexts, text and audio created are easy to capture, and discourse analysis constitutes a possible form of enquiry.

Susan Herring developed a computer-mediated discourse analysis (CMDA) approach, which 'adapts methods from the study of spoken and written discourse to computer-mediated communication data' (Herring, 2007, n.p.). Her classification scheme includes what she calls medium factors; these include synchronicity, message transmission, persistence of transcript, size of message buffer, channels of communication, anonymous messaging, private messaging, filtering, quoting, and message format. The situation factors consist of participation structure, participant characteristics, purpose, topic or theme, tone, activity, norms and code. She illustrates this approach by applying it to two samples of computer-mediated discourse (taken from different types of blogs) and comparing them. Herring herself admits that the scheme is limited by being based mainly on textual CMC and ignoring other channels of communication. Since then, however, other studies have gone beyond the examination of written CMC. Thus Hampel and Stickler (2012), for example, have looked at the interplay between spoken language and written text chat in a video conferencing environment.

Herring's scheme also does not go beyond classifying the discourse found – which is where critical discourse analysis may offer a more comprehensive view on what happens in online communication and why. As van Dijk (2001, p. 354) points out, '[l]anguage use, discourse, verbal interaction, and communication belong to the microlevel of the social order. Power, dominance, and inequality between social groups are typically terms that belong to a macrolevel of analysis'. This is reflected in Androutsopoulos's (2006, p. 419) description of 'the move from the "language of CMC" to socially situated computer-mediated discourse; its grounding in the notion of online community; and the application of sociolinguistic methodologies to its study'.

Discourse analysis requires the collection of written texts and/or the recording and transcription of interaction. If the focus of a study goes beyond verbal language, transcripts need to include other modes such as body language, actions taken in the online environment, visual representations used. As Flewitt and her colleagues (2014) show, this requires choosing what to include in a transcription and how to represent it.

## Conclusion

This chapter began by showing how sociocultural theory helps to see learning as a social practice that takes place in and is shaped by a particular context. Online language teachers thus not only have to take account of the tasks they use and the role that learners play, but also need to consider how a particular environment and the modes that it offers for communication and interaction mediate learning. In its second part, this chapter focused on three different language pedagogies that are compatible with sociocultural theory – that is, task-based language learning and teaching, telecollaborative and intercultural learning, and mobile language learning, with their project-based, collaborative and real-world focus. The third and final part examined various methodologies that are potentially suited to the exploration by teachers themselves or by other researchers interested in different pedagogical aspects. These qualitative approaches to research also tie in with the overall theoretical, sociocultural approach taken in this book.

## Reflective task

If you teach online, are there any aspects related to your practice that you would like to investigate and possibly improve? Areas that link to the topics outlined under 'Pedagogical approaches' above are:

- Task design and implementation: comparing your expectations as a teacher (task-as-workplan) with what happens in class (task-as-process).
- Telecollaboration, e-tandem or e-twinning project: examining possible tensions between groups and improving interaction and intercultural learning.
- Learner interaction using a synchronous or asynchronous CMC tool (e.g. Skype, chat, wiki, blog): investigating what could be done to improve interaction.

If you don't teach online but would like to start, you could introduce a new activity into your teaching and carry out a small action research study to evaluate its success. Examples could be:

- Introduction of a quasi-telecollaborative online exchange with a neighbouring school or class to practise the target language.
- Using CMC to offer learners the opportunity to interact online with speakers of the L2 (e.g. writing a Wikipedia entry, using Twitter or creating a class blog).
- Devising a task that makes use of students' mobile devices to go out in to the real world, gather information and share it with other learners (this only works if your students are not L1 speakers of the country they live or study in).

- Using an online tool to develop collaborative student writing (e.g. wiki or blog).

You need to think about what you want to find out or change and which methodology would help you with this. Who will be your research participants and/or co-investigators and what kind of data are you going to collect? How will you record and process the data? And how will you analyse the data? More information on practitioner research as well as possible projects can be found in Lamy and Hampel (2007).

# 10
## Developing Online Teaching Skills: The DOTS Project

*Mateusz-Milan Stanojević*

### Introduction

Language teachers, whether they teach in formal, non-formal or informal contexts, often feel the need (or the pressure) to use information and communication technology (ICT) in their teaching. Over half of the teachers in a survey conducted in 2010 report that they have received formal training in using ICT in their teaching (Beaven et al., 2010); nevertheless, they and the other teachers surveyed feel the need for 'high quality, appropriate and ongoing forms of training' (Chapter 2) to become aware of the range of available online tools (for a review of open educational resources see Chapters 6 and 7). Moreover, teachers report that the training should be hands-on and include a social element, allowing them to share experiences with other teachers (Emke & Stickler, 2015). In addition, it is crucial that teachers are able to use ICT tools for specific pedagogic purposes (see Chapter 5 for an overview of skills that teachers need in order to use ICT in teaching), and that their training is time efficient and just-in-time (see Chapter 3). Finally, as shown in Chapter 4, learners also consider it important that teachers are competent users of the available IT tools.

This chapter describes the 'Developing Online Teaching Skills' project (DOTS; http:/dots.ecml.at/) supported by the European Centre for Modern Languages (http://www.ecml.at/), which is an attempt to respond to the needs identified above. In this 2008–2011 project within the programme entitled 'Empowering Language Professionals' (http://www.ecml.at/Programme/Programme20082011/tabid/154/language/en-GB/Default.aspx), an international team of eight experts[1] developed a set of self-training activities for language teachers designed to help them implement a range of ICT tools in their classrooms. The activities are available online through a Moodle workspace and in a downloadable format. The Moodle workspace (http://moodle.dots.ecml.at/) also gives language practitioners the opportunity to share their experiences.

This chapter starts with a discussion of the main characteristics of the activities and the workspace, which features a range of communication tools that enable teachers to discuss pedagogical or technological issues with their colleagues. The second part of the chapter discusses how these practical characteristics came about from a hands-on bottom-up approach undertaken by the team in their development which was based on socio-constructivist theory and a belief that integration of pedagogy and technology is crucial. The chapter concludes with a set of practical suggestions for how teachers may apply such an approach in their particular context.

## The DOTS activities and the DOTS Moodle workspace

The self-training activities feature ten tools (for example, blogs, wikis, Surveymonkey; see http:/dots.ecml.at/ for details). The activities are designed to bring together pedagogy and technology: rather than giving detailed descriptions of technical characteristics of a tool, they concentrate on what the teacher needs to know technologically to use the tool in a pedagogically-sound way. Such an approach is in line with the second level of the adapted skills pyramid shown in Chapter 5 and with teachers' expressed wishes (see Chapter 2). For instance, rather than listing the technical options that various blogging websites offer (such as customization, blog theme and comments), the DOTS activity on blogs lists reasons and a pedagogical rationale for why blogs could be used in teaching (for example, for reading, to disseminate student-generated content, for sustained writing, to increase interaction outside the classroom and as a portfolio; see http://dots.ecml.at/TrainingKit/Activities/Blogs/tabid/2809/language/en-GB/Default.aspx).

All the activities follow the same modular template: they provide practical pedagogical guidelines and an example of a lesson plan for immediate implementation in the language classroom, and they encourage teachers to reflect on the use of the tool in their own context and share their practice with others. They are also open – that is, free to be reused and adapted to particular contexts.

The modular template means that each of the ten activities consists of three parts, with each part being divided into a number of subsections. For example, part 1 explains briefly what the tool is and lists some pedagogical reasons why teachers might use it in their classroom, providing a teacher-oriented overview of the tool that enables teachers to understand its potential uses at a glance. Whereas part 1 is meant as an introduction for those who may be unfamiliar with the tool or as a way of finding initial ideas on how to use it (for example, to decide whether it is appropriate for their class), part 2 of each activity may be useful if a teacher is familiar with the tool and would like to implement it in his/her teaching, and part 3 focuses on reflection and sharing. Each part is designed to be 'bite-sized', in that it can be completed in around 30 minutes. Modularity allows teachers to choose their own way of going through an activity. Some may want to read through the entire activity before trying it out, others may want to look at parts and try it out as they go along, while others still may be interested in finding only particular technical or pedagogical information or ideas for their next class. All this is in line with the needs reported by both full-time and part-time language teachers (see Chapters 2 and 3, respectively).

The activities are designed to enable immediate implementation, rather than providing lengthy (and often unnecessary) technological descriptions which may be of little use to teachers. Thus, the technical descriptions in part 2 are framed with a pedagogical purpose in mind, and each activity provides an example of a lesson plan. For instance, the activity on YouTube gives a short checklist of things a teacher needs to do in order to show a video in a face-to-face classroom, as well as some techniques of sharing a video with students outside the classroom. The lesson plan features an activity where a YouTube video is used as part of a lesson designed to help students at the B2/C1 level of the Common European Framework of Reference to develop their presentation skills in English (see http://dots.ecml.at/Portals/31/training-kit/PagsEN/Files_EN/Using_YouTube_in_class.pdf). Overall, part 2 of every activity provides some technological advice from a teaching perspective, explaining key characteristics that may be of importance to teachers, and giving practical pointers (with a pedagogical rationale) on how to use the tool. This is precisely what the teachers report they need (see Chapters 2 and 3). Therefore, immediate implementation is the central characteristic of part 2, allowing the teacher to put the tool into practice in his/her language classroom straight away.

As argued and exemplified throughout this book, a crucial aspect of any teaching is reflection about one's own teaching practice. In the DOTS activities, the focus on reflection is evident in part 3. This part invites teachers to reflect on their understanding of the tool through a series of 'can-do' statements (such as, 'I can describe <tool> to somebody else (e.g. a colleague)' or 'I can set up a language learning activity around <tool>'), linking to the appropriate sections of the activity in case the user does not feel confident in one of the aspects highlighted in the question. This is followed by two sets of questions/statements to guide the user's reflection: one to be done after the teacher has completed the activity, and one after he/she has attempted using the tool in his/her classroom. The next section of this part (Protecting students' privacy) is intended to raise awareness about privacy issues (if any) when using a tool. For example, when using a blog or registering for any social website there are potential risks connected with providing personal information (such as, address, telephone number and photographs), which teachers should be aware of and should warn their students about (for more information check the DOTS workspace http://moodle.dots.ecml.at/). All these sections encourage teachers to reflect on their use of the tool, both with respect to the affordances of the tool, its constraints and possibilities for language learning (Hampel, 2014; also see Chapter 5), and with respect to the particularities of their own context (for example, their learners, support and similar issues).

Given that for some teachers reflectivity works better by using others as their virtual mirror or reflection aid, reflective activities include the invitation to teachers for sharing. This is featured in the 'Explore and share' section of each activity, which contains some ideas on how teachers might want to build on their current practice and share their ideas with others, both online and offline. For instance, the blog activity suggests making a shared class blog for two groups with a colleague, which minimizes the risk of making a fully public blog, while still providing an external audience.

The DOTS workspace also promotes sharing through a number of forums and wikis, as a way to encourage teachers to form communities of practice (see Chapter 8) as well as to promote peer learning, in line with sociocultural principles of learning (see Chapters 1 and 9). For instance, the 'Explore and share' forum contains posts with examples of how particular tools have been used by teachers, frequently with links to activities they have created based on the particular tool. Sharing is also done through a wiki (http://moodle.dots.ecml.at/mod/wiki/view.php?id=24), where teachers are invited to upload sample activities under an existing category or create a category themselves. The activities posted by teachers range from ideas that are quick and easy to implement (for example, using the News Forum in the Moodle environment to post news about assignments) to project descriptions incorporating the use of online tools (such as the use of video-conferencing to promote intercultural education in the multilingual and multicultural

environment of Turku, Finland; see http://moodle.dots.ecml.at/mod/
wiki/view.php?pageid=24).

Finally, to support the widest possible usage of the activities, as well
as their easiest implementation in a variety of contexts, the project is
guided by the principle of openness on a variety of levels (for a discussion of the various senses of openness see Chapter 7). Firstly, the
DOTS workspace is open to all, and offers self-enrolment. Being based
on Moodle, the interface is available in multiple languages, and most
of the activities have been translated into different languages (for
example, German, Spanish, Turkish, and Croatian). Secondly, openness
refers to the fact that the activities are freely available to all, both in an
online and in a downloadable form, which allows teachers to access
them in a way that is easiest for them (some teachers may prefer to
save them for later use because they may not have continuous internet access). Thirdly, all ten tools featured in the activities have been
selected because they are free. Fourthly, all activities are licensed under
a Creative Commons Attribution 3.0 Unported License (http://creative
commons.org/licenses/by/3.0/), which means that anyone is free to copy
and redistribute the material in any medium or format, transform it
for any purpose, as long as they give appropriate credit, and indicate if
changes were made. In accordance with this, the activities have been or
are being reused as the basis of training in different contexts (such as in
Andorra, Poland, Austria; see Chapter 11 for an example from Turkey).
Thus, the DOTS materials follow the principle of openness, making
them available to the widest possible online and offline audience.

## A hands-on bottom-up approach to DOTS

The characteristics of modularity, immediate implementation, reflectivity, sharing and openness evident in the DOTS activities and on the
DOTS workspace are based on sociocultural and socio-constructivist
theories of learning (see Chapter 9 for an overview), whereby it is crucial
that learners can explore a new environment and engage with it, supported by carefully designed materials, timely constructive feedback and
continuous peer support (Emke & Stickler, 2015). Moreover, in order for
teachers to institute a change towards the use of online technologies,
teachers' beliefs must be taken into account. This particularly refers to
the effectiveness of ICT and its possible influence on other higher-level
goals as well as to the teacher's ability and resources (Beaven et al., 2010,
pp. 9–10; Zhao & Cziko, 2001). In other words, the project is based on
the principles of collaborative learning and community building in

order for teachers to develop their own teaching style in the online medium (see Chapter 5).[2]

So as to ensure the application of these theoretical principles, the DOTS team followed a bottom-up approach to the construction of the workspace and the activities, loosely based on the action research spiral (see Chapter 9). The process involved identifying teachers' needs by enquiry and observation, creating DOTS activities and templates, piloting and collecting feedback, building the DOTS workspace, piloting it (along with receiving feedback), as well as disseminating and cascading.

The first step was to identify teachers' needs with regard to online teaching, based on observation and needs analysis during a hands-on workshop held in Graz in December 2008. The participants in the workshop (26 teachers and teacher trainers from 25 countries) took part in a range of activities centred on online teaching, including hands-on group activities using a variety of online tools, discussing their prior experience as well as their current and future needs, showcasing their best practices and considering the benefits and challenges of online teaching. Finally, they completed a needs analysis questionnaire which helped the project team in the selection of tools for DOTS activities and the design of the activities (see Chapter 2 for the results).

Based on these expressed needs the project team developed self-training activities for three tools identified as the most interesting by the participants, and at the same time suitable for practising different skills and using different pedagogies: YouTube (listening comprehension, the use of authentic materials), wikis (collaborative writing, reading), and audio-/video-conferencing (speaking, authentic communication). These were presented to 16 online language teaching experts during a regional workshop in Barcelona, Spain, held in December 2009. The experts provided feedback on the activities, indicating, among other things, the importance of making activities immediately usable, of providing examples of best practices accompanied by a lesson plan, taking into account the varying computer skills of teachers and a clear structure of the activity.

This feedback was implemented by the team in the creation of the remaining seven activities, as well as the construction of the Moodle workspace. The workspace and the activities were piloted and evaluated by a group of 40 teachers, teacher trainers and decision makers during a workshop held in March 2011 in Graz. The workshop was attended by participants who were experienced in using ICTs in their professional practice as well as others with expertise in teacher education and policy but very little ICT knowledge. In addition to populating the workspace with participants' comments and experiences, the team gathered feedback on the overall design of the workspace and a detailed evaluation of the activities. This led to a change in the structure of the activities, a reduction in the amount of text and the addition of certain functionalities on the workspace (such as a glossary and a feedback forum). Moreover, taking into account the views of a range of stakeholders (students, teachers, teacher trainers and decision makers) enabled the team to incorporate a variety of points of view into the activities while maintaining an overall coherence. The workspace was opened to the public during the Closing conference of the 3rd programme of ECML activities (http://www.ecml.at/Home/Conference2011/tabid/663/language/en-GB/Default.aspx ) in September 2011.

The dissemination of the DOTS project, cascading its materials, results and training, has continued in a number of initiatives undertaken by the project team, specifically running blended workshops and launching two follow-up projects. The team offered a series of 11 workshops to Austrian language practitioners in cooperation with the Verein ECML (http://verein.ecml.at/), as well as four national workshops within the ECML format of training and consultancy (http://www.ecml.at/ECMLtrainingandconsultancyformemberstates/tabid/1055/language/en-GB/Default.aspx) held in Poland, Norway, Malta and Austria. These workshops (attended by over 350 participants) were designed to raise awareness about the use of ICT and disseminate an approach which integrates pedagogy and technology in teaching with ICT. Further development continued under two follow-up projects. The first one, 'Using open resources to develop online teaching skills' (http://dots.ecml.at/M5/tabid/2893/language/en-GB/Default.aspx), was funded by the ECML from 2012 to 2013 under their programme 'Learning through languages'.[3] It sought to provide pedagogical and technological support for the use of ICT in language teaching to individuals who work as language teachers (in formal, non-formal or informal contexts), but who may not have the necessary skills of using language pedagogy or online technology (for example a Red Cross volunteer working with immigrants to help them integrate into the labour market in their new country). With such a goal in mind, the existing DOTS activities were adapted to introduce some basic aspects of language pedagogy (such as learning objectives and learning strategies, which had been taken for granted in the original DOTS activities), and explicitly start with the objective the teacher has in mind. The second follow-up project, entitled 'Use of ICT in Support of Language Teaching and Learning' (http://ict-rev.ecml.at/en-us/), is a two-year project (May 2013–August

2015) within the framework of a cooperation agreement between the ECML and the European Commission (http://www.ecml.at/Programme/ ECMLECCooperation/tabid/1461/language/en-GB/Default.aspx).[4] Its aims are twofold. Firstly, it cascades the DOTS principles and activities to teachers and teacher trainers through blended workshops. Such workshops took place in 2013/14 in seven EU/ECML member countries (namely, UK, Croatia, Finland, Hungary, Norway, Slovenia and Belgium). This is an effort to promote the dissemination of DOTS principles and to strengthen the community of practice aspect on the national and international level by inviting participants to share their experience face-to-face (during the workshop) and online (in the DOTS workspace) prior to, during and after the workshop (see also Chapter 8). The second aim of the project is to extend the existing list of online tools for which training activities are available on the DOTS workspace. With this in mind, the team created a searchable inventory of open tools organized according to a variety of pedagogical and practical criteria (including, for example, the language skill which can most easily be practised using the tool, the type of interaction the tool facilitates, how user-friendly the tool is for the teacher, and a number of other criteria). The first version of the inventory was launched in October 2014. This includes a range of aspects that will help develop the community of practice aspect, with users being able to add, tag and rate new tools, providing examples of their use, thus keeping the inventory up-to-date.

Importantly, all aspects of the training workshops and follow-up projects were based on the same approach as the DOTS project, following the action research spiral of establishing participants' needs and pre-workshop communication, individualizing training materials (prior to the workshop), a hands-on approach to training in a blended environment with a significant part of the workshop dedicated to sharing experiences and best practices and creating immediately implementable classroom activities, a feedback phase and follow-up (in the DOTS workspace). Moreover, the feedback from each workshop fed into not only the subsequent workshops but also the training materials.

## Review and prospects

Working on the basis of the action research spiral and the inclusion of the various stakeholders in every step of the planning and implementation of the project (for instance, the design features of the activities and the workspace) proved to be the strongest points of the project. The excellent cooperation among the team members was especially evident in the face-to-face workshops: in their post-workshop evaluations, the participants regularly noted the productive but also relaxed atmosphere. This made the workshops a place of sharing among peers in a person-centred fashion. Therefore, the participant feedback concerning the workspace and the activities (which was part of the workshop schedule) was always something that both the participants and the project team felt they owned, making the feedback process constructive and non-threatening.

Some aspects of the activities and the workspace, nevertheless, need to be further improved. Specifically, the community of practice formed during face-to-face workshops did continue on the online workspace for brief periods of time. However, as shown in Chapter 8, a moderator is crucial for a small community of practice to work, and it was difficult for the team to maintain the momentum because of the time needed to prepare the following workshops and other work on the project. In other words, full long-term self-sustainability of the online community has not yet been achieved.

With this in mind, there are several directions the team is planning to explore in the future. Firstly, there are steps that can be taken to make the workspace more interactive than it currently is. For instance, the inclusion of a comment and rating feature linked directly to the online activity (for example on the bottom of the page and not, as currently, only in the forum) might allow users to feel more ownership of the content of the workspace. This could be strengthened by making some workspace content available without login, and reserving login authentication to, for instance, individualization. This might result in an increase in registered users, making the online community larger where moderation might not be as crucial. Thirdly, a step towards mobile learning (both in terms of optimizing the workspace for mobile and handheld devices, and in terms of including the mobile learning aspect in the activities themselves) is another important prospect, especially taking into consideration the increase in mobile learning with its potential to promote learner autonomy, just-in-time learning and spontaneity in learning (Ferreira et al., 2013, pp. 50–51), which corresponds to the principles that the DOTS project is built on. Finally, face-to-face dissemination is planned through workshops targeting teacher trainers rather than teachers, as a way to achieve a cascading effect, raise the number of users, as well as to get more feedback on those features of the workspace and the activities that can be further improved.

## Applying the DOTS approach: practical suggestions to teachers

As teachers, we may be tempted to use an online tool because we like it (or because we think our students will like it) or because of the received wisdom that it is 'the' tool for a particular activity (for example, using wikis for collaborative writing). Indeed, this may be a great start, because it might be motivating for us (in that we like the tool, and hence we want to use it with our students) or because it would allow us to tap into numerous activities available on the web with suggestions on how to use this tool. However, in the DOTS approach reflection is a crucial step in deciding on an online tool and all other parts of the process, which includes assessing the potential added value of doing the task online with regard to the context, the characteristics of the tool, the characteristics of communication in the online medium and the time/support needed. Here is a list of issues for reflection (most of these appear in all the DOTS activities):

- Is this tool/resource relevant for your course?
  - o Does it fit with your teaching approach and aims?
  - o Does it add more linguistically and culturally relevant material to what you are already doing?
- Is this tool appropriate for your learners (age, level, interest ...)?
  - o Is the level appropriate for the intended users?
- Can the tool accommodate learners with a range of levels?
- Is the language used in the instructions and reference material suitable?
- For which skills and activities do you think this tool/resource is best used?
  - o Does it allow for interactive activities to maintain student interest?
  - o Are there a variety of exercises and tasks that can be built with this tool?
- How user-friendly is the tool?
  - o Is the tool/resource clear and easy to use for your students?
  - o Does the tool/resource necessitate some training activities for your students?
- Communication-related considerations
  - o If the communication is oral: Does it have a visual element (e.g. video-conferencing)? Does it allow simultaneous speech by both parties? What will this mean for the communication and the task? Are there any specific turn-taking techniques required? Will the speaker be able to receive instant backchannel information from

his/her collocutors and in what way (such as emoticons, text chat)? Are there any other communication facilities that the tool has and do they require specific consideration?

- o If the communication is written: Is the communication synchronous or asynchronous? What will this mean for the communication and the task? Are there any special ways to include your attitudes (e.g. emoticons, text highlighting)? Are there any other communicational facilities that the tool has and do they require specific consideration?
- • Technical considerations
  - o What equipment and technical support is required?
  - o Is this available in your institution?
  - o What on-going costs are involved (e.g. licences for software)?

The DOTS approach also includes sharing the team's experience with others, which is a way to improve our teaching practice, as well as help the professional development of others (see Chapter 7 for a review of benefits of sharing and some online spaces where you can share). If sharing online, it is easy to start small; a single sentence about an activity or the use of a tool can give a colleague an idea for his/her next class. Keep in mind that when sharing online, you are potentially sharing with the entire world (increasing the risk of possibly unkind reactions), so it may be best to start with an online environment that is designed specifically for teachers and that requires user login to view and post comments. See the DOTS workspace (http://moodle.dots.ecml.at/) for more ideas on what and how to share.

If you are training other teachers face-to-face, it is crucial to listen to the needs of your colleagues and their experience, keep in mind that success hinges on matching pedagogy and technology, and providing opportunities for hands-on work. A good place to start might be the phases used in the DOTS project – needs analysis, sharing and feedback. These should feed into the preparation of your face-to-face training sessions (even if they are individual and not very formal) and the use of hands-on activities (exploring rather than reading about). Some ideas for face-to-face activities that may be useful in such a context are available on the DOTS workspace.

## Conclusion

This chapter presented the Developing Online Teaching Skills project, whose aim was to develop self-training activities for language teachers, designed to help them implement a range of ICT tools in their classroom, and provide them with a platform to share their experiences through Moodle. The main characteristics of the activities are that they are modular and designed for immediate implementation in the language classroom, they foster teacher reflection and sharing with others and they are open. These characteristics are a result of a bottom-up approach based on socio-constructivist principles. A needs analysis conducted among teachers provided the basis for building the activities and the workspace, which were then piloted. In each stage of the piloting, feedback was collected among teachers, teacher trainers and decision makers from the ECML member states, and was built into the activities during a series of hands-on workshops. The ideas behind the project were extended through a number of workshops and two follow-up projects which followed the same cycle of constant revision based on feedback. Overall, the approach is based on continuous reflection about one's own practice, as a crucial part of project development and, more importantly, as a vital part of the use of ICT in one's teaching. Teachers should, therefore, keep in mind the interaction between the learning goals and objectives, the characteristics of the tool and the online environment, and their context (including students, support and time). Another crucial aspect of the project is sharing, both online and offline.

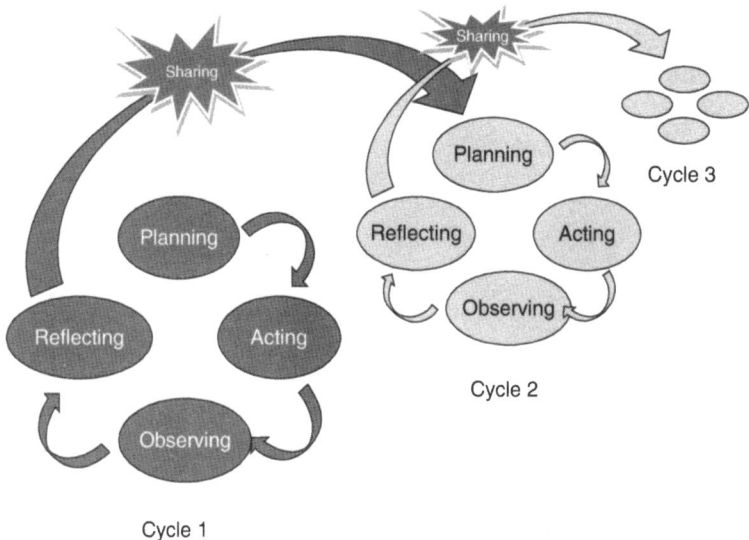

*Figure 10.1* Modified action research spiral

## Reflective task

Use the modified action research spiral (taken from Chapter 9) to plan and institute a change in your teaching practice. For some ideas of activities you could introduce, visit the DOTS workspace (http://moodle.dots. ecml.at/). Share your ideas with others (Figure 10.1).

## Notes

1. Ursula Stickler (coordinator), Tita Beaven, Martina Emke, Pauline Ernest, Joseph Hopkins, Aline Germain-Rutherford, Regine Hampel and Mateusz-Milan Stanojević.
2. For a more detailed account of these theoretical principles and how they correspond with the project principles, see Emke & Stickler (2015) and Stickler and colleagues (2010).
3. Mateusz-Milan Stanojević (coordinator), Martina Emke, Pauline Ernest, Aline Germain-Rutherford, Regine Hampel, Joseph Hopkins and Ursula Stickler.
4. Mateusz-Milan Stanojević and Martina Emke (coordinators), Pauline Ernest, Aline Germain-Rutherford, Regine Hampel, Joseph Hopkins and Ursula Stickler, with collaboration from Aiko Nakamura.

# 11
## Using DOTS Materials for the Professional Development of English Teachers in Turkey: Teachers' Views

*Süleyman Başaran, Emrah Cinkara and Neşe Cabaroğlu*

### Introduction

Teaching and learning in the 21st century demands a new skillset and mindset (Johnson, 2012, p. 113). In this rapidly changing age, increased opportunities created by information and computer technologies (ICT) have resulted in a positive change in the range of activities, approaches and applications in language learning and teaching. In simple terms, this innovation has brought a shift from traditional textbooks to innovative forms of multimodal use of technological tools in classrooms, which has also brought a change in the curriculum and the ecology of language teaching and learning (Blyth, 2009). Fully online and distance courses have been attracting ever more people into higher education; and in 2009 the growth of online higher education degree programmes in the world was reported to be much higher than that of traditional programmes (Allen & Seaman, 2010). According to OSYM (Student Selection and Placement Centre for Higher Education in Turkey, 2013), most Turkish universities now offer online higher education programmes. With these facts in mind and to help teachers of English in Turkey adapt to the new circumstances and gain new ICT-related skills, we became part of the Developing Online Teaching Skills (DOTS) project (see Chapter 10 in this volume and Stickler, 2011 for an overview) and translated the DOTS materials into Turkish. We held a meeting with Turkish teachers of English to promote the use of the materials. We also organized three workshop sessions for two groups of teachers (total number: 35) on some of the DOTS tools; namely YouTube, blogs, wikis, and podcasts and the development of language teaching tasks based on these tools. This chapter is an account of the work we undertook and its impacts on participant teachers.

## ICT in teaching and learning

The uses and implications of ICT for teachers and learners have been extensively studied (Bransford et al., 2000). Through the use of ICT, enriched curricula based on authentic materials have been introduced into schools. With the emergence of task-based language teaching, authentic materials have gained importance. Nunan (1989, p. 54) describes authentic material as any material that is 'not specifically produced for the purposes of language teaching'. After a long history of language teaching, from the 1890s to the late 1970s, the authenticity of language teaching materials gained a more important role in language classrooms with the introduction of Communicative Language Teaching (Gilmore, 2007). The presentation of authentic materials is also reported to improve students' motivation and confidence (Peacock, 1997). Thanks to the wide range of options and ease of online access to real-world materials, learners can access examples of the target language on demand. Together with the use of various ICT tools, students can also be provided with tasks in which they can see how their language skills relate to real-life language use. Furthermore, by utilizing tools such as YouTube, teachers can easily integrate authentic videos into their courses.

Teaching students with different backgrounds, skills, interests and levels of motivation poses challenges in terms of the achievement of curriculum objectives. Therefore, individualization of the learning process can be considered as an essential step in order to meet the students' learning needs. Web 2.0 has created opportunities for more individualized instruction and self-study at the learners' own pace. As facilitators, teachers are an integral part of ICT-enabled or virtual classrooms (Egbert et al., 2009). With the availability of a wide selection of tools with many diverse functions based on different methodologies, teachers today have the means to create customized lessons in a way that has probably not been possible before (Cennamo et al., 2010), provided they have the skills necessary for teaching languages online (for a description of these skills see Chapter 5). Through a balanced combination of the right web 2.0 tools for the audience, virtual learning environments (VLE) can be turned into online teaching and learning spaces in which one can execute almost all processes including enrolling on courses, attending online courses, accessing course content, receiving and completing homework and assessment, doing quizzes, checking grades and many others. By having a Learning Management System, such as Moodle, on a school server, a teacher can easily offer these resources and activities and invite his/her students to be a part of the virtual learning space.

A further opportunity created by the wider use of ICT is in the way it can facilitate feedback and aid reflection on teaching and learning. In a study with EFL teachers, it was stated that reflective practice could be enhanced through mutual feedback between teachers and students, and that this form of practice is helpful to both (Brandt, 2008). For the teachers, reflection was reported to raise their awareness about teaching, and to enable deeper understanding of the variables related to teaching, which led to a positive change in teaching practice (Liou, 2001). Moreover, in a more recent and extensive study, Fatemi and colleagues (2011) studied 1,000 EFL learners and 100 EFL teachers in order to explore the effect of the teachers' reflection on their learners' writing achievement. Their results suggested that reflection significantly affects EFL learners' writing achievement. Real-time interactive functionalities afforded by ICT tools and platforms give students and teachers more opportunities for feedback, reflection and revision. Student performance is positively affected by appropriate teacher and peer feedback in language classes (Han, 2002). However, the most striking drawback of providing 'public' feedback to students in face-to-face classrooms is the risk of creating learner anxiety. With the appropriate use of certain online ICT tools, teachers and students can enjoy privacy when they are giving feedback and providing comments on each other's performance.

Nevertheless, there are some criticisms of ICT in education. Initially, introducing ICT practices might result in reduced face-to-face communication with students (Bushati et al., 2012). When students are assigned online tasks, the actual face-to-face conversation time among students may decrease. Moreover, when institutions start using ICT technologies, they have to invest in training their teachers to encourage the use of these technologies. However, the task of in-service training of teachers can be difficult, as some teachers might be resistant to ICT technologies (Bakker, 2008; Başaran & Cabaroğlu, 2014). Even if they learn and start using them, they need to be highly motivated to update their course content. In addition, the availability of a vast number of resources may complicate the teachers' material selection process. Loucky (2010, p. 225) describes the users who have such wide range of resources at their disposal as being 'almost spoiled for choice'. Finally, as ICT hardware and software are expensive, education institutions and students could have financial difficulty in starting up and maintaining them. In a recent study, a lack of adequate investments and financial challenges, among other factors, were stated as the main challenges regarding ICT use in education (Vajargah et al., 2010). Therefore, some financially disadvantaged institutions and students do not have equal opportunities in an ICT-based educational setting. This notion has been described as a digital divide between people who are fully integrated into the new technology and those who have not yet reached this stage (Hilbert, 2014). However, it should be recognized that this negative divide is declining as mobile devices become more popular in educational settings.

In order to meet the very significant need for providing equal opportunities for all, as is the case in Turkey, governments may revise their educational policies regarding the use of ICT in education. As part of a new national education policy to keep pace with the latest developments in educational technology, the Ministry of National Education (MONE) in Turkey has launched new projects and initiatives to enrich the classroom ecology with the use of ICT. The most influential of these projects is Movement of Enhancing Opportunities and Improving Technology (FATİH), which started in 2010 (MONE, 2014). The project consists of five components. The first is to equip schools and classrooms with required hardware as well as software. The second consists of preparation and management of course content on the learning platform. Integration of ICT in education programmes is the third component. In the fourth component, the purpose is to provide in-service training to teachers and, finally, the last component is to ensure a dependable, manageable, measurable and sustainable use of ICT in education. The project works simultaneously on each of these components. As part of the first stage, MONE aims to equip 570,000 classrooms with the latest information technologies, transforming them into computerized or 'smart' classes by the end of 2014. These smart classes will have smart boards, tablet computers for students, software and educational e-content, and there will be in-service training of the teachers. Also, 675,000 tablet computers have been distributed to ninth-graders and their teachers.

Considering the size and scope, FATİH is one of the most extensive ICT developments in the history of Turkish education. There is pressure on administrators and teachers to improve the quality of education by implementing ICT applications effectively. For this reason, organising a workshop for the local directorate of MONE and participants, who participated voluntarily, with no financial compensation, was an important initiative. In this period of educational reform in Turkey and at a time when training in teaching languages with ICT was much needed we became part of the DOTS project, and held a meeting and a workshop to introduce DOTS materials and improve teachers' ICT-related skills and thus promote the use of DOTS materials. A detailed account of the DOTS project is given in Chapter 10 of this book. The following section gives details about the meeting, the workshop and participants in Turkey.

## DOTS workshop and data collection

The DOTS Moodle workspace, which was created as an output of a project supported by the European Centre for Modern Languages, is an online platform for delivering teacher training at a distance. As the project partners in Turkey (three researchers from Dicle University, Çukurova University and Gaziantep University), we translated the material produced in the context of the DOTS project into Turkish in order to make it more accessible to English language teachers in Turkey. The translated material was uploaded to the Moodle webpage of the DOTS project.

The next step was to hold a face-to-face meeting with teachers of English to introduce the DOTS materials and promote their use. 211 teachers working in Turkish primary and secondary schools, who responded to an invitation sent out to all schools in Diyarbakır, participated in the meeting. Two project leaders from the UK (Open University) and Spain (Universitat Oberta de Catalunya) contributed to the meeting and gave an overview of the DOTS project via Skype. The meeting presentations focused on why ICT is important for English language teaching, the problems teachers usually have to face when teaching, and how materials produced by the DOTS project can be used to address those problems. Another aim of the meeting was to collect data about English teachers, their problems, the facilities they had and the frequency of ICT use in their classes. A survey given to the teachers after the meeting also collected biographical data from the 189 who completed it. Data were tabulated, analyzed and utilized in the preparation stage of the DOTS workshop which followed the meeting.

The 211 teachers of English that participated in the initial meeting were also invited to take part in the workshop about using the DOTS materials to teach English, and 35 (27 female and eight male) teachers of English working at state schools in Diyarbakır accepted. The participants were divided into two groups according to their preference, and each group joined a workshop consisting of three sessions of 90 minutes each. Participation was voluntary and the teachers were not paid to attend. As we were not interested in gender-related correlations (and generalizations) we did not try to secure a balance between the number of male and female participants. Also, such an imbalance in the number of male and female teachers of English is typical in Turkish schools where female English teachers outnumber male teachers. After the workshop a separate questionnaire was given to the 35 English teachers in order to answer the following questions:

1. What are the attitudes of English teachers towards the use of ICT tools?
2. What are the views of English teachers towards the effectiveness of the workshop?
3. What do English teachers think about the DOTS materials?
4. What are English teachers' views about the effectiveness of the tools used during the workshop?

The DOTS workshop was conducted for the two groups of teachers on two consecutive days with the cooperation of the Faculty of Education at Dicle University and the Provincial Directorate of MONE. The workshop was structured in three consecutive sessions with three different trainers introducing YouTube, wikis, blogs and podcasts and their use in language classrooms. Each tool was presented in detail and the participants were asked to do related tasks in which they practised what had been presented. The trainers (who were also part of the team that carried out the study and authored this chapter) had prepared presentations with DOTS materials accessible at http://moodle.dots.ecml.at/ and focused on the benefits of and techniques required for using each of the tools before engaging the participating teachers in related tasks. In the first session, one of the trainers described the criteria for selecting YouTube videos for language classes, showed the teachers how to upload, link and embed videos, and asked them to do this themselves. In the second session, another trainer focused on pedagogical issues concerning wikis and blogs. He demonstrated how to start a wiki on wikispaces.com. Following the instructions, each participant created her/his own wikispace. The third session involved an introduction of podcasts and podcasting, and highlighted technical issues such as selecting, downloading and uploading podcasts. The trainer stressed that podcasts provide flexibility in time and location, and opportunities for self-paced learning. He suggested that teachers could design tasks based on podcasts that they could find at http://www.bbc.co.uk/podcasts, http://learnenglish.british council.org/en/elementary-podcasts or www.elllo.org among others. Alternatively they could use Audacity to make high-quality recordings, provide feedback on homework or ask students to produce podcasts on a given theme. For hands-on experience, the participating teachers were asked to find and subscribe to podcasts on iTunes and prepare a class-room activity around one of the podcasts. They were asked to reflect on whether the level of the podcast was appropriate for their students, whether there were any support materials and how they could integrate the podcast into their classes.

As mentioned earlier, two different data collection tools were employed. In the initial meeting, a questionnaire was given to the participants. The questionnaire had 40 items, nine of which investigated participants' demographic characteristics and their institution's technological infra-structure, while 16 items explored their attitudes towards the use of ICT tools in language classes. In the second questionnaire, which followed participation in the workshop and which was administered online, the participants were asked further questions about their attitudes, and for their evaluation of the workshop and the DOTS materials.

The survey data collected after the initial meeting that aimed to promote use of DOTS materials showed that among the meeting par-ticipants 52% were below the age of 30, 23% were between the ages of 31 and 35, 16% were between 36 and 40; and 3% were 46 and above. 42.5% (80) of the participants had been working as teachers for less than five years, while 28.2% (53) of them had teaching experience of more than ten years. These ratios are typical of the situation in Turkish schools in general. (Please note that the percentages given here and elsewhere were calculated for each item according to the number of participants who replied to that particular item.)

## Challenges, facilities and ICT use

Analyses of the survey data collected after the initial meeting also showed that most of the teachers did not have the basic motivation, knowledge and means to use ICT tools in their language classes. They reported that the classrooms were too crowded and that they did not have up-to-date computers and fast internet connections. 75 teachers (40.8%) reported that the number of students in their classes was between 31 and 40, while 66 teachers (35.9%) replied that they had more than 40 students in the English classes. There are techniques to cope with large classes, but the lack of ICT tools seems to be an overwhelming challenge. Figure 11.1 shows the scarcity of technological facilities English teachers can use.

Nearly half of the participants claimed that they did not have an Internet connection at their school, whereas 58 participants (31%) asserted that they had an Internet connection, with 26 participants reporting that they had access to the Internet but that it was very slow.

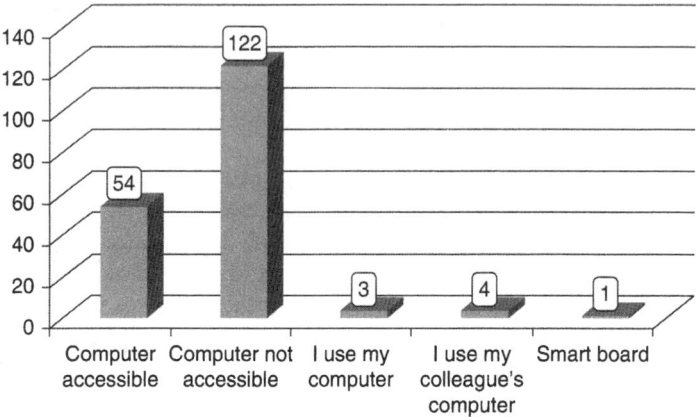

*Figure 11.1*   Accessibility of computer and smart board at state schools in Diyarbakır

Figure 11.2 shows that out of the 211 teachers who responded to this item, 123 teachers (58%) did not have projectors in the classrooms where they taught. Only 59 teachers (28%) reported that they could utilize this equipment while teaching. For 29 teachers (14%) projectors could be provided on demand.

Figure 11.3 shows that only 58 teachers (31%) out of 189 have regular Internet access in the classroom while 26 of them (14%) have a regular but a relatively slow Internet connection. Six of the teachers (3%) can connect to the Internet in the school libraries only. 99 teachers (52%), however, do not have regular access to the Internet in the classroom. This shows that despite major projects, such as FATİH, carried out by the Turkish Ministry of Education, many schools still do not have regular Internet access.

In terms of Learning Management System (LMS) or Virtual Learning Environment (VLE) use, as shown in Figure 11.4, 47%, or about half of the teachers (out of a total of 183 participants who responded to the related item in the questionnaire) reported that their institution had its own management system, while a slightly higher percentage of the teachers (51%) stated that they did not use any kind of management system in their schools. Only 2% of responding teachers reported using the management systems of other institutions. Knowing that VLE use is not common in Turkish state schools, most probably this questionnaire item was not clear to some of the participant teachers. It is possible that they mistook the VLE for the national online system of the Ministry of Education, where teachers enter students' marks and attendance details.

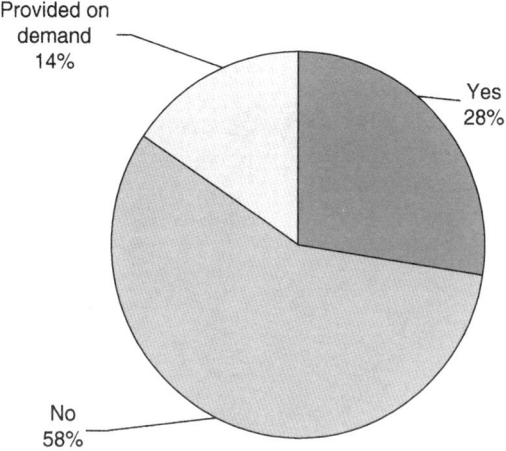

*Figure 11.2*   Availability of projectors in classrooms

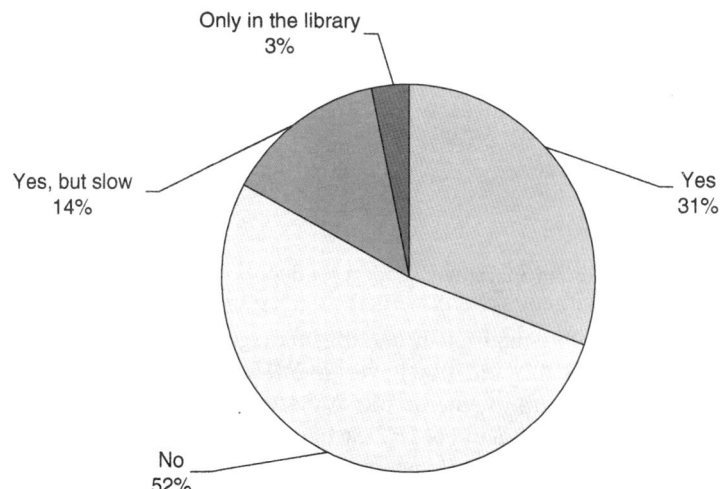

*Figure 11.3*   Availability of regular access to the Internet in classrooms

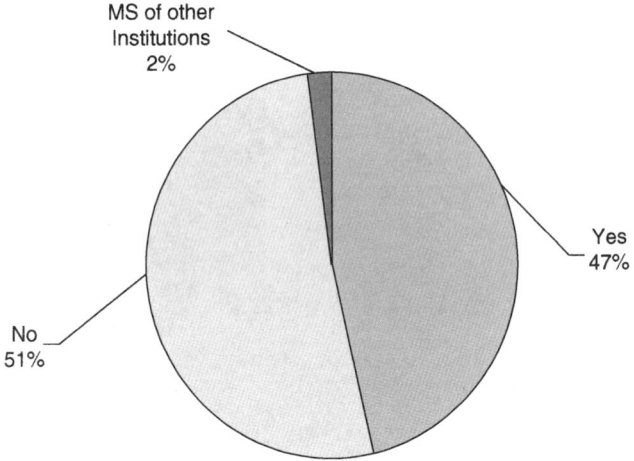

*Figure 11.4*   Availability of Learning Management System

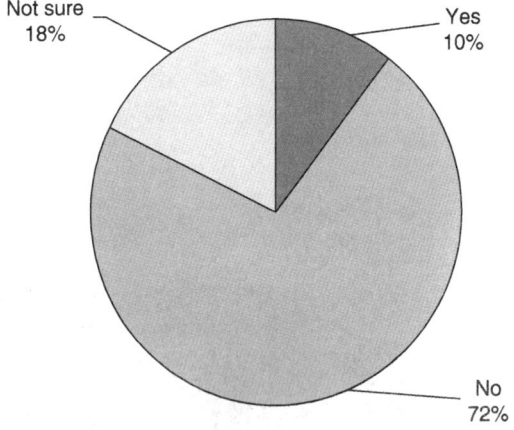

*Figure 11.5*   School management support for development of ICT skills

The teachers who reported using the management systems of other institutions probably did not have an Internet connection and used other schools' set-up to enter marks and attendance.

Figure 11.5 shows that out of 182 teachers, the majority (72%) stated that their school's management did not give any incentive for the improvement of teachers' ICT skills. 18% of the teachers were not sure whether their school's management was supportive in the area. 10% of the teachers were of the opinion that their school's management supported them in terms of developing their ICT skills.

## Impact of the DOTS workshops: views of Turkish participants

After the workshop the participating teachers (N = 35) were asked to complete an online questionnaire about the usefulness and effectiveness of the workshop and the DOTS materials used. The analysis showed that most of the participants found the workshop very useful. Out of 29 teachers who responded to this item, 72% thought that the workshop was very useful, and 17% of participants thought that it was extremely useful (Figure 11.6). Similar questionnaire results collected in various European countries can be found in Chapter 2.

Analysis of the qualitative data collected through open questions within the online questionnaire verified the findings outlined above. Most of the participants commented that the workshop had been very useful and that they had learnt much that they could apply in their classes. During the workshop, it was emphasized that some of the material (for example, YouTube videos and podcasts) could be downloaded and used offline. From participants' practical experience, other ideas emerged to mitigate the lack of Internet connection. For example, some participants suggested that they could use the Internet connection on

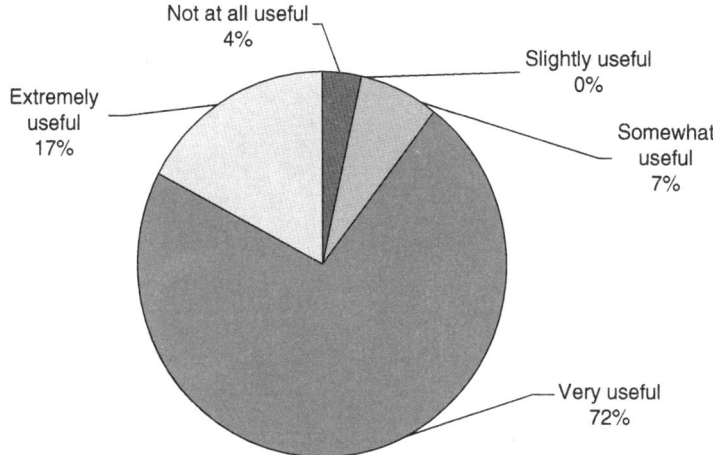

*Figure 11.6*  Overall rating of the workshop

their mobile phones or on their PC via Wi-Fi sharing in the classroom. Therefore, it was clear that even teachers who were not provided with an Internet connection by their school could utilize some of the tools presented in the workshop. One participant wrote:

> I learned useful and important things which I can use in my ELT class. (Participant # 20)

However, there were also some shortcomings. Some participants pointed to the fact that the workshop duration was short and that they needed more training, while others mentioned that the Internet connection was rather slow for those who participated on the first day. All in all, participants' evaluation of the workshop was quite positive and this is supported by responses to further questions.

The questionnaire included items about more specific benefits of the workshop. Replies to those items were also very positive in general. For instance, 71% of the 31 participants who responded to this item agreed with the assertion that they had improved their knowledge and confidence in using ICT in the classroom, while 23% of the participants strongly agreed that they had done so. Only 6% of the participants disagreed that they had improved their knowledge of and confidence in using ICT in the classroom (see Figure 11.7). Participant teachers were

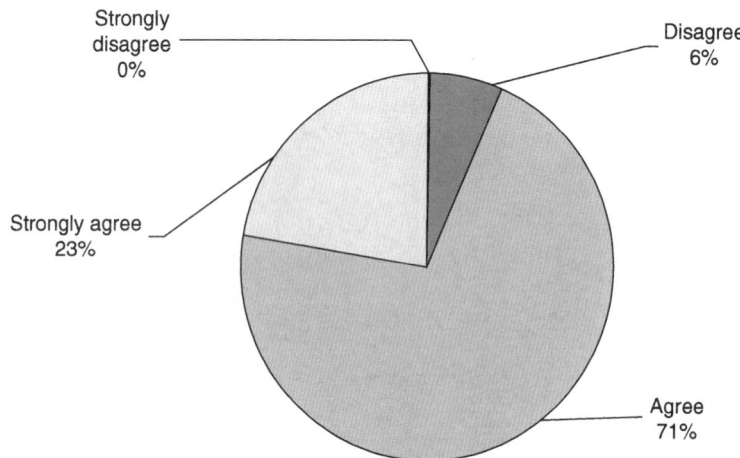

*Figure 11.7* Improved confidence in and knowledge of using ICT in the classroom

asked to do tasks such as downloading a YouTube video or a podcast and developing a lesson or a worksheet about it. The lessons and worksheets they produced and their comments during the workshop provided clear evidence that they had improved their knowledge and confidence.

Responding to an item asking whether they would use ICT tools more frequently after the workshop, most participants (84%) out of 31 either agreed or strongly agreed that they intended to use ICT tools in language education on a more frequent basis. 13% of the participants reported that they neither agreed nor disagreed and only 3% disagreed (see Figure 11.8). Given the shortcomings, challenges and lack of facilities the teachers had to cope with at their schools, this finding is very interesting. The fact that participants noted that they could use some of the tools offline and the encouragement and the practical examples provided during the workshops seemed to have a strong effect.

The answers to the open ended questions included many responses that support the finding that most of the participants intended to use ICT in their classes more often. For example, participants wrote:

> The workshop was quite satisfying I think. I'll use podcasts and dots more in my lessons. (Participant # 12)

> Now I have more courage to use technology in my classes if I have [the] opportunity. (Participant # 13)

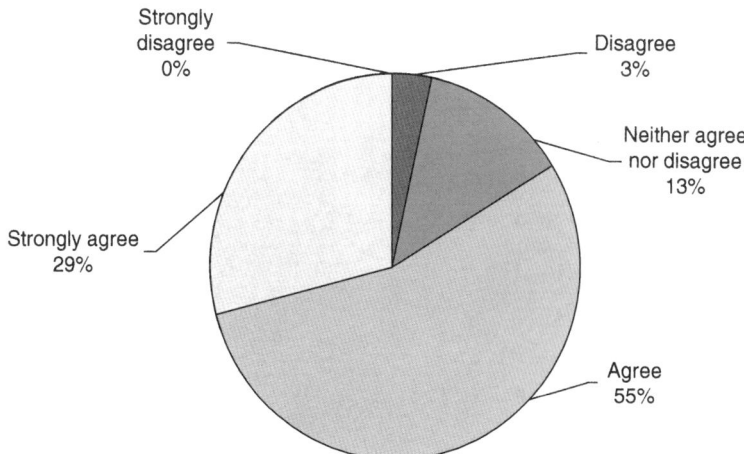

*Figure 11.8* Willingness to use ICT after the workshop

> With this education … I learned more things about technologies used in the classroom I have learned some important pages which can be used for teaching techniques thank you. (Participant # 27)

The influence of encouragement and practical examples is also apparent in Figure 11.9. Out of 31, most of the teachers (93%) were found to be very motivated by the workshop to keep up with technological development. As mentioned earlier, at the initial meeting teachers appeared demoralized due to too many teaching hours and lack of ICT tools and access to the Internet. Therefore, it seems reasonable to conclude that the DOTS workshop increased the motivation of those teachers who participated to use online resources.

We also included an item that examined participant teachers' ability to identify and apply appropriate ICT tools in their specific contexts. As Figure 11.10 shows, 87% of the participants (out of 31) asserted that they had expanded their ability to identify and apply appropriate ICT tools at the workshops. Some answers to open-ended questions included clues confirming this finding:

> First of all I want to thank you all for this short education. I have learned more things for developing techniques used in the classroom. (Participant # 27)

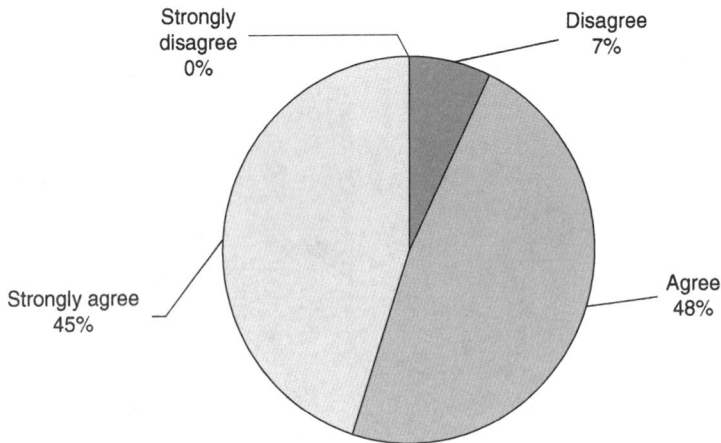

*Figure 11.9* Willingness to keep up with technological development after the workshop

Concerning the capability of acting as multipliers, 74% participants either agreed or strongly agreed that they could act as a multiplier and promote the use of ICT tools to others in the field. As a speculative explanation we can offer that the fact that 26% of the participants neither agreed nor disagreed might have resulted from an ambiguity about the phrase 'acting as a multiplier' or not knowing what this might entail (see Figure 11.11). This finding implies that several participants felt that

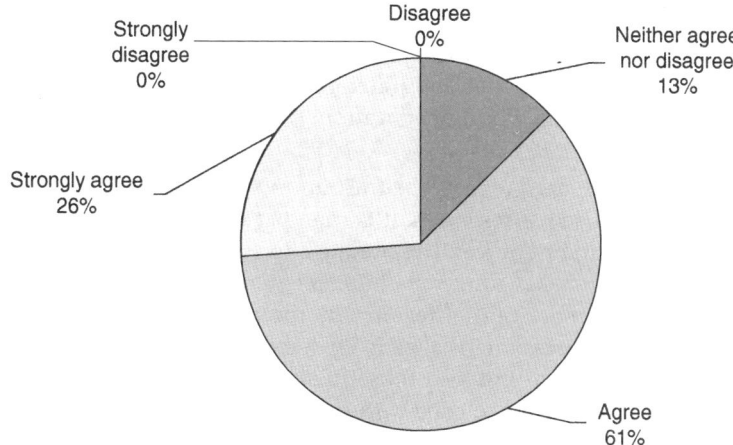

*Figure 11.10*   Skills in identifying and applying appropriate ICT tools

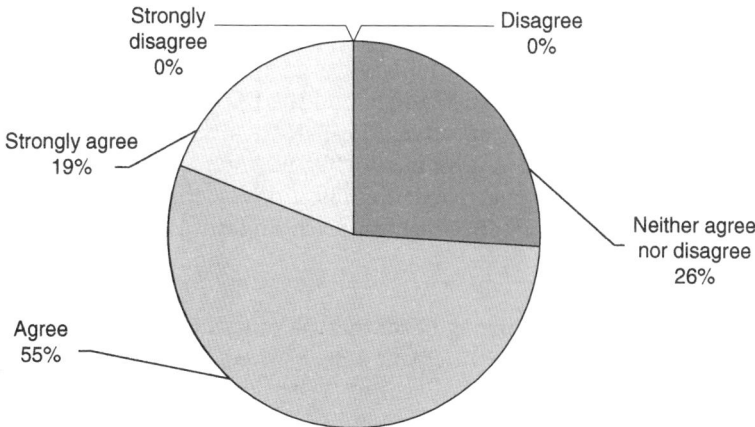

*Figure 11.11*   Capability to act as a multiplier and promote the use of ICT tools to others

they needed more training before they could feel capable of helping others with ICT tools. This may also be a result of the lack of facilities reported by some participants. Two participant teachers wrote:

> I have improved my knowledge but I am hopeless about using them in the classroom. (Participant # 29)

> The activities you suggest us in the presentations are not very applicable in every type of schools. If you give me 10 students in a private school environment with computers and projectors I can do all of these. But in our world these are not applicable as I work in a village school with no internet and illiterate students. I wish you a happy life in your dream world of education. (Participant # 14)

The second statement reflects the frustration that some teachers might feel due to the lack of resources. It is true that not all schools have the same facilities and resources. Despite the efforts of the Turkish Ministry of Education, it takes longer to implement initiatives in rural areas compared with more central regions. By the time the initiatives reach villages, the resources might already be depleted or outdated. Not only schools in rural areas but also those in suburbs of large cities such as Diyarbakır usually have to cope with such problems.

The participants held similar views concerning their capability to identify and apply appropriate DOTS materials. Regarding whether they feel better able to identify and apply appropriate DOTS tools, 78% of the participant teachers (out of 31 who replied to this item) either agreed or strongly agreed, whereas only 3% disagreed (see Figure 11.12). Qualitative data verify this finding. Answers to open-ended questions show that most of the participants found the DOTS workshop and the material presented very effective. The participants asserted they had not known that there were so many effective tools available to teachers free of charge, or that popular applications, such as YouTube and wikis, could be used so effectively to teach English. For example, one participant wrote:

> I think it gives us a strong belief that we can also use these ICT elements in our classes. (Participant # 8)

Most training programmes in the field focus either on the promotion of latest technologies or teaching techniques and strategies. That is why both the DOTS project meeting and the DOTS workshops were

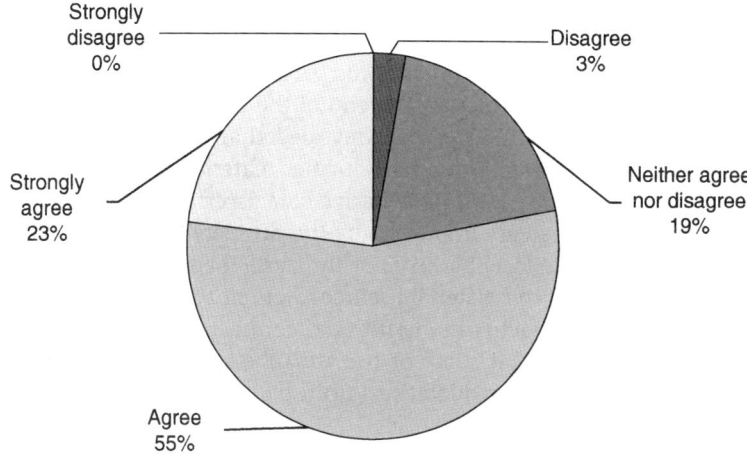

*Figure 11.12* Enhanced ability to identify and apply appropriate DOTS tools

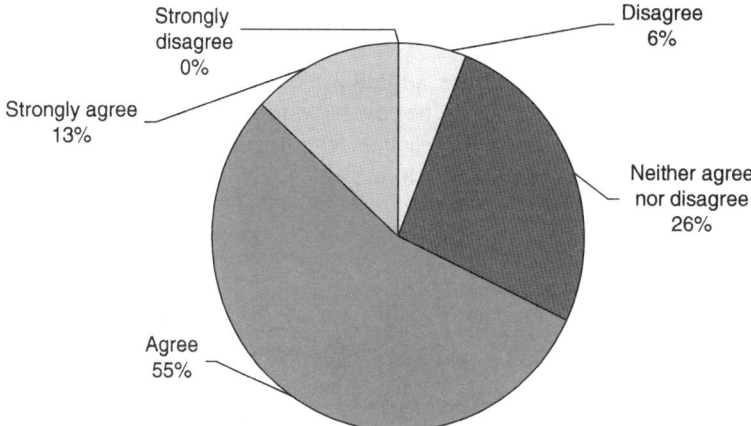

*Figure 11.13* The ability to promote the use of DOTS tools

specifically based on how to use available technologies to teach English in the context of the pedagogy of language teaching.

As with the idea of acting as a multiplier and promoting the use of ICT tools, some participants felt intimidated by the idea of getting others in the field to use DOTS tools. 32% of the participants were found to be not so confident in multiplying and promoting the use of the DOTS tools, whereas 68% of the participants either agreed or strongly agreed that they felt capable of doing so (see Figure 11.13). The short duration of the workshop (three sessions of 90 minutes for each group), participants' diverse backgrounds, and the reported scarcity of ICT tools at schools seem to have prevented some participants from developing a stronger sense of self-efficacy by the end of the DOTS workshop.

The analysis of quantitative data revealed that 71% of the participants were satisfied with the quality of the material provided for the workshops (see Figure 11.14). Qualitative data ascertained that most of the participants were very impressed by the diversity and usefulness of DOTS materials. The fact that 29% of the participants (out of 31 who replied) did not find the material useful or were not sure, might at least partly be due to the fact that the Internet connection was rather slow on the first day and that some of the YouTube-based tasks could not be done effectively. A few quotations from participants' comments are given below:

Very useful work. Thank you. (Participant # 7)

Due to time constraints we couldn't do everything as much as I would love to, but main topics were clear and effective. (Participant # 16)

Besides podcasts, YouTube and blogs other technologies such as Facebook and Twitter could be covered during training. Anyway, the training was very useful for teachers who learnt about such things for the first time. (Participant # 18)

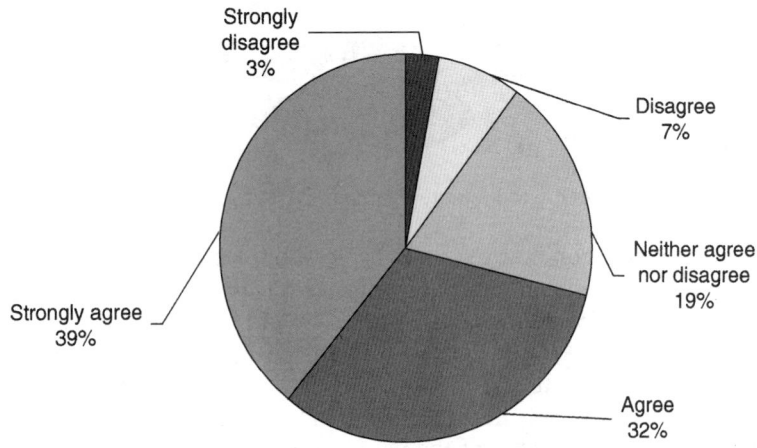

*Figure 11.14*  Perceived quality of materials provided during the workshop

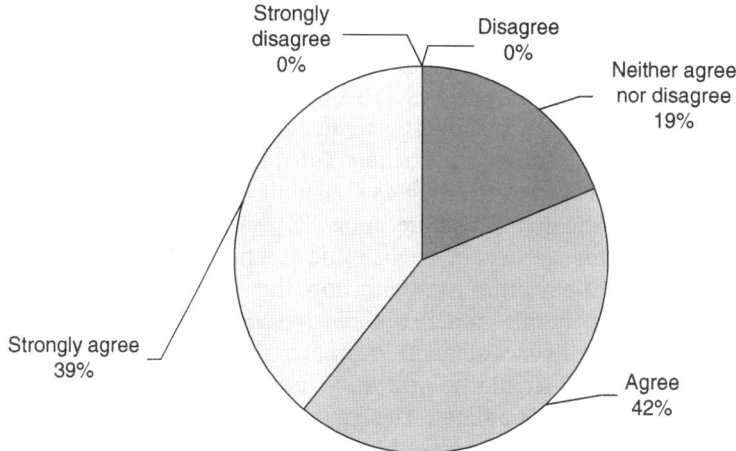

*Figure 11.15* Perceived quality of DOTS materials provided during the workshop

Two of the trainers had taken part in the translation of the DOTS materials into Turkish and all three trainers were well-prepared for both the promotion of the materials produced under the DOTS project and the hands-on experience of developing real classroom tasks based on the DOTS materials. Therefore, it was not surprising to find that most of the participants (94%) believed that the quality of the trainers was very good.

The positive response to the materials is supported by the findings presented in Figure 11.15. A total of 81% of the participants either agreed or strongly agreed that the DOTS tools promoted and utilized during the workshops were very useful. This finding is also supported by qualitative data collected through open-ended questions. One participant wrote:

> I like it and I think I will use the things I have learnt here in my classroom from now on. (Participant # 15)

## Conclusion

In this chapter we have given an account of our experience of a meeting with 211 Turkish teachers of English to introduce and promote DOTS materials, and of running a DOTS workshop to train 35 teachers in using the DOTS materials accessible at http://moodle.dots.ecml.at/ free of charge. Answers to the questionnaire distributed at the end of the workshop showed that most of the participants had positive views about the effectiveness of DOTS materials and the tools provided during the workshop sessions. The training sessions increased their motivation to use ICT in language teaching. This shows that despite the impediments and challenges reported by some teachers, the DOTS workshop was effective in motivating teachers and indeed prompted some to think of practical ways to overcome some of the challenges that they face in their teaching. Therefore, more ICT-related workshops should be organized for teachers of English and teachers should be provided with training about other tools and how they could be used, such as SurveyMonkey, forums, audio-conferencing and Moodle. Finally, participants' positive views about DOTS materials suggest that outputs of the DOTS project should be utilized in undergraduate and in-service teacher training programmes. The guidelines and practical examples given in the DOTS modules are easy to apply and this had a significant impact on the participant teachers' attitudes. These free tools can be utilized to train pre-service and in-service teachers of English working in similar circumstances. Future studies might focus on the potential of other DOTS tools for teacher training purposes. Also, a follow-up survey would be valuable to gauge how teachers have applied their new skills.

## Reflective task

In your own teaching environment, what are the contributing factors to enabling or hindering the use of ICT for language learning?

Either respond to the questions used in the Turkish DOTS workshop or design your own simple questionnaire and survey colleagues in your institution(s).

This concludes the Reflective Tasks for the book. Do you feel ready now to put your thoughts into practice?

# Bibliography

Allen, E. I., & Seaman, J. (2010). *Learning on demand: Online education in the United States, 2009*. Babson Survey Research Group, The Sloan Consortium. Retrieved from www.sloanconsortium.org/publications/survey/pdf/learningondemand.pdf

Almeida d'Eça, T., & Gonzáles, D. (2006). Becoming a webhead: Bridging the gap from classroom to blended or online teaching. *CALICO Journal, 23*(3), 569–580. doi:10.11139/cj.23.3.569-580

Androutsopoulos, J. (2006). Introduction: Sociolinguistics and computer-mediated communication. *Journal of Sociolinguistics, 10*(4), 419–438. doi:10.1111/j.1467-9841.2006.00286.x

Androutsopoulos, J. (2008). Potentials and limitations of discourse-centred online ethnography. *Language@Internet, 5*, article 8. Retrieved from http://www.languageatinternet.org/articles/2008/1610

Androutsopoulos, J. (2013). Networked multilingualism: Some language practices on Facebook and their implications. *International Journal of Bilingualism*, 1367006913489198. doi:10.1177/1367006913489198

Antoniadou, V., Canals, E., Mohr, C., & Zourou, K. (2011). *Young people with fewer opportunities learning languages informally: Perceptions and uses of and social media* (Study operated by the network 'Language learning and social media: 6 key dialogues'). Retrieved from www.openeducationeuropa.eu/en/download/file/fid/23485

Attwell, G. (2010, April 4). Informal learning and why the training model does not work. Retrieved from http://www.pontydysgu.org/2010/04/informal-learning-and-why-the-training-model-does-not-work/

Aydin, S. (2014). Foreign language learners' interactions with their teachers on Facebook. *System, 42*, 155–163. doi:10.1016/j.system.2013.12.001

Bakker, S. C. (2008). *BYU students' beliefs about language learning and communicative language teaching activities* (Unpublished master's thesis). Center for Language Studies, Brigham Young University. Retrieved from http://hdl.lib.byu.edu/1877/etd2202

Barkhuizen, G., & Wette, R. (2008). Narrative frames for investigating the experiences of language teachers. *System, 36*(3), 372–387. doi:10.1016/j.system.2008.02.002

Barkhuizen, G., Benson, P., & Chik, A. (2013). *Narrative inquiry in language teaching and learning research*. New York, Abingdon: Routledge.

Başaran, S., & Cabaroğlu, N. (2014). Language learning podcasts and learners' belief change. *TESL-EJ, 17*(4). Retrieved from http://www.tesl-ej.org/wordpress/issues/volume17/ej68/ej68a5/

Baumann, U., Shelley, M. A., Murphy, L. M., & White, C. J. (2008). New challenges, the role of the tutor in the teaching of languages at a distance. *Distances et Savoirs, 6*(3), 365–392. doi:10.3166/ds.6.365-392

Bax, S. (2003). CALL – past, present and future. *System, 31*(1), 13–28. doi:10.1016/S0346-251X(02)00071-4

Bax, S. (2011). Normalisation revisited: The effective use of technology in language education. *International Journal of Computer-Assisted Language Learning and Teaching, 1*(2), 1–15. doi:10.4018/ijcallt.2011040101

Beasley-Murray, J. (2008). Was introducing Wikipedia to the classroom an act of madness leading only to mayhem if not murder? [Wiki]. Retrieved August 23, 2014, from http://en.wikipedia.org/wiki/User:Jbmurray/Madness

Beaven, T., Comas-Quinn, A., Hauck, M., de los Arcos, B., & Lewis, T. (2013). The Open Translation MOOC: Creating online communities to transcend linguistic barriers. *Journal of Interactive Media in Education.* Retrieved from http://jime. open.ac.uk/jime/article/view/2013-18

Beaven, T., Emke, M., Ernest, P., Germain-Rutherford, A., Hampel, R., Hopkins, J., Stanojević, M.-M., & Stickler, U. (2010). Needs and challenges for online language teachers – The ECML project DOTS. *Teaching English with Technology, 10*(Special Issue 2), 5–20. Retrieved from http://www.tewtjournal. org/VOL%2010/ISSUE%202/volume_10_issue_02-03_article_1.pdf

Beetham, H., Falconer, I., McGill, L., & Littlejohn, A. (2012). *Open practices: Briefing paper.* JISC. Retrieved from https://oersynth.pbworks.com/w/ page/51668352/OpenPracticesBriefing

Beggan, A. (2010). *Exploring institutional attitudes to open learning, the Berlin experience.* Paper presented at the OER10 Conference, Cambridge. Retrieved from https://googledrive.com/host/0Bx_VhBlh4p_jQnhtMXI2WHRvT2s/ abstracts/1003.html

Belz, J. A. (2003). Linguistic perspectives on the development of intercultural competence in telecollaboration. *Language Learning & Technology, 7*(2), 68–117. Retrieved from http://llt.msu.edu/vol7num2/belz/default.html

Bennett, S., & Marsh, D. (2002). Are we expecting online tutors to run before they can walk? *Innovations in Education and Teaching International, 39*(1), 14–20. doi:10.1080/13558000110097055

Black, R. W. (2005). Access and affiliation: The literacy and composition practices of English language learners in an online fanfiction community. *Journal of Adolescent & Adult Literacy, 49*(2), 118–128. doi:10.1598/JAAL.49.2.4

Blake-Plock, S. (2013, December 16). Moving PD forward beyond videos. Retrieved August 24, 2014, from https://www.edsurge.com/n/2013-12-16-opinion-how-to-move-pd-forward

Block, D. (2003). *The social turn in second language acquisition.* Edinburgh: Edinburgh University Press.

Blurton, C. (1999). *New directions of ICT-Use in education* (UNESCO's World Communication and Information Report 1999). United Nations Educational, Scientific and Cultural Organization: UNESCO. Retrieved from http://www. unesco.org/education/lwf/dl/edict.pdf

Blyth, C. (2009). From textbook to online materials: The changing ecology of foreign-language publishing in the era of ICT. In M. Evans (Ed.), *Education and digital technology: Foreign language learning with digital technology* (pp. 174–202). London: Continuum International Publishing.

Borau, K., Ullrich, C., Feng, J., & Shen, R. (2009). Microblogging for language learning: Using Twitter to train communicative and cultural competence. In M. Spaniol, Q. Li, R. Klamma, & R. W. H. Lau (Eds), *Advances in web based learning – ICWL 2009* (pp. 78–87). Berlin, Heidelberg: Springer. doi:10.1007/978-3-642-03426-8_10

Borg, S. (2003). Teacher cognition in language teaching: A review of research on what language teachers think, know, believe, and do. *Language Teaching*, *36*(02), 81–109. doi:10.1017/S0261444803001903

Borg, S. (2006). The distinctive characteristics of foreign language teachers. *Language Teaching Research*, *10*(1), 3–31. doi:10.1191/1362168806lr182oa

Borthwick, Kate. (2012). *The FAVOR project* (Final report). JISC. Retrieved from https://www.llas.ac.uk/sites/default/files/nodes/6505/FAVOR-Final-report.pdf

Borthwick, K., & Gallagher-Brett, A. (2014). 'Inspiration, ideas, encouragement': Teacher development and improved use of technology in language teaching through open educational practice. *Computer Assisted Language Learning*, *27*(2), 163–183. doi:10.1080/09588221.2013.818560

Boyatzis, R. E. (1998). *Transforming qualitative information: Thematic analysis and code development.* Thousand Oaks, CA: Sage.

Brandt, C. (2008). Integrating feedback and reflection in teacher preparation. *ELT Journal*, *62*(1), 37–46. doi:10.1093/elt/ccm076

Bransford, J. D., Brown, A. L., & Cocking, R. R. (Eds). (2000). *How people learn: Brain, mind, experience, and school* (Expanded Edition). Washington, DC: National Academies Press.

Breuer, F. (2003). Subjekthaftigkeit der sozial-/wissenschaftlichen Erkenntnistätigkeit und ihre Reflexion: Epistemologische Fenster, methodische Umsetzungen. *Forum Qualitative Sozialforschung / Forum: Qualitative Social Research*, *4*(2). Retrieved from http://nbn-resolving.de/urn:nbn:de:0114-fqs0302258

Browne, T., Holding, R., Howell, A., & Rodway-Dyer, S. (2010). The challenges of OER to academic practice. *Journal of Interactive Media in Education*, *2010*(01). Retrieved from http://jime.open.ac.uk/jime/article/view/2010-3

Buchberger, F., Campos, B. P., Kallos, D., & Stephenson, J. (Eds). (2000). *Green paper on teacher education in Europe: High quality teacher education for high quality education and training.* Umeå: Thematic Network on Teacher Education in Europe, Umeå universitet. Retrieved from http://tntee.umu.se/publications/greenpaper.html

Buiskool, B.-J., Van Lakerveld, J., & Broek, S. (2009). Educators at work in two sectors of adult and vocational education: An overview of two European research projects. *European Journal of Education*, *44*(2), 145–162. doi:10.1111/j.1465-3435.2009.01378.x

Bushati, J., Barolli, E., Dibra, G., & Haveri, A. (2012). Advantages and disadvantages of using ICT in education. In *International conference on educational sciences*. Hëna e Plotë Bedër University. Retrieved from http://bederweb.majdanoz.net/Conferences/ICES%202012/FULL%20ARTICLE/Bushati_Barolli_Dibra_Haveri_Advantages%20and%20disadvantages%20of%20using%20ICT%20in%20education.pdf

Byington, T. A. (2011). Communities of practice: Using blogs to increase collaboration. *Intervention in School and Clinic*, *46*(5), 280–291. doi:10.1177/1053451210395384

Cabaroğlu, N. (2014). Professional development through action research: Impact on self-efficacy. *System*, *44*, 79–88. doi:10.1016/j.system.2014.03.003

Caena, F. (2011). *Literature review: Quality in Teachers' continuing professional development* (Education and Training 2020: Thematic Working Group 'Professional Development of Teachers'). Brussels: European Commission. Retrieved from http://ec.europa.eu/education/policy/strategic-framework/doc/teacher-development_en.pdf

Cambridge, D., Kaplan, S. & Suter, V. (2005) Community of Practice Design Guide: A Step-by-Step Guide for Designing & Cultivating Communities of Practice in Higher Education. http://net.educause.edu/ir/library/pdf/nli0531.pdf

CARLA. (n.d.). Introduction to technology integration for language learning. Retrieved August 24, 2014, from http://www.carla.umn.edu/technology/modules/intro/index.html

Cennamo, K., Ross, J. D., Ertmer, P. A., & International Society for Technology in Education. (2010). *Technology integration for meaningful classroom use: A standards-based approach* (1st edition.). Belmont, CA: Wadsworth, Cengage Learning.

Charmaz, K. (2000). Grounded theory methodology: Objectivist and constructivist qualitative methods. In N. K. Denzin, & Y. S. Lincoln (Eds), *Handbook of qualitative research* (2nd ed., pp. 509–535). Thousand Oaks, CA: Sage.

Comas-Quinn, A. (2011). Learning to teach online or learning to become an online teacher: An exploration of teachers' experiences in a blended learning course. *ReCALL, 23*(Special Issue 3), 218–232. doi:10.1017/S0958344011000152

Comas-Quinn, A., de los Arcos, B., & Mardomingo, R. (2012). Virtual learning environments (VLEs) for distance language learning: Shifting tutor roles in a contested space for interaction. *Computer Assisted Language Learning, 25*(2), 129–143. doi:10.1080/09588221.2011.636055

Compton, L. K. L. (2009). Preparing language teachers to teach language online: A look at skills, roles, and responsibilities. *Computer Assisted Language Learning, 22*(1), 73–99. doi:10.1080/09588220802613831

Conole, G. (2012). Fostering social inclusion through open educational resources (OER). *Distance Education, 33*(2), 131–134. doi:10.1080/01587919.2012.700563

Conole, G. (2013). *Designing for learning in an open world.* New York. Heidelberg, Dordrecht, London: Springer.

Cook, V. (1999). Going beyond the native speaker in language teaching. *TESOL Quarterly, 33*(2), 185–209. doi:10.2307/3587717

Cook, V. (2005). Basing teaching on the L2 user. In E. Llurda (Ed.), *Non-Native language teachers: Perceptions, challenges and contributions to the profession* (pp. 47–61). New York: Springer.

Cook, V. (2008). *Second language learning and language teaching* (4th edition.). Abingdon, New York: Routledge.

Cook, V. (2013). *Second language learning and language teaching* (4 ed.). Abingdon: Routledge.

Cornwall, A. (1996). Towards participatory practice: Participatory rural appraisal and the participatory process. In K. De Koning, & M. Martin (Eds), *Participatory research in health: Issues and experiences* (pp. 94–107). London: Zed Books.

Cox, M., Preston, C., & Cox, K. (1999, September 2). *What factors support or prevent teachers from using ICT in their classrooms?* Paper presented at the British Educational Research Association Annual Conference, Brighton. Retrieved from http://www.leeds.ac.uk/educol/documents/00001304.htm

Craft, A., Cremin, T., Hay, P., & Clack, J. (2014). Creative primary schools: Developing and maintaining pedagogy for creativity. *Ethnography and Education, 9*(1), 16–34. doi:10.1080/17457823.2013.828474

Cross, J. (2010). 'They had people called professors...!' Changing worlds of learning: Strengthening informal learning in formal institutions? In U.-D. Ehlers &

D. Schneckenberg (Eds), *Changing cultures in higher education: Moving ahead to future learning* (pp. 43–54). Berlin, Heidelberg: Springer.

Cummins, J. (2000). Academic language learning, transformative pedagogy, and information technology: Towards a critical balance. *TESOL Quarterly, 34*(3), 537–548. doi:10.2307/3587742

Cutrim Schmid, E. (2011). Video-stimulated reflection as a professional development tool in interactive whiteboard research. *ReCALL, 23*(Special Issue 3), 252–270. doi:10.1017/S0958344011000176

Cutrim Schmid, E., & Whyte, S. (2012). Interactive whiteboards in state school settings: Teacher responses to socio-constructivist hegemonies. *Language Learning & Technology, 16*(2), 65–86. Retrieved from http://llt.msu.edu/issues/june2012/cutrimschmidwhyte.pdf

Dahlstrom, E., Walker, J. D., & Dziuban, C. (2013). *ECAR study of undergraduate students and information technology, 2013* (Research report). Louisville, CO: EDUCASE Center for Analysis and Research. Retrieved from http://net.educause.edu/ir/library/pdf/ERS1302/ERS1302.pdf

Daniel, B., Schwier, R. A., & McCalla, G. (2003). Social capital in virtual learning communities and distributed communities of practice. *Canadian Journal of Learning and Technology / La Revue Canadienne de l'Apprentissage et de La Technologie, 29*(3). Retrieved from http://cjlt.csj.ualberta.ca/index.php/cjlt/article/view/85

Dausien, B., & Schwendowius, D. (2009). Professionalisation in general adult education in Germany – an attempt to cut a path through a jungle. *European Journal of Education, 44*(2), 183–203. doi:10.1111/j.1465-3435.2009.01387.x

Davies, D., Jindal-Snape, D., Collier, C., Digby, R., Hay, P., & Howe, A. (2013). Creative learning environments in education – A systematic literature review. *Thinking Skills and Creativity, 8*, 80–91. doi:10.1016/j.tsc.2012.07.004

Dooly, M. (2011). Divergent perceptions of telecollaborative language learning tasks: Tasks-as-workplan vs. task-as-process. *Language Learning & Technology, 15*(2), 69–911. Retrieved from http://llt.msu.edu/issues/june2011/dooly.pdf

Doughty, C. J., & Long, M. H. (2003). Optimal psycholinguistic environments for distance foreign language learning. *Language Learning & Technology, 7*(3), 50–80. Retrieved from http://llt.msu.edu/vol7num3/doughty/default.html

Dougiamas, M. (1998). *A journey into constructivism.* Retrieved from http://www.researchgate.net/publication/200022404_A_journey_into_constructivism

Downes, S. (2007, February 3). What connectivism is [Blog post]. Retrieved from http://halfanhour.blogspot.com/2007/02/what-connectivism-is.html

Downes, S. (2011, July 14). Open educational resources: A definition [Blog post]. Retrieved from http://halfanhour.blogspot.it/2011/07/open-educational-resources-definition.html

Eckert, P. (2006). Communities of practice. In K. Brown (Ed.), *Encyclopedia of language & linguistics* (2nd edition, pp. 683–685). Amsterdam: Elsevier.

Edwards, M., Perry, B., & Janzen, K. (2011). The making of an exemplary online educator. *Distance Education, 32*(1), 101–118. doi:10.1080/01587919.2011.565499

Egbert, J., Huff, L., McNeil, L., Preuss, C., & Sellen, J. (2009). Pedagogy, process, and classroom context: Integrating teacher voice and experience into research on technology-enhanced language learning. *The Modern Language Journal, 93* (Issue Supplement s1), 754–768. doi:10.1111/j.1540-4781.2009.00971.x

Ellis, R. (2000). Task-based research and language pedagogy. *Language Teaching Research, 4*(3), 193–220. doi:10.1177/136216880000400302

Ellis, R. (2003). *Task-based language learning and teaching.* Oxford: Oxford University Press.

Emke, M., & Stickler, U. (2015). Teaching and learning online – developing your own skills to develop others. In H. Krings & B. Kühn (Eds), *Fremdsprachliche Lernprozesse.* Erträge des 4. Bremer Symposions zum Fremdsprachenlehren und -lernen an Hochschulen. Band 48 in der Reihe FREMDSPRACHEN IN LEHRE UND FORSCHUNG (FLF), pp.199–209.

Ernest, P., Guitert Catasús, M., Hampel, R., Heiser, S. L., Hopkins, J., Murphy, L. M., & Stickler, U. (2013). Online teacher development: Collaborating in a virtual learning environment. *Computer Assisted Language Learning, 26*(4), 311–333. doi:10.1080/09588221.2012.667814

Ertmer, P. A., Ottenbreit-Leftwich, A., Sadik, O., Sendurur, E., & Sendurur, P. (2012). Teacher beliefs and technology integration practices: Examining the alignment between espoused and enacted beliefs. In J. König (Ed.), *Teachers' pedagogical beliefs: Definition and operationalisation – connections to knowledge and performance – development and change* (pp. 149–170). Münster: Waxmann.

European Commission (2013). The Opening up Education initiative. Retrieved August 24, 2014, from http://www.openeducationeuropa.eu/en/initiative

European Commission, Education Audiovisual and Culture Executive Agency, & Eurydice (2013). *Key data on teachers and school leaders in Europe* (2013 Edition. Eurydice Report). Luxembourg: Office of the European Union. Retrieved from http://eacea.ec.europa.eu/education/eurydice/documents/key_data_series/151EN.pdf

European Parliament, & Council of the European Union (2006). *Recommendation of the European Parliament and of the Council of 18 December 2006 on key competences for lifelong learning.* Retrieved from http://eur-lex.europa.eu/legal-content/EN/TXT/?uri=uriserv:OJ.L_.2006.394.01.0010.01.ENG

Fatemi, A. H., Shirvan, M. E., & Rezvani, Y. (2011). The effect of teachers' self-reflection on EFL learners' writing achievement. *Cross-Cultural Communication, 7*(3), 177–183. doi:10.3968/j.ccc.1923670020110703.250

Felix, U. (2002). The web as a vehicle for constructivist approaches in language teaching. *ReCALL, 14*(01), 2–15. doi:10.1017/S0958344002000216

Felix, U. (2005). What do meta-analyses tell us about CALL effectiveness? *ReCALL, 17*(02), 269–288. doi:10.1017/S0958344005000923

Ferreira, J. B., Klein, A. Z., Freitas, A., & Schlemmer, E. (2013). Mobile learning: Definition, uses and challenges. In L. A. Wankel, & P. Blessinger (Eds), *Increasing student engagement and retention using mobile applications: Smartphones, Skype and texting technologies* (Vol. 6, pp. 47–82). Bingley: Emerald.

Firth, A., & Wagner, J. (1997). On discourse, communication, and (some) fundamental concepts in SLA research. *The Modern Language Journal, 81*(3), 285–300. doi:10.1111/j.1540-4781.1997.tb05480.x

Firth, A., & Wagner, J. (2007). Second/foreign language learning as a social accomplishment: Elaborations on a reconceptualized SLA. *The Modern Language Journal, 91*, 800–819. doi:10.1111/j.1540-4781.2007.00670.x

Flewitt, R. S., Hampel, R., Hauck, M., & Lancaster, L. (2014). What are multimodal data and transcription? In C. Jewitt (Ed.), *The Routledge handbook of multimodal analysis* (2nd ed., pp. 40–53). London: Routledge.

Fraga-Cañadas, C. P. (2011). Building communities of practice for foreign language teachers. *The Modern Language Journal, 95*(2), 296–300. doi:10.1111/j.1540-4781.2011.01183.x

Freire, P. (1982). Creating alternative research methods: Learning to do it by doing it. In B. Hall, A. Gillette, & R. Tandon (Eds), *Creating knowledge: A monopoly? Participating research in development* (pp. 29–37). New Delhi, India: Society for Participatory Research in Asia.

Fryer, L., & Carpenter, R. (2006). Emerging technologies: Bots as language learning tools. *Language Learning & Technology, 10*(3), 8–14. Retrieved from http://llt.msu.edu/vol10num3/pdf/emerging.pdf

Furstenberg, G., Levet, S., English, K., & Maillet, K. (2001). Giving a virtual voice to the silent language of culture: The CULTURA project. *Language Learning & Technology, 5*(1), 55–102. Retrieved from http://llt.msu.edu/vol5num1/furstenberg/default.html

Gallardo, M., Heiser, S. L., & Nicolson, M. (2011). Teacher development for blended contexts. In M. Nicolson, L. M. Murphy, & M. Southgate (Eds), *Language teaching in blended contexts* (pp. 219–231). Edinburgh, U.K.: Dunedin Academic Press.

Garrison, D. R., & Arbaugh, J. B. (2007). Researching the community of inquiry framework: Review, issues, and future directions. *The Internet and Higher Education, 10*(3), 157–172. doi:10.1016/j.iheduc.2007.04.001

Garrison, D. R., Anderson, T., & Archer, W. (2010). The first decade of the community of inquiry framework: A retrospective. *The Internet and Higher Education, 13*(1–2), 5–9. doi:10.1016/j.iheduc.2009.10.003

Garrison, D. R., Cleveland-Innes, M., & Fung, T. S. (2010). Exploring causal relationships among teaching, cognitive and social presence: Student perceptions of the community of inquiry framework. *The Internet and Higher Education, 13*(1–2), 31–36. doi:10.1016/j.iheduc.2009.10.002

Gass, S. M., & Mackey, A. (2000). *Stimulated recall methodology in second language research*. Mahwah, N.J.: Lawrence Erlbaum Associates.

Gilmore, A. (2007). Authentic materials and authenticity in foreign language learning. *Language Teaching, 40*(02), 97–118. doi:10.1017/S0261444807004144

Glaser, B. G., & Strauss, A. L. (2008). *The discovery of grounded theory: Strategies for qualitative research*. New Brunswick, London: Transaction Publishers.

Glasersfeld, E. von. (2007). Learning as a constructive activity. In M. Larochelle (Ed.), *Key works in radical constructivism*. Rotterdam, Taipei: Sense Publishers.

Golonka, E. M., Bowles, A. R., Frank, V. M., Richardson, D. L., & Freynik, S. (2014). Technologies for foreign language learning: A review of technology types and their effectiveness. *Computer Assisted Language Learning, 27*(1), 70–105. doi:10.1080/09588221.2012.700315

Gonzáles, D., & St. Louis, R. (2008). The use of Web 2.0 tools to promote learner autonomy. *Independence, 43*, 28–32.

Gotto IV, G. S., Turnbull, A., Summers, J. A., & Blue-Banning, M. (2008). *Community of practice development manual: A step-by-step guide for designing and developing a community of practice*. Austin, Texas: SEDL.

Guldberg, K., & Mackness, J. (2009). Foundations of communities of practice: Enablers and barriers to participation. *Journal of Computer Assisted Learning, 25*(6), 528–538. doi:10.1111/j.1365-2729.2009.00327.x

Hammersley, M., & Atkinson, P. (2007). *Ethnography: Principles in practice* (3rd edition.). Abingdon: Routledge.

Hampel, R. (2006). Rethinking task design for the digital age: A framework for language teaching and learning in a synchronous online environment. *ReCALL, 18*(01), 105–121. doi:10.1017/S0958344006000711

Hampel, R. (2010). Task design for a virtual learning environment in a distance language course. In M. Thomas, & H. Reinders (Eds), *Task-Based language learning and teaching with technology* (pp. 131–153). London: Continuum.

Hampel, R. (2014). Making meaning online: Computer-mediated communication for language learning. In A. Peti-Stantić, & M.-M. Stanojević (Eds), *Language as information: Proceedings from the CALS Conference 2012* (pp. 89–106). Frankfurt am Main: Peter Lang.

Hampel, R., & de los Arcos, B. (2013). Interacting at a distance: A critical review of the role of ICT in developing the learner – Context interface in a university language programme. *Innovation in Language Learning and Teaching, 7*(2), 158–178. doi:10.1080/17501229.2013.776051

Hampel, R., & Pleines, C. (2013). Fostering student interaction and engagement in a virtual learning environment: An investigation into activity design and implementation. *CALICO Journal, 30*(3), 342–370. doi:10.11139/cj.30.3.342-370

Hampel, R., & Stickler, U. (2005). New skills for new classrooms: Training tutors to teach languages online. *Computer Assisted Language Learning, 18*(4), 311–326. doi:10.1080/09588220500335455

Hampel, R., & Stickler, U. (2012). The use of videoconferencing to support multimodal interaction in an online language classroom. *ReCALL, 24*(02), 116–137. doi:10.1017/S095834401200002X

Hanson-Smith, E., & Bauer-Ramazani, C. (2004). Professional development: The electronic village online of the TESOL CALL interest section. *TESL-EJ, 8*(2). Retrieved from http://www.tesl-ej.org/wordpress/issues/volume8/ej30/ej30int/

Han, Z. H. (2002). Rethinking the role of corrective feedback in communicative language teaching. *RELC Journal, 33*(1), 1–34. doi:10.1177/003368820203300101

Hanna, B.E. & de Noy, J. (2009). *Learning language and culture via public internet discussion forums.* New York: Palgrave Macmillan.

Harmeier, M. (2009). *'Für die Teilnehmer sind wir die VHS': Selbstverständnis von Kursleitenden und ihr Umgang mit Qualifizierungsmaßnahmen* (Vol. 6). Bielefeld: Bertelsmann.

Healey, D., Hegelheimer, V., Hubbard, P., Ioannou-Georgiou, S., Kessler, G., & Ware, P. (2008). *TESOL technology standards framework.* Alexandria: Teachers of English to Speakers of Other Languages, Inc. (TESOL). Retrieved from http://www.tesol.org/docs/books/bk_technologystandards_framework_721.pdf

Heiser, S. L., Stickler, U., & Furnborough, C. (2013). Ready, steady, speak-online: Student training in the use of an online synchronous conferencing tool. *CALICO Journal, 30*(2), 226–251. doi:10.11139/cj.30.2.226-251

Herring, S. C. (2007). A faceted classification scheme for computer mediated discourse. *Language@Internet, 4*(1), 1–37. Retrieved from http://www.languageatinternet.org/articles/2007/761

Hilbert, M. (2014). Technological information inequality as an incessantly moving target: The redistribution of information and communication capacities between 1986 and 2010. *Journal of the Association for Information Science and Technology, 65*(4), 821–835. doi:10.1002/asi.23020

Hilton, J. L. I., Lutz, N., & Wiley, D. (2012). Examining the reuse of open textbooks. *The International Review of Research in Open and Distance Learning,*

*13*(2), 45–58. Retrieved from http://www.irrodl.org/index.php/irrodl/article/view/1137

Hinckey, D. T. (1997). Motivation and contemporary socio-constructivist instructional perspectives. *Educational Psychologist, 32*(3), 175–193.

Hinkelman, D., & Gruba, P. (2012). Power within blended language learning programs in Japan. *Language Learning & Technology, 16*(2), 46–64. Retrieved from http://llt.msu.edu/issues/june2012/hinkelmangruba.html

Horwitz, E. K., Horwitz, M. B., & Cope, J. (1986). Foreign language classroom anxiety. *The Modern Language Journal, 70*(2), 125–132. doi:10.1111/j.1540-4781.1986.tb05256.x

Hubbard, P. (2008). CALL and the future of language teacher education. *CALICO Journal, 25*(2), 175–188. doi:10.11139/cj.25.2.175-188

Hubbard, P. (2009). General introduction. In P. Hubbard (Ed.), *Computer-Assisted Language Learning* (Vols. 1–4, Vol. 1: Foundations of Call, pp. 1–20). New York: Routledge.

Hubbard, P., & Levy, M. (2006a). Introduction. In P. Hubbard & M. Levy (Eds), *Teacher education in CALL* (pp. ix–xi). Amsterdam, Philadelphia: John Benjamins.

Hubbard, P., & Levy, M. (2006b). The scope of CALL education. In P. Hubbard & M. Levy (Eds), *Teacher education in CALL* (pp. 3–20). Amsterdam, Philadelphia: John Benjamins.

Huntemann, H., & Reichart, E. (2013). *Volkshochschul-Statistik* (No. 51. Folge, Arbeitsjahr 2012). Bonn: Deutsches Institut für Erwachsenenbildung, Leibniz-Zentrum für Lebenslanges Lernen e.V. Retrieved from http://www.die-bonn.de/doks/2013-volkshochschule-statistik-01.pdf

Hurd, S. (2006). Towards a better understanding of the dynamic role of the distance language learner: Learner perceptions of personality, motivation, roles, and approaches. *Distance Education, 27*(3), 303–329. doi:10.1080/01587910600940406

Hurd, S. (2008). Affect and strategy use in independent language learning. In S. Hurd, & T. Lewis (Eds), *Language learning strategies in independent settings* (pp. 218–236). Bristol: Multilingual Matters. Retrieved from http://www.google.com/books?hl=hr&lr=&id=zHJjBQNGXUoC&oi=fnd&pg=PA218&dq=Affect+and+strategy+use+in+independent+language+learning&ots=tmVc3BiW8f&sig=aXlFc1PLhHoqBVPchrcYNhRFo9k

ICT Cluster (2010). *Learning, innovation and ICT. Lessons learned by the ICT Cluster Education & Training 2010 programme.* International Council for Open and Distance Education. Retrieved from http://www.icde.org/filestore/Resources/Reports/KeyLessonsICTclusterReport.pdf

International Society for Technology in Education (2000). *ISTE standards.* Retrieved from http://www.iste.org/docs/pdfs/nets_for_teachers_2000.pdf?sfvrsn=2

International Society for Technology in Education (2008). *ISTE standards.* Retrieved from http://www.iste.org/docs/pdfs/20-14_ISTE_Standards-T_PDF.pdf

Jephcote, M., & Salisbury, J. (2009). Further education teachers' accounts of their professional identities. *Teaching and Teacher Education, 25*(7), 966–972. doi:10.1016/j.tate.2009.05.010

Johnson, D. (2012). *The classroom teacher's technology survival guide* (1st ed.). Hoboken, NJ: Jossey-Bass.

Johnson, K. E. (2006). The sociocultural turn and its challenges for second language teacher education. *TESOL Quarterly, 40*(1), 235–257. doi:10.2307/40264518

Jones, C. M., & Youngs, B. L. (2006). Teacher preparation for online language instruction. In P. Hubbard, & M. Levy (Eds), *Teacher education in CALL* (pp. 267–280). Amsterdam, Philadelphia: John Benjamins. Retrieved from http://public.eblib.com/EBLPublic/PublicView.do?ptiID=623195

Joyce, A. (2006). *OECD study of OER: Forum report*. Paris: International Instituted for Educational Planning. Retrieved from https://oerknowledgecloud.org/content/oecd-study-oer-forum-report

Karavas-Doukas, E. (1996). Using attitude scales to investigate teachers' attitudes to the communicative approach. *ELT Journal, 50*(3), 187–198. doi:10.1093/elt/50.3.187

Kemmis, S., & McTaggart, R. (2000). Participatory action research. In N. K. Denzin, & Y. S. Lincoln (Eds), *Handbook of qualitative research* (2nd ed., pp. 567–605). Thousand Oaks, CA: Sage.

Kennedy, A. (2005). Models of Continuing Professional Development: A framework for analysis. *Journal of In-Service Education, 31*(2), 235–250. doi:10.1080/13674580500200277

Kern, R. (2006). Perspectives on technology in learning and teaching languages. *TESOL Quarterly, 40*(1), 183–210. doi:10.2307/40264516

Kern, R., Ware, P., & Warschauer, M. (2004). Crossing Frontiers: New directions in online pedagogy and research. *Annual Review of Applied Linguistics, 24*, 243–260. doi:10.1017/S0267190504000091

Koehler, M., & Mishra, P. (2009). What is Technological Pedagogical Content Knowledge (TPACK)? *Contemporary Issues in Technology and Teacher Education, 9*(1), 60–70. Retrieved from http://www.citejournal.org/vol9/iss1/general/article1.cfm

Kopcha, T. J. (2012). Teachers' perceptions of the barriers to technology integration and practices with technology under situated professional development. *Computers & Education, 59*(4), 1109–1121. doi:10.1016/j.compedu.2012.05.014

Kozar, O. (2012). Use of synchronous online tools in private English language teaching in Russia. *Distance Education, 33*(3), 415–420. doi:10.1080/01587919.2012.723164

Krashen, S. D. (1985). *The input hypothesis: Issues and implications*. Harlow: Longman.

Kukulska-Hulme, A. (2012) Language learning defined by time and place: A framework for next generation designs. In: Díaz-Vera, J.E. (Ed.) *Left to My Own Devices: Learner Autonomy and Mobile Assisted Language Learning.* Innovation and Leadership in English Language Teaching, 6. Bingley, UK: Emerald Group Publishing Limited, pp. 1–13.

Kumaravadivelu, B. (2008, e-Edition). *Understanding language teaching: From method to post-method.* Mahwah, New Jersey; London: Lawrence Erlbaum Associates. Retrieved from http://search.ebscohost.com/login.aspx?direct=true&scope=site&db=nlebk&db=nlabk&AN=158596

Lai, C., & Li, G. (2011). Technology and task-based language teaching: A critical review. *CALICO Journal, 28*(2), 498–521. doi:10.11139/cj.28.2.498-521

Lam, W. S. E. (2000). L2 literacy and the design of the self: A case study of a teenager writing on the internet. *TESOL Quarterly, 34*(3), 457–482. doi:10.2307/3587739

Lamy, M.-N., & Hampel, R. (2007). *Online communication in language learning and teaching*. Houndmills: Palgrave Macmillan.

Language Educators Community (2010). Retrieved August 25, 2014, from http://community.actfl.org/communities/viewcommunities/communitydetails/?CommunityKey=e6b76e7b-b0aa-4f53-a06e-4b456e9a5339

Lantolf, J. P. (2006). Sociocultural theory and L2: State of the art. *Studies in Second Language Acquisition, 28*(01), 67–109. doi:10.1017/S0272263106060037

Lave, J. (1991). Situating learning in communities of practice. In L. B. Resnick, J. M. Levine, & S. D. Teasley (Eds), *Perspectives on socially shared cognition* (pp. 63–82). Washington, DC: American Psychological Association.

Lave, J., & Wenger, E. C. (1991). *Situated learning: Legitimate peripheral participation*. Cambridge: Cambridge University Press.

Les Compagnons du Tour de France (n.d.). Qui peut être candidat pour partir sur le Tour de France. Retrieved August 25, 2014, from http://compagnonsdutourdefrance.org/fncmb/qui_peut_etre_candidat

Levine, T. H., & Marcus, A. S. (2010). How the structure and focus of teachers' collaborative activities facilitate and constrain teacher learning. *Teaching and Teacher Education, 26*(3), 389–398. doi:10.1016/j.tate.2009.03.001

Levy, M., Wang, Y., & Chen, N.-S. (2009). Developing the skills and techniques for online language teaching: A focus on the process. *Innovation in Language Learning and Teaching, 3*(1), 17–34. doi:10.1080/17501220802655417

Lewin, K. (1946). Action research and minority problems. *Journal of Social Issues, 2*(4), 34–46. doi:10.1111/j.1540-4560.1946.tb02295.x

Lindsay, H. F. (2013). *Patterns of learning in the accountancy profession: The roles of continuing professional development and lifelong learning* (Unpublished doctoral dissertation). The Open University, Milton Keynes.

Liou, H.-C. (2001). Reflective practice in a pre-service teacher education program for high school English teachers in Taiwan. *System, 29*(2), 197–208. doi:10.1016/S0346-251X(01)00011-2

Long, M. H., & Robinson, P. (1998). Focus on form: Theory, research, and practice. In C. Doughty, & J. Williams (Eds), *Focus on form in classroom second language acquisition* (pp. 15–41). Cambridge: Cambridge University Press.

Loucky, J. P. (2010). Constructing a roadmap to more systematic and successful online reading and vocabulary acquisition. *Literary and Linguistic Computing, 25*(2), 225–241. doi:10.1093/llc/fqp039

Maclure, M. (1993). Arguing for Your Self: Identity as an organising principle in teachers' jobs and lives. *British Educational Research Journal, 19*(4), 311–322. doi:10.1080/0141192930190401

Maier-Gutheil, C., & Hof, C. (2011). The development of the professionalism of adult educators: A biographical and learning perspective. *European Journal for Research on the Education and Learning of Adults, 2*(1), 75–88. doi:10.3384/rela.2000-7426.rela0024

Martínez-Arboleda, A. (2013). Discovering Spanish voices abroad in a digital world. In A. Beaven, A. Comas-Quinn, & B. Sawhill (Eds), *Case studies of openness in the language classroom* (pp. 176–188). Dublin, Viollans: Research publishing.net. Retrieved from http://research-publishing.net/publication/chapters/978-1-908416-10-0/MartinezArboleda_119.pdf

Masterman, L., Wild, J., White, D., & Manton, M. (2011). The impact of OER on teaching and learning in UK universities: Implications for Learning Design. In L. Cameron & J. Dalziel (Eds), *Proceedings of the 6th International LAMS & Learning Design Conference 2011: Learning design for a changing world* (pp. 135–144).

Sydney: LAMS Foundation. Retrieved from http://lamsfoundation.org/lams 2011sydney/docs/RP/Masterman_Wild.pdf

McDonald, K. (2007). Wikipedia projects for language learning. Forum article. *Computer Assisted Language Learning – Electronic Journal, 9*(1). Retrieved from http://callej.org/journal/9-1/mcdonald.html

McGill, L., Currier, S., Duncan, C., & Douglas, P. (2008). *Good intentions: Improving the evidence base in support of sharing learning materials* (Final report). JISC. Retrieved from http://repository.jisc.ac.uk/265/1/goodintentionspublic.pdf

Mercer, N. (1995). *The guided construction of knowledge: Talk amongst teachers and learners.* Clevedon: Multilingual Matters.

Middlebury Interactive Languages (2013, January 14). MIL, Middlebury College Vermont World Language Initiative. Retrieved August 25, 2014, from http://www.middlebury.edu/newsroom/archive/524638/node/442588

Middlebury Interactive Teachers Community (2013). Retrieved August 25, 2014, from http://middleburyinteractiveteachers.ning.com

Millard, D. E., Borthwick, K., Howard, Y., McSweeney, P., & Hargood, C. (2013). The HumBox: Changing educational practice around a learning resource repository. *Computers & Education, 69,* 287–302. doi:10.1016/j.compedu.2013.07.028

MONE (2014). Fatih Projesi. Retrieved August 31, 2014, from http://fatihprojesi.meb.gov.tr/tr/index.php

Montoro Sanjosé, C. R. (2012). *The language learning activity of individual learners using online tasks* (Unpublished doctoral dissertation). Open University, Milton Keynes.

Motteram, G. (Ed.). (2013). *Innovations in learning technologies for English language teaching.* London: British Council. Retrieved from http://www.teachingenglish.org.uk/sites/teacheng/files/C607%20Information%20and%20Communication_WEB%20ONLY_FINAL.pdf

Mruck, K., & Mey, G. (2007). Grounded theory and reflexivity. In A. Bryant, & K. Charmaz (Eds), *The Sage handbook of grounded theory* (pp. 515–538). Thousand Oaks, CA: Sage.

Murday, K., Ushida, E., & Chenoweth, N. A. (2008). Learners' and teachers' perspectives on language online. *Computer Assisted Language Learning, 21*(2), 125–142. doi:10.1080/09588220801943718

Murillo, E. (2008). Searching Usenet for virtual communities of practice: Using mixed methods to identify the constructs of Wenger's theory. *Information Research, 13*(4). Retrieved from http://www.informationr.net/ir/13-4/paper386.html

Murphy, L. M., Shelley, M. A., & Baumann, U. (2010). Qualities of effective tutors in distance language teaching: Student perceptions. *Innovation in Language Learning and Teaching, 4*(2), 119–136. doi:10.1080/17501220903414342

Murphy, L. M., Shelley, M. A., White, C. J., & Baumann, U. (2011). Tutor and student perceptions of what makes an effective distance language teacher. *Distance Education, 32*(3), 397–419. doi:10.1080/01587919.2011.610290

Nelson, I., & Pozo-Gutiérrez, A. (2013). The OpenLIVES project: Alternative narratives of pedagogical achievement. In A. Beaven, A. Comas-Quinn, & B. Sawhill (Eds), *Case studies of openness in the language classroom* (pp. 162–175). Dublin, Viollans: Research publishing.net. Retrieved from http://research-publishing.net/publication/chapters/978-1-908416-10-0/Nelson_PozoGutierrez_118.pdf

Nielsen, J. (2006, October 9). Participation inequality: Encouraging more users to contribute. Retrieved August 25, 2014, from http://www.nngroup.com/articles/participation-inequality/

Nikitina, L., & Furuoka, F. (2006). Re-Examining Horwitz's Beliefs About Language Learning Inventory (BALLI) in the Malaysian context. *Electronic Journal of Foreign Language Teaching, 3*(2), 209–219. Retrieved from http://e-flt. nus.edu.sg/v3n22006/nikitina.pdf

Nishino, T. (2012). Multi-membership in communities of practice: An EFL teacher's professional development. *TESL-EJ, 16*(2), 1–21. Retrieved from http://www.tesl-ej.org/wordpress/issues/volume16/ej62/ej62a1/

Norton, B. (1997). Language, identity, and the ownership of English. *TESOL Quarterly, 31*(3), 409–429. doi:10.2307/3587831

Nunan, D. (1989). *Designing tasks for the communicative classroom.* Cambridge: Cambridge University Press.

Nunan, D., & Lamb, C. (1996). *The self-directed teacher: Managing the learning process.* Cambridge: Cambridge University Press.

O'Dowd, R. (2006). *Telecollaboration and the development of intercultural communicative competence.* Berlin and München: Langenscheidt.

O'Dowd, R., & Ritter, M. (2006). Understanding and working with 'failed communication' in telecollaborative exchanges. *CALICO Journal, 23*(3), 623–642. doi:10.11139/cj.23.3.623-642

OECD (2007). Recognition of non-formal and informal learning. Retrieved August 24, 2014, from http://www.oecd.org/education/skills-beyond-school/recognitionofnon-formalandinformallearning-home.htm

Official Journal of the European Union (2006). Recommendation of the European Parliament and of the Council of 18 December 2006 on key competences for lifelong learning. (2006/962/EC). pp. 10–18.

OER Synthesis and Evaluation Project (2012). JISC/HE Academy OER Programme Synthesis and Evaluation Project wiki [Wiki]. Retrieved August 24, 2014, from https://oersynth.pbworks.com/w/page/29595671/OER%20Synthesis%20and%20Evaluation%20Project

OpenLIVES project blog (2014, January 3). OpenLIVES inspires Spanish singer/songwriter [Blog post]. Retrieved from http://openlives.wordpress. com/2014/01/03/openlives-inspires-spanish-singersongwriter/

Open Society (n.d.). The Cape Town Open Education Declaration. Open Society Foundations and Shuttleworth Foundation. Retrieved from http://www.capetowndeclaration.org/read-the-declaration

OSYM (Student Selection and Placement System) (2013). Student Guide 2013. Retrieved from http://dokuman.osym.gov.tr/pdfdokuman/2013/OSYS/2013%20%C3%96SYS%20KONT%20KILAVUZU%20BASKI%20%28Tablo%204%29_KB.pdf

Parker Webster, J., & Marques da Silva, S. (2013). Doing educational ethnography in an online world: Methodological challenges, choices and innovations. *Ethnography and Education, 8*(2), 123–130. doi:10.1080/17457823.2013.792508

Park, P. (2006). Knowledge and participatory research. In P. Reason, & H. Bradbury (Eds), *Handbook of action research* (pp. 83–93). London: Sage.

Parry, D. (2011). Mobile perspectives: On teaching. Mobile literacy. *EDUCAUSE Review, 46*(2). http://net.educause.edu/ir/library/pdf/ERM1120.pdf

Pasfield-Neofitou, S. (2011). Online domains of language use: Second language learners' experiences of virtual community and foreignness. *Language Learning & Technology, 15*(2), 92–108. Retrieved from http://llt.msu.edu/issues/june2011/pasfieldneofitou.pdf

Peacock, M. (1997). The effect of authentic materials on the motivation of EFL learners. *ELT Journal, 51*(2), 144–156. doi:10.1093/elt/51.2.144

Pegler, C. (2012). Herzberg, hygiene and the motivation to reuse: Towards a three-factor theory to explain motivation to share and use OER. *Journal of Interactive Media in Education, 2012*(01). Retrieved from http://www-jime.open.ac.uk/jime/article/view/2012-04

Pegrum, M. (2011). Modified, multiplied and (re-)mixed: Social media and digital literacies. In M. Thomas (Ed.), *Digital education: Opportunities for social collaboration* (pp.9–35). New York: Palgrave Macmillan.

Pellerin, M. (2013). E-Inclusion in early French immersion classrooms: Using technologies to support inclusive practices that meet the needs of all learners. *Canadian Journal of Education/Revue Canadienne de L'éducation, 36*(1), 44–70. Retrieved from http://journals.sfu.ca/cje/index.php/cje-rce/article/view/1186

Pellerin, M. (2014). Language tasks using touch screen and mobile technologies: Conceptualizing task-based CALL for young language learners. *Canadian Journal of Learning and Technology / La Revue Canadienne de L'apprentissage et de La Technologie, 40*(1), 1–23. Retrieved from http://www.cjlt.ca/index.php/cjlt/article/viewFile/803/385

Petrides, L., & Jimes, C. (2008). Building open educational resources from the ground up: South Africa's free high school science texts. *Journal of Interactive Media in Education, 2008*(1). Retrieved from http://jime.open.ac.uk/jime/article/view/2008-7

Petrides, L., Jimes, C., Middleton-Detzner, C., & Howell, H. (2010). OER as a model for enhanced teaching and learning. In *Open ED 2010 proceedings*. Barcelona: UOC, OU, BYU. Retrieved from http://hdl.handle.net/10609/4995

Preece, J. (2004). Etiquette, empathy and trust in communities of practice: Stepping-stones to social capital. *Journal of Universal Computer Science, 10*(3), 294–302. doi:10.3217/jucs-010-03-0294

Probst, G., & Borzillo, S. (2008). Why communities of practice succeed and why they fail. *European Management Journal, 26*(5), 335–347. doi:10.1016/j.emj.2008.05.003

Reed, P. (2012, November 21). Is OER actually open? Gratis vs libre.... [Blog post]. Retrieved from http://www.scieng-elearning.blogspot.com.es/2012/11/is-oer-actually-open-gratis-vs-libre.html

Research voor Beleid, PLATO (2008). *ALPINE – Adult Learning Professions in Europe: A study of the current situation, trends, and issues* (Final report). US: Zoetermeer: European Commission.

Richards, J. C. (2013). Creativity in language teaching. *Iranian Journal of Language Teaching Research, 1*(3), 19–43.

Richards, J. C., & Lockhart, C. (1994). *Reflective teaching in second language classrooms*. Cambridge: Cambridge University Press.

Rodríguez, A. G., & McKay, S. (2010). *Professional development for experienced teachers working with adult English language learners* (CAELA Network Briefs). Washington, DC: Center for Adult English Language Acquisition. Retrieved from http://www.cal.org/caelanetwork/pdfs/ExpTeachersFinalWeb.pdf

Ruggles Gere, A. (2010, November). Teacher learning communities: A policy research brief produced by the national council of teachers of English. *The*

*Council Chronicle*, 1–4. Retrieved from http://www.ncte.org/library/NCTEFiles/ Resources/Journals/CC/0202-nov2010/CC0202Policy.pdf

Sarramona, J., Vázquez, G., & Colom, A. J. (1998). *Educación no formal*. Barcelona: Ariel.

Satar, M. H. (2010). *Social presence in online multimodal communication: A framework to analyse online interactions between language learners* (Unpublished doctoral dissertation). The Open University, Milton Keynes.

Sawhill, B. (2013). Communicating out in the open: The Wordpress Class Blogs Plug-in Suite and language learning. In A. Beaven, A. Comas-Quinn, & B. Sawhill (Eds), *Case studies of openness in the language classroom* (pp. 11–22). Dublin, Viollans: Research publishing.net. Retrieved from http://research-publishing. net/publication/chapters/978-1-908416-10-0/Sawhill_106.pdf

Scanlon, E., Gaved, M., Jones, A., Kukulska-Hulme, A., Paletta, L., & Dunwell, I. (2014). Representations of an incidental learning framework to support mobile learning. *10th International Conference on Mobile Learning 2014*, 28 February - 02 March 2014, Madrid, Spain, IADIS Press, pp. 238–242.

Scheerens, J. (2010). *Teachers' professional development: Europe in international comparison: an analysis of teachers' professional development based on the OECD's Teaching and Learning International Survey (TALIS)*. Luxembourg: Office for Official Publications of the European Union.

Schlager, M. S., & Fusco, J. (2004). Teacher professional development, technology, and communities of practice: Are we putting the cart before the horse? In S. A. Barab, R. Kling, & J. H. Gray (Eds), *Designing for virtual communities in the service of learning* (pp. 120–153). Cambridge: Cambridge University Press.

Schön, D. A. (1983). *The reflective practitioner: How professionals think in action*. London: Temple Smith.

Selvi, A. F. (2011). The non-native speaker teacher. *ELT Journal, 65*(2), 187–189. doi:10.1093/elt/ccq092

Shea, P., Sau Li, C., & Pickett, A. (2006). A study of teaching presence and student sense of learning community in fully online and web-enhanced college courses. *The Internet and Higher Education, 9*(3), 175–190. doi:10.1016/j. iheduc.2006.06.005

Shelley, M. A., Murphy, L. M., & White, C. J. (2013). Language teacher development in a narrative frame: The transition from classroom to distance and blended settings. *System, 41*(3), 560–574. doi:10.1016/j.system.2013. 06.002

Shelley, M. A., White, C. J., Baumann, U., & Murphy, L. M. (2006). 'It's a unique role!' Perspectives on tutor attributes and expertise in distance language teaching. *The International Review of Research in Open and Distance Learning, 7*(2). Retrieved from http://www.irrodl.org/index.php/irrodl/article/view/297

Siemens, G. (2005). Connectivism: A learning theory for the digital age. *International Journal of Instructional Technology & Distance Learning, 2*(1). Retrieved from http:// www.itdl.org/journal/jan_05/article01.htm

Smith, M. S., & Casserly, C. M. (2006). The promise of open educational resources. *Change: The Magazine of Higher Learning, 38*(5), 8–17. doi:10.3200/ CHNG.38.5.8-17

Son, J.-B. (2011). Online tools for language teaching. *TESL-EJ, 15*(1). Retrieved from http://www.tesl-ej.org/wordpress/issues/volume15/ej57/ej57int/

Steel, C. H., & Levy, M. (2013). Language students and their technologies: Charting the evolution 2006–2011. *ReCALL, 25*(03), 306–320. doi:10.1017/S0958344013000128

Stevens, A. (2009). *Study on the impact of Information and Communications Technology (ICT) and new media on language learning* (Final report No. EACEA 2007/09). Education, Audiovisual & Culture Executive Agency. Retrieved from http://eacea.ec.europa.eu/llp/studies/documents/study_impact_ict_new_media_language_learning/final_report_en.pdf

Stickler, U. (2011). The DOTS project: Developing online teaching skills. *Language Teaching, 44*(03), 403–404. doi:10.1017/S0261444811000255

Stickler, U., & Hampel, R. (2010). CyberDeutsch: Language production and user preferences in a Moodle virtual learning environment. *CALICO Journal, 28*(1), 49–73. doi:10.11139/cj.28.1.49-73

Stickler, U., Batstone, C., Duensing, A., & Heins, B. (2007). Distant classmates: Speech and silence in online and telephone language tutorials. *European Journal of Open, Distance and E-Learning, 2007*(II). Retrieved from http://www.eurodl.org/?p=archives&year=2007&halfyear=2&article=277

Stickler, U., Beaven, T., Emke, M., Ernest, P., Germain-Rutherford, A., Hampel, R., Hopkins, J., & Stanojević, M.-M. (Eds). (2010a). Developing Online Teaching Skills. *Teaching English with Technology, 10*(Special Issue 2). Retrieved from http://www.tewtjournal.org/pastissues2010.htm

Stickler, U., Beaven, T., Emke, M., Ernest, P., Germain-Rutherford, A., Hampel, R., Hopkins, J., & Stanojević, M.-M. (2010b). From the editors: Stepping stones to teaching languages with technology. *Teaching English with Technology, 10*(Special Issue 2), 1–4. Retrieved from http://www.tewtjournal.org/VOL%2010/ISSUE%202/volume_10_issue_02-02_from_the_editor.pdf

Stickler, U., Ernest, P., Beaven, T., Emke, M., Germain-Rutherford, A., Hampel, R., Hopkins, J., & Stanojević, M.-M. (2010). Joining the DOTS. A collaborative approach to online teacher training. *The EuroCALL Review, 16*, 2–6. Retrieved from http://www.eurocall-languages.org/wordpress/wp-content/uploads/2014/01/review16.pdf

Stockwell, G. (Ed.) (2012). *Computer-assisted language learning: Diversity in research and practice*. Cambridge, UK; New York: Cambridge University Press.

Suber, P. (2008, August 2). Gratis and libre open access [Newsletter]. Retrieved August 24, 2014, from http://legacy.earlham.edu/~peters/fos/newsletter/08-02-08.htm

Tait, A. (2000). Planning student support for open and distance learning. *Open Learning: The Journal of Open, Distance and E-Learning, 15*(3), 287–299. doi:10.1080/713688410

Tarmizi, H., de Vreede, G.-J., & Zigurs, I. (2007). Leadership challenges in communities of practice: Supporting facilitators via design and technology. *International Journal of E-Collaboration, 3*(1), 18–39. doi:10.4018/jec.2007010102

TESConnect (2014). Retrieved August 24, 2014, from http://www.tes.co.uk/

Thomas, A. (2014, February 25). Economics of learning materials [Blog post]. Retrieved from http://fragmentsofamber.wordpress.com/2014/02/25/economicslm/

Thomas, M., & Reinders, H. (Eds) (2010). *Task-based language learning and teaching with technology*. London: Continuum.

Thoms, J. J., & Thoms, B. L. (2014). Open educational resources in the United States: Insights from university foreign language directors. *System, 45*, 138–146. doi:10.1016/j.system.2014.05.006

Thorne, S. L. (2003). Artifacts and cultures-of-use in intercultural communication. *Language Learning & Technology, 7*(2), 38–67. Retrieved from http://llt. msu.edu/vol7num2/pdf/thorne.pdf

Thorne, S. L., Black, R. W., & Sykes, J. M. (2009). Second language use, socialization, and learning in Internet interest communities and online gaming. *The Modern Language Journal, 93*(Issue Supplement s1), 802–821. doi:10.1111/j.1540-4781.2009.00974.x

TNS Infratest Sozialforschung, van Rosenbladt, B., & Thebis, F. (2004). *Berufliche und soziale Lage von Lehrenden in der Weiterbildung* (Bericht zur Pilotstudie). Bonn, Berlin: Bundesministerium für Bildung und Forschung.

Tomás, C. (2011). *Language Open Resources Online (LORO): Environmental assessment.* JISC. Retrieved from http://loro.open.ac.uk/1976/

Touriñán, J. M. (1983). Análisis teórico del carácter formal, no formal e informal de la educación. *Papers d'Educació, 1*, 105–127.

Trilla, J. (1997). Relaciones entre la educación formal, la no formal y la informal. In J. Trilla, B. Gros, F. López, & J. M. Martín (Eds), *La educación fuera de la escuela: ámbitos no formales y educación social* (pp. 187–196). Barcelona: Ariel.

Truman, C., & Raine, P. (2001). Involving users in evaluation: The social relations of user participation in health research. *Critical Public Health, 11*(3), 215–229. doi:10.1080/09581590110066667

UNESCO. (2010). Compagnonnage, network for on-the-job transmission of knowledge and identities. Retrieved August 27, 2014, from http://www.unesco. org/culture/ich/en/RL/00441

Vajargah, K. F., Jahani, S., & Azadmanesh, N. (2010). Application of ICTs in teaching and learning at university level: The case of Shahid Beheshti University. *Turkish Online Journal of Educational Technology – TOJET, 9*(2), 33–39. Retrieved from http://tojet.net/articles/v9i2/924.pdf

Van Dijk, T. (2001). Critical discourse analysis. In D. Schiffrin, D. Tannen, & H. E. Hamilton (Eds), *The handbook of discourse analysis* (pp. 352–371). Oxford: Blackwell.

Vardi, M. Y. (2012). Will MOOCs destroy academia? *Communications of the ACM, 55*(11), 5. doi:10.1145/2366316.2366317

Vater, S., & Zwielehner, P. (2013). *27. KEBÖ-Statistik (Arbeitsjahr 2012).* Wien: Konferenz der Erwachsenenbildung Österreichs. Retrieved from http://files. adulteducation.at/statistik/berichte/Keb%C3%B6%2027.pdf

Vescio, V., Ross, D., & Adams, A. (2008). A review of research on the impact of professional learning communities on teaching practice and student learning. *Teaching and Teacher Education, 24*(1), 80–91. doi:10.1016/j.tate.2007. 01.004

Vygotsky, L. S. (1978). *Mind and society: The development of higher mental processes.* Cambridge, Massachusetts: Harvard University Press.

Wajnryb, R. (1992). *Classroom observation tasks: A resource book for language teachers and trainers.* Cambridge: Cambridge University Press.

Wallace, M. J. (1998). *Action research for language teachers.* Cambridge: Cambridge University Press.

Wang, Y.-C. (2014). Using wikis to facilitate interaction and collaboration among EFL learners: A social constructivist approach to language teaching. *System, 42*, 383–390. doi:10.1016/j.system.2014.01.007

Wang, Y., Chen, N.-S., & Levy, M. (2010). Teacher training in a synchronous cyber face-to-face classroom: Characterizing and supporting the online teachers' learning process. *Computer Assisted Language Learning, 23*(4), 277–293. doi:10.1080/09588221.2010.493523

Ware, P. (2005). 'Missed' communication in online communication: Tensions in a German-American telecollaboration. *Language Learning & Technology, 9*(2), 64–89. Retrieved from http://llt.msu.edu/vol9num2/pdf/ware.pdf

Weller, M. (2010). Big and little OER. In *Open ED 2010 proceedings*. Barcelona: UOC, OU, BYU. Retrieved from http://openaccess.uoc.edu/webapps/o2/bit stream/10609/4851/6/Weller.pdf

Weller, M. (2011). *The digital scholar: How technology is changing academic practice*. London: Bloomsbury Academic.

Wenger, E. C. (1998). *Communities of practice: Learning, meaning, and identity*. Cambridge: Cambridge University Press.

Wenger, E. C. (2010). Communities of practice and social learning systems: The career of a concept. In C. Blackmore (Ed.), *Social learning systems and communities of practice* (pp. 179–198). London: Springer.

Wenger, E. C., & Snyder, W. M. (2000, January). Communities of practice: The organizational frontier. *Harvard Business Review*, 139–145.

Wenger, E. C., McDermott, R. A., & Snyder, W. M. (2002). *Cultivating communities of practice: A guide to managing knowledge*. Boston, MA: Harvard Business School Press.

Wenger-Trayner, E. (2006). Communities of practice: A brief introduction. Retrieved August 27, 2014, from http://wenger-trayner.com/theory/

Wertsch, J. V. (1991a). A sociocultural approach to socially shared cognition. In L. B. Resnick, J. M. Levine, & S. D. Teasley (Eds), *Perspectives on socially shared cognition* (pp. 85–100). Washington, DC: American Psychological Association.

Wertsch, J. V. (1991b). *Voices of the mind: A sociocultural approach to mediated action*. London: Harvester Wheatsheaf.

Wertsch, J. V. (1998). *Mind as action*. Oxford: Oxford University Press.

White, C. J. (2003). *Language learning in distance education*. Cambridge: Cambridge University Press.

White, C. J., Murphy, L. M., Shelley, M. A., & Baumann, U. (2005). Towards an understanding of attributes and expertise in distance language teaching: Tutor maxims. In T. Evans, P. Smith, & E. Stacey (Eds), *Research in distance education 6: Revised papers from the sixth Research in Distance Education conference* (pp. 83–97). Melbourne: Research Institute for Professional & Vocational Education & Training, Deakin University.

Wiley, D. (2009, November 16). Defining 'open' [Blog post]. Retrieved from http://opencontent.org/blog/archives/1123

Wiley, D. (2013, October 10). On quality and OER [Blog post]. Retrieved from http://opencontent.org/blog/archives/2947

Wiley, D. (2014, March 5). The access compromise and the 5th R [Blog post]. Retrieved from http://opencontent.org/blog/archives/3221

Wiley, D., & Gurrell, S. (2009). A decade of development... *Open Learning: The Journal of Open, Distance and E-Learning, 24*(1), 11–21. doi:10.1080/02680510802627746

Woods, R., & Ebersole, S. (2003). Becoming a 'communal architect' in the online classroom – Integrating cognitive and affective learning for maximum effect in web-based learning. *Online Journal of Distance Learning Administration, 6*(1), 1–24. Retrieved from http://www.westga.edu/~distance/ojdla/spring61/woods61.htm

Wozney, L., Venkatesh, V., & Abrami, P. (2006). Implementing computer technologies: Teachers' perceptions and practices. *Journal of Technology and Teacher Education, 14*(1), 173–207. Retrieved from http://www.editlib.org/p/5437

WSF – Wirtschafts- und Sozialforschung (2005). *Erhebung zur beruflichen und sozialen Lage von Lehrenden in Weiterbildungseinrichtungen* (Schlussbericht). Kerpen. Retrieved from http://www.bmbf.de/pubRD/berufliche_und_soziale_lage_von_lehrenden_in_weiterbildungseinrichtungen.pdf

Yang, S.-H. (2009). Using blogs to enhance critical reflection and community of practice. *Educational Technology & Society, 12*(2), 11–21. Retrieved from http://www.ifets.info/journals/12_2/2.pdf

Zhao, Y., & Cziko, G. A. (2001). Teacher adoption of technology: A perceptual control theory perspective. *Journal of Technology and Teacher Education, 9*(1), 5–30.

Zheng, D., Li, N., & Zhao, Y. (2008). *Learn Chinese in Second Life Chinese school.* Paper presented at the CALICO 2008, San Francisco. Retrieved from https://calico.org/p-399-%20...html

# Index

access to ICT, 2, 7, 17, 30, 79, 97, 116, 169–71, 175, 178, 180
action research, 3, 6, 8, 9, 10, 30, 31, 32, 78–9, 135, 142, 143, 144–5, 148, 157
action research spiral, 144, 155, 157, 161–2
adaptive teaching, 9
adult education, 28–29, 31, 39
affect, 47, 116, 117–8
  *see also* learner support functions
affordances, 5, 9, 59, 64, 65, 68–69, 77, 89, 92, 137, 153
agency, 31, 136, 143
American Council on the Teaching of Foreign Languages' Language Educators Community, 120, 121–4, 130
assessment, 9, 13, 17, 84, 85, 101, 104
Audacity, 17, 102, 168
audio-conferencing, 45, 50, 53, 62, 71, 155, 182
authenticity, 2, 5, 13, 16, 17, 25, 68, 70, 74, 85, 104, 138, 139, 148, 155, 164
autonomy, 5, 16, 17, 25, 78, 92, 136, 138, 158, 182

blended learning and teaching, 6, 12, 14, 18, 25, 37, 42, 45–6, 47, 49, 51–2, 60, 61, 66, 67, 121, 124, 145, 156–7
blog, 16–7, 71, 35, 38, 44, 62, 71, 79, 81, 86, 87–89, 92, 101, 102, 104, 113, 124, 141, 147, 148, 149, 151, 153, 163, 168, 180
body language, 59, 71, 147

Cape Town Open Education Declaration, 101
collaboration, 3, 4, 5, 8, 9, 16, 17, 18, 25, 48, 60, 63, 65, 66, 67, 70–1, 75, 85, 89, 93, 94, 100, 101, 102, 103, 104, 113–4, 116, 117, 119, 122, 124, 125–6, 136, 138, 149, 154, 155, 159
communication, 5, 8, 9, 12, 13, 17, 18, 20, 32, 48, 54, 56, 59, 60, 62, 63, 66, 68, 70–2, 73, 75, 76, 77, 86, 119–20, 126, 135, 137–8, 140, 142, 147, 148, 155, 159, 160
communicative competence, 5, 60, 66, 68, 70–2, 76–7
communication tools, 4, 7, 68–9, 85, 116, 140, 151
communicative approach, 19, 118, 133, 137, 164
communities of practice, 3, 4, 7–8, 15, 30, 40, 42, 79, 80, 81, 83, 89–91, 93, 94, 95, 106, 113–33, 136, 153, 157, 158
  characteristics of, 115, 132
  definition, 114–5
  design principles, 119–20, 132
  life cycle, 126
  liveliness and relevance, 126, 131, 133
  typical activities, 122–3, 132
  virtual communities of practice, 116–7
community building, 60, 155
Community of Inquiry framework, 48–9, 54, 55–62
*Compagnonage*, 114, 133
computer-mediated communication (CMC), 30, 135, 137, 147, 148
construction of knowledge, 3, 70, 75, 80, 119, 136
constructivism, 3, 48, 72
Content-Language-Integrated Learning (CLIL), 84
course management system (CMS), *see* learning management system
Creative Commons, 97, 109, 154
creativity, 5, 59, 64, 65, 66, 68, 72–5, 76–7

critical pedagogy, 142
critical thinking, 5, 17, 73–4, 102, 137
cultural awareness, 12, 16
cultures-of-use, 69

Developing Online Teaching Skills
  (DOTS) project, 2–3, 5, 8, 14–26,
  32–42, 43, 69, 75, 81–2, 121,
  126–30, 133, 150–62, 163–82
  Croatian Regional Online
    Community, 126–30
  Moodle workspace with activities,
    43, 151–6, 157, 160, 162, 167,
    168, 181–2
  related projects, 14–5, 116, 133,
    156–7, 162
  teacher training in Turkey, 4, 8,
    163–82
  tool inventory, 157
digital divide, 166
digital literacy, 12, 17, 73–4, 96, 99, 138
digital storytelling, 83
discourse analysis, 135, 142, 146–7
  computer-mediated discourse
    analysis, 147
  critical discourse analysis, 147
distance language learning and
    teaching 46–7, 49–61, 138, 139,
    163

ecological approaches, 136, 163, 166
Electronic Village Online, 38, 81,
    83–4, 91
ethnography, 8, 135, 142, 145–6
  methods, 146
  online ethnography, 146
European Centre for Modern
    Languages (ECML), 2, 5, 8, 10,
    14, 15, 19, 113, 133, 150, 156,
    161, 167
European Commission, 2, 5, 12, 27,
    30, 96, 133, 157
experiential learning, 2, 18, 47, 67,
    150, 154–7, 160, 161, 168, 181

feedback, 40, 43, 47, 53, 69, 72, 73, 74,
    90, 93, 100, 103, 109, 113, 133,
    138, 154–7, 158, 160–1, 165, 168
FlashMeeting, 70

forum, 16, 37, 53, 61, 62, 68, 69, 71,
    72, 76–7, 80, 81, 83, 84, 90–1,
    120, 121–4, 127, 130, 146, 153,
    156, 182
FutureLearn, 98, 107, 110

grammar teaching, 20, 53, 54
grounded theory, 33
group cohesion, 48, 54, 56, 72

ICT and language learning reports, 5,
    12–4, 16–7, 18, 26,
ICT-REV project, 14, 116, 133, 156
ICT user profiles, 23–5, 26–7
identity of learners, 133, 136, 141
identity of teachers, 29, 30, 31–2, 33,
    37, 39–42, 47, 74, 101, 115, 114,
    118, 131, 133
informal learning, 6, 12, 13, 27, 31,
    35, 40, 42, 78, 79, 102, 115, 119,
    141–2, 156
  definition, 27
input, 68, 135, 136, 138
input hypothesis, 135
integration of pedagogy and
    technology, 1–2, 5, 9, 13, 66,
    68–70, 80–1, 82–3, 85, 89, 100,
    134, 150–1, 156, 159–60
interaction, 17, 20, 55, 60, 70–2, 80,
    81, 92, 100, 115, 117, 119, 120,
    122, 124, 130, 133, 135, 137, 140,
    141, 142, 146–7, 148, 151, 157,
    165, 181
interaction hypothesis, 135
intercultural awareness, 64, 68, 75, 117
intercultural learning, 68, 137–8,
    139–41, 148, 153
International Society for Technology
    in Education (ISTE), 68
interpretative approaches to research,
    135, 142

knowledge society, 12

learner anxiety, 47, 72, 165,
learner-centred approach, 10, 36
learning design, 70
learner expectations, 4, 6, 7, 45–62,
    140

learner support functions, 46, 48, 49, 54–60
  affective function, 56–7
  cognitive function, 57–60
  systemic function, 54–6
learning management system (LMS), 16, 18, 86, 109, 164, 170, 172
learning strategy, 156,
learning style, 20, 22, 25, 41, 53, 54, 57
learning theories, 8,
learning to learn, 12
legitimate peripheral participation, 8, 114
lifelong learning, 12, 99
listening skills, 16, 18, 155
literacy, 17, 62, 71, 73, 74, 137, 138, 146
LORO (Languages Open Resources Online), 96, 98, 100, 110

mash-up, 73–4, 98
massive multiplayer online games (MMOGs), 70, 146
massive open online courses (MOOCs), 81–2, 84–5, 92, 93, 94, 98, 107
mediation, 114, 135–6, 137, 140, 148
Middlebury Interactive Teaching Community, 121, 124–6, 130, 133
mobile learning, 9, 84, 137, 141–2, 143, 148, 158, 166, 174
moderation, 1, 72, 125, 130, 158
modes of communication, 71, 72, 147, 148, 159–60
Moodle, 16, 18, 68, 70, 84, 102, 151–4, 155, 164, 182
motivation of learners, 16, 17, 20, 47, 68, 93, 104, 136, 140, 164, 169, 176
motivation of teachers, 39–40, 41, 42, 47, 68, 104, 169, 176, 182
multilingualism, 10, 13, 63, 153
multimedia, 16, 83, 84, 99
multimodality, 63, 73, 163

narrative frames, 23, 33
negotiating online spaces, 7, 66, 74–5, 76
netiquette, 72, 75, 116–7

online reference tools, 15–6, 70, 86
online socialization, 5, 60, 64, 65, 66, 70–2, 76–7, 146
online teaching skills models, 65–7
  *see also* skills pyramid, Technological Pedagogical Content Knowledge framework
OpenLearn, 80, 107, 108, 111
Open Education Europa, 96, 107, 111
open educational resources (OER), 2, 3, 4, 7, 8, 79, 80, 96–112, 150, 154
  access, 97, 154
  adaptation, 97
  definition
  discoverability, 107
  distribution, 97
  open licensing, 97–8, 154
  openness, 98, 154
  repositories, 104–7, 108
  usability, 80
  utility, 99
open educational practice (OEP), 3, 4, 7, 96–112
  open learning, 101–2
  open pedagogies, 101–2
  open scholarship and research, 101–2
  open technologies for education, 101–3, 104
Open University, The, 4, 45, 49, 63, 100, 107, 110, 111
oral skills, 18, 143, 159
output, 68, 136

Paris OER Declaration, 96
participatory research, 135, 142–3, 145
  methods, 143
  modes of participation in research, 143
podcasting, 16, 17, 36, 84, 88, 111, 163, 168–9, 173, 175, 180
portfolios, 89, 151
presence (cognitive, social, teaching), 48–9, 54–62, 63, 71
presentation tools, 15, 86
privacy, 69, 74–5, 94, 120, 124, 132, 147, 153, 165

problem-based learning, 16
problem solving, 122–3, 132
professional development, 1, 8, 14,
    19, 21, 22, 28–44, 78–80, 92,
    96–7, 100–1, 103, 104, 106, 108,
    113–33, 143, 145, 160, 163–82
    models, 30, 31, 41
psycholinguistic approaches, 4, 135,
    138

qualitative approaches to research,
    10, 14, 25, 33, 54–7, 135, 142,
    145, 148

re-mix, 73–4, 75
reading skills, 151, 155
reflective practice 2, 6, 7, 8, 16, 31,
    144–5, 152–3, 154, 159, 161, 165
resistance to technology, 14, 25

second language acquisition (SLA), 3,
    4, 65, 135
Second Life, 146
self-directed development, 78–80, 91,
    92
self-reflection, *see* reflective practice
self-training modules and workshops,
    7, 81, 82–4, 92, 93, 95
self-training plan, 80, 93
    *see also* Developing Online Teaching
    Skills (DOTS) project
shared cognition, 136
skills pyramid, 4–5, 7, 46–7, 58–61,
    64, 65–77, 151
Skype, 69, 71, 148
smart classes, 166
social bookmarking, 73–4, 86, 94–95
social media, 9, 12, 13, 68–9, 77, 86,
    102, 108, 115, 116, 148, 180
social practice, 114, 136, 144, 146, 147
social responsibility, 97
social turn, 4
socio-constructivism, 3–4, 6, 65, 75,
    117, 136, 151, 154, 161
sociocultural theory, 3–4, 10, 32, 64,
    115, 134–5, 135–8, 147–8, 153,
    154
speaking, 71, 72, 76, 143, 155
SurveyMonkey, 43, 151, 182

task-based language learning and
    teaching, 16, 81, 84–5, 92, 137,
    138–9, 148, 164
teacher attitudes and beliefs, 6, 13–4,
    18–21, 23, 26, 31, 32, 35, 37,
    38, 41, 100, 154, 168, 169,
    178, 182
teacher expectations, 4, 6, 12–27, 143,
    148
teacher needs analysis, 4, 5, 6, 8–9,
    27, 12–27, 28–44, 155, 161
teacher roles, 36, 45–62, 134, 137
teaching strategies, 37, 122, 130,
    178
teaching style, 21, 47, 58, 64, 65, 72,
    155
Technological Pedagogical Content
    Knowledge framework, 65
telecollaboration, 83, 137, 139–41,
    148
text chat, 16, 70, 77, 147, 160, 148,
    160
tool directories, 81, 85–6, 92, 93, 94
tools training sites, 81, 86–9, 92, 93,
    95
    *see also* Developing Online Teaching
    Skills (DOTS) project
transformation, 21, 30, 32, 41, 45, 49,
    60–61, 63–77, 104, 117, 126, 131,
    136, 137
translation, 74, 98, 99, 102, 112, 121,
    154, 163, 167, 181
translation tools, 70, 74

virtual learning environment (VLE),
    see learning management
    system
video-conferencing, 16, 61, 147, 153,
    155, 159
voice recording, 102
voicethread, 72, 76
*Volkshochschule*, 28–9, 39
Vygotsky, Lev Semyonovich, 3, 80,
    115, 136

Web 2.0, 17, 81, 87, 116, 164, 189
web quest, 16, 27, 83
Webheads, 4, 38, 81, 91
whiteboard, 16, 34

widening participation, 97
wiki, 16, 62, 68, 76, 86, 92, 102, 148,
    149, 151, 153, 155, 159, 163, 168,
    178
Wikipedia, 68, 70, 74, 102, 148, 184,
    194
Wikispaces, 92, 168

WordPress, 92
writing, 68–9, 71, 72, 74, 88, 89, 94,
    102, 107, 148, 149, 151, 155, 159,
    165

YouTube, 16, 17, 69, 70, 73, 102, 152, 155,
    163, 164, 168, 173, 175, 178, 180